Air Wars

Air Wars

TELEVISION ADVERTISING IN ELECTION CAMPAIGNS, 1952–2008

FIFTH EDITION

Darrell M. West
The Brookings Institution

CQ PRESS

A Division of SAGE
Washington, D.C.

CQ Press
2300 N Street, NW, Suite 800
Washington, DC 20037

Phone: 202-729-1900; toll-free, 1-866-4CQ-PRESS (1-866-427-7737)

Web: www.cqpress.com

Cover design: Diane Buric

♾ The paper used in this publication exceeds the requirements of the American National Standard for Information Sciences—Permanence of Paper for Printed Library Materials, ANSI Z39.48-1992.

Printed and bound in the United States of America

13 12 11 10 09   1 2 3 4 5

Library of Congress Cataloging-in-Publication Data

West, Darrell M.
    Air wars : television advertising in election campaigns, 1952–2008 / Darrell M. West.—5th ed.
        p.   cm.
    Includes bibliographical references and index.
    ISBN 978-0-87289-778-6 (alk. paper)
    1. Advertising, Political—United States. 2. Television in politics—United States. 3. Political campaigns—United States. 4. United States—Politics and government—1945–1989. 5. United States—Politics and government—1989– I. Title.

JF2112.A4W47 2009
324.7'3'097309045—dc22   2008055473

To Karin Rosnizeck,
for all the ways she has enriched my life

————————————————

Contents

Tables and Figures

Preface

Since the publication of the fourth edition of this book, several new developments have occurred: an unpopular war in Iraq; a financial meltdown; a Democratic takeover of the House and Senate in 2006; and the election of America's first African American president, Barack Obama. My goal in this edition is to make sense of the 2008 elections and put the use of advertising and mass media in historical context. Throughout the book, I present new data from the 2008 campaign, including material on ad buys; a review of candidate, party, and group advertising; content analyses of campaign ads and media coverage of ads; and case studies of ad appeals during the recent campaign. This information allows me to discuss changes in the use and effects of campaign advertising. New material on ads in congressional elections also has been included, and all of the chapters have been thoroughly revised and updated.

Chapter 1 discusses how ads are put together. It emphasizes several key advertising principles (such as stereotyping, association, demonization, and code words) and the attention media consultants pay to music, color, editing techniques, audio voice-overs, visual text, and images when developing campaign commercials. Chapter 2 shows how candidates buy air time. These decisions, called ad buys, are the most fundamental decisions made in any campaign, and examination of them shows how commercials are used to advance the strategic goals of candidates. Chapter 3 reviews the messages presented in ads broadcast over the air as well as on the Internet. Chapter 4 looks at the relationship between ads and the news, focusing in particular on how reporters cover and evaluate political ads. Chapters 5–8 investigate the impact of ads on viewers, looking at what citizens learn about the candidates through ads; how ads affect the agenda; how candidates attempt, through advertising, to shift the standards voters use to assess contestants; and how candidates play the blame game to shift responsibility for negative campaigning to their opponents. Chapter 9 studies ads in congressional races, and chapter 10 puts advertising within the framework of democratic elections.

Many people deserve thanks for their assistance with this project. David Barker of the University of Pittsburgh, David Kimball of the University of Missouri–St. Louis, and Scott McClurg of Southern Illinois University at Carbondale made a number of helpful comments on earlier editions. The staff members at CQ Press deserve a big thank you. I am grateful to Brenda Carter, executive director of college publishing; chief acquisitions editor Charisse Kiino; and development editor Allison McKay for their help in making this edition possible. Lorna Notsch did an excellent job copyediting the manuscript. Their advice made this a better book. Ken Goldstein of the University of Wisconsin at Madison provided very helpful data on ad buys from the presidential campaign.

The John Hazen White Sr. Public Opinion Laboratory and the A. Alfred Taubman Center for Public Policy and American Institutions at Brown University facilitated this analysis by providing research support for data collection. In the middle of this project, I moved to the Brookings Institution to become vice president and director of governance studies. I am grateful for the support provided by Brookings during the fall stage of the presidential campaign. Jenny Lu provided terrific research assistance in collecting ads and other materials for this project. None of these individuals or organizations is responsible for the analyses or interpretations presented in this book.

Television Advertising in Election Campaigns: A History in Pictures

1964

Lyndon Johnson's "Daisy" ad shocked viewers in 1964.

1984

Ronald Reagan's "Bear in the Woods" ad was the most remembered spot in 1984.

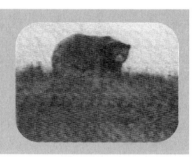

1988

George H. W. Bush's "Revolving Door" ad was one of the most notorious spots of 1988.

1990

Jesse Helms's 1990 spot, "White Hands," helped him win reelection.

1992

Bill Clinton pioneered ads with footnotes to document his claims in 1992.

1992

In 1992, Ross Perot attacked Clinton's job-creation record in Arkansas.

1992

George H. W. Bush used a desolate landscape in 1992 to argue Clinton was too big of a risk.

1993

"Harry and Louise" helped undermine support for Clinton's health care reform in 1993.

1996

In 1996, Clinton surrounded himself with police officers to buttress his credentials as a leader who is tough on crime.

1996

Democrats turned Bob Dole and Newt Gingrich into Siamese twins in the 1996 campaign.

1996

The Republican National Committee attacked Democrats across the country in 1996 for "being too liberal."

1996

Dole's "American Hero" ad documented his war wounds.

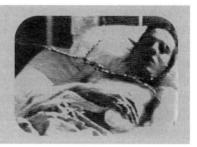

2000

Vice President Al Gore complained that George W. Bush was not ready to lead the nation.

2000

Bush's commercials portrayed Gore as a partisan political figure.

2004

John Kerry attacked George W. Bush and Dick Cheney on Iraq, the economy, and health care.

2004

Bush claimed Kerry did not take terrorism very seriously.

2004

Ads by the Swift Boat Veterans for Truth argued that Kerry was not trustworthy.

2008

John McCain said that Barack Obama stood for higher taxes and more spending, and was not ready to lead.

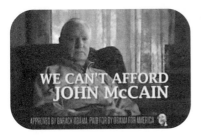

2008

Obama compared McCain to Bush and said his GOP rival wanted to tax health benefits and cut Medicare.

Chapter 1

Overview of Ads

It was a historic election. After defeating Sen. Hillary Clinton for the Democratic nomination and triumphing over Republican nominee John McCain, Sen. Barack Obama made history by becoming America's first African American president. Noting that the country was mired in a financial meltdown and engulfed in controversial wars in Iraq and Afghanistan, Obama broadcast advertisements explaining that he represented "Change We Can Believe In." His commercials linked McCain to unpopular GOP President George W. Bush with the slogan "More of the Same." Employing McCain's own words from the nominating process, Obama put forth that the Arizona senator supported Bush 90 percent of the time on legislative votes.

For his part, McCain ran a scorched earth strategy that characterized Obama as a vacuous celebrity similar to Paris Hilton and Britney Spears, then as someone who palled around with domestic terrorists, and finally as a tax-and-spend liberal whose philosophy bordered on socialism. One ad hammered Obama with the attack of "Higher Taxes. More Spending. Not Ready." In the end, though, people's fears about the national economy led Obama to a 52 percent to 46 percent margin win over his Republican rival.

As illustrated throughout the campaign, advertisements are a major component of political races. In recent presidential campaigns, campaign spots accounted for the largest item in total fall expenditures.[1] Commercials are used to shape citizens' impressions and affect news coverage.[2] As such, they represent a major strategic tool for campaigners. However, not all spots produce the same results. Some ads work; others do not. To determine which spots are effective, analysts must look at production techniques, ad buys (the frequency and location of ad broadcasting), opposition responses, news coverage, and citizens' predispositions. Through detailed studies of ad campaigns since the 1950s, this book shows how to assess ad messages, media coverage of ads, and ad impact on voters.

The History of Ads

From the earliest days of the Republic, communications devices have been essential to political campaigns. In 1828, handbills distributed by Andrew Jackson's supporters portrayed John Quincy Adams as "driving off with a horsewhip a crippled old soldier who dared to speak to him, to ask an alms." A circular distributed by Adams's forces, meanwhile, attacked Jackson for "ordering other executions, massacring Indians, stabbing a Samuel Jackson in the back, murdering one soldier who disobeyed his commands, and hanging three Indians."[3]

The method, though perhaps not the tone, of communicating with the electorate has changed dramatically since 1828. Handbills have virtually disappeared. Radio became the most popular vehicle in the 1920s and 1930s. After World War II, television emerged as the advertising medium of choice for political candidates. And now, in the twenty-first century, the media marketplace has fragmented into a bewildering variety of communication channels from cable television and talk radio to late-night entertainment shows and the World Wide Web. A new Internet-based lexicon has appeared that distinguishes banner ads (large boxes that span the top of a Web site), interstitial ads (spots that flash while a Web site is being loaded), pop-up ads (spots that appear after a Web site is loaded), transactional ads (spots that allow viewers to make a purchase or request information), and rich media ads (spots that have audio, video, or motion embedded within them).[4] Somehow, in this multifaceted situation, candidates must figure out how to reach voters who will decide key election contests.

The 1952 presidential campaign was the first one to feature television ads. In that year, each party ran television and print ads evoking World War II memories. Republicans, in an effort to support Gen. Dwight Eisenhower and break two decades of Democratic control, reminded voters in a *New York Times* ad that "one party rule made slaves out of the German people until Hitler was conquered by Ike." Not to be outdone, Democratic ads informed voters that "General Hindenburg, the professional soldier and national hero, [was] also ignorant of domestic and political affairs. . . . The net result was his appointment of Adolf Hitler as Chancellor."[5]

In the 1960s, television spots highlighted differences in candidates' personal traits. The 1964 presidential campaign with Lyndon Johnson and Barry Goldwater was one of the most negative races since the advent of television. Johnson's campaign characterized Goldwater as an extremist not to be trusted with America's future. One five-minute ad, "Confession of a Republican," proclaimed, "This man scares me. . . . So many men with strange ideas are working for Goldwater."[6] Johnson's "Daisy" ad made a similar point in a more graphic manner. Along with speeches and news coverage, the visual image of a mushroom cloud rising behind a little girl picking daisies in a meadow helped raise doubts about Goldwater's fitness for office in the nuclear age, even though a firestorm of protest forced the ad off the air after only one showing.

Ads in the 1970s and 1980s took advantage of public fear about the economy. When the United States started to experience the twin ills of inflation and unemployment, a phenomenon that led experts to coin a new word, *stagflation,* campaign commercials emphasized economic themes. In 1980, Republican challenger Ronald Reagan effectively used ads to criticize economic performance under President Jimmy Carter. When the economy came roaring back in 1984, Reagan's serene "Morning in America" ad communicated the simple message that prosperity abounded and the United States was at peace.

The 1988 presidential contest was the zenith of attack politics in the post–World War II period. This campaign illustrated the powerful ability of ads to alter impressions of a candidate who was not well known nationally. Early in the summer of 1988, Massachusetts governor Michael Dukakis held a 17-percentage-point lead over his Republican rival, then vice president George H. W. Bush. Women preferred Dukakis over Bush by a large margin, and the governor was doing well among blacks, elderly citizens, and Democrats who previously had supported Reagan.

Meanwhile, Republicans were test marketing new advertising material. Over Memorial Day weekend in Paramus, New Jersey, Bush aides Jim Baker, Lee Atwater, Roger Ailes, Robert Teeter, and Nicholas Brady stood behind a one-way mirror observing a small group of so-called Reagan Democrats. Information concerning Willie Horton, a convicted black man who—while on furlough from a Massachusetts prison—brutally raped a white woman, was being presented, and the audience was quite disturbed. Atwater later boasted to party operatives, "By the time this election is over, Willie Horton will be a household name."[7] Bush went on to beat Dukakis 53 percent to 46 percent.

The 1992 campaign represented the dangers of becoming overly reliant on attack ads and the power of thirty-minute "infomercials" by Reform Party candidate Ross Perot. Throughout the race, Bush used ads to attack Democratic nominee Bill Clinton's character and his record as governor of Arkansas. But unlike in his 1988 race, Bush did not prevail. The poor economy, the backlash that developed against Bush's advertising attacks, and Clinton's quick responses to criticisms led to Clinton beating Bush 43 percent to 38 percent. Perot finished in third place with 19 percent, the best showing for a third-party candidate since Theodore Roosevelt in 1912.

In 1996, President Clinton coasted to reelection through the help of ads broadcast more than a year before the election. With the advice of political strategist Dick Morris, Clinton defied the conventional wisdom arguing against early advertising. He ran ads both on television and over the Internet that positioned him as the bulwark against GOP extremism. Linking Republican nominee Bob Dole to unpopular House Speaker Newt Gingrich, Clinton portrayed the Republican Party as insensitive to women, children, and minorities and not to be trusted with important issues such as Social Security, Medicare, and education.

In 2000, Al Gore and George W. Bush ran in the closest presidential election in decades. Featuring cautious advertising that played to undecided voters, each candidate, along with outside groups, ran commercials that challenged the integrity and experience of the other. Bush emphasized education reform, whereas Gore focused on health care and Social Security. One Bush ad, popularly known as "RATS," featured the first use of a subliminal message in presidential campaign history when the word *RATS* was superimposed over a few frames criticizing Gore's prescription drug plan.[8] The election even saw a remake of the infamous 1964 "Daisy" ad ("Daisy II"), when a group of Texans paid for an ad with an image of a girl plucking petals off a daisy while an announcer complained that because of Clinton–Gore deals with "communist Red China" in return for campaign contributions, Democrats had compromised the country's security and made the nation vulnerable to Chinese missile attacks.

In 2004, Bush used images of firefighters carrying victims away from the World Trade Center to explain how he was a "tested" individual who could provide steady leadership in turbulent times. At the same time, he characterized his opponent, Democrat John Kerry, as an unprincipled and untrustworthy "flip-flopper." The campaign produced a commercial showing Senator Kerry wind-surfing while a narrator intoned, "In which direction would John Kerry lead? Kerry voted for the Iraq War, opposed it, supported it, and now opposes it again. . . . John Kerry: Whichever way the wind blows."[9] Kerry, meanwhile, attacked Bush's economic record and complained about Bush's foreign policy. One advertisement said "only Herbert Hoover had a worse record on jobs." Another spot showed a picture of Saudi Crown Prince Abdullah and suggested that "the Saudi royal family gets special favors, while our gas prices skyrocket."[10]

The 2008 presidential campaign represented one of the most wide-open races in decades. There was no incumbent or heir-apparent on the ballot of either major party. The result was that eight Democrats and nine Republicans sought their party's nomination. This included a woman (Hillary Clinton), an African American (Barack Obama), a Hispanic (Bill Richardson), a Mormon (Mitt Romney), and a former prisoner of war (John McCain). Between the primaries and the general election, the airwaves were saturated with political commercials. In the fall, McCain attacked Obama in terms of policy vision, lack of foreign policy experience, and personal associations. Obama, meanwhile, said McCain represented "Bush's Third Term" and that his GOP rival was not the party maverick he claimed to be.

Throughout these elections, commercials were a valuable lens on the inner workings of each campaign. Candidates revealed crucial aspects of their vision, leadership style, and substantive positions. As stated by Elizabeth Kolbert, then a news reporter for the *New York Times,* "Every advertising dollar spent represents a clue to a campaign's deepest hopes and a potential revelation about its priorities."[11]

Principles of Advertising

Strategists use the principles of stereotyping, association, demonization, and code words to influence the electorate. A *stereotype* refers to a common portrait or an oversimplified judgment that people hold toward groups or sets of individuals. For example, Republicans are often portrayed as strong on defense, but not very compassionate toward poor people. Democrats are viewed as caring and compassionate toward the downtrodden, but overly eager to raise taxes. Because television ads are brief, generally no more than thirty seconds, campaigners evoke stereotypes knowing they appeal to voters' prejudices and commonly held views.

However, ads cannot create perceptions that do not already exist in people's minds. There must be a kernel of truth in the stereotype for these types of appeals to be effective. If people do not already think that college professors are absent-minded, nurses are caring, or car salespeople are sleazy, it is hard for election ads to play to these kinds of sentiments.

Association is based on linking a candidate or cause to some other idea or person. Politicians love to connect themselves to widely esteemed popular objects while tying their opponents to things that are unpopular, controversial, or divisive. Flags, patriotism, and prominent celebrities are examples of objects with which candidates surround themselves. In contrast, opponents are pictured with unpopular causes or organizations or cast in a light that bonds them to unfavorable objects such as higher taxes, funding cuts for social programs, and ties to fringe groups or corporate "big money."[12]

During the Cold War, it was popular to portray leftist-leaning candidates as communist sympathizers having allegiance to foreign powers. When Kerry received the Democratic nomination, opponents sought to tie him to controversial Vietnam War protester, actress Jane Fonda. The Swift Boat Veterans for Truth ran an ad entitled "Friends" that asserted, "even before Jane Fonda went to Hanoi to meet with the enemy and mock America, John Kerry secretly met with enemy leaders in Paris. . . . Jane Fonda apologized for her activities, but John Kerry refuses to."[13]

In the campaign for the 2008 Democratic presidential nomination, Hillary Clinton used association techniques to tie Obama to controversial African American minister Jeremiah Wright, Obama's hometown minister at Trinity United Church of Christ in Chicago. Using videos of Wright complaining that America was "the No. 1 killer in the world" and that the U.S. government had "started the AIDS virus," she suggested that Obama was outside the political meanstream because he associated with such a controversial speaker.[14]

The 2008 general election saw a similar tactic on the part of McCain. The GOP nominee attempted to link Obama to former 1960s radical William Ayers. Noting that Ayers had admitted to participating in a police station bombing in 1970 and that Obama had held a benefit coffee at Ayers's home in 1995 during his first run for public office, McCain said that this personal link between the men proved that Obama was too extreme for America and not to be trusted.

However, after endorsements by Warren Buffett and Colin Powell, Obama ran spots touting support by these prominent Americans and used these associations to make the point that he represented a safe choice for America. Combined with his own calm demeanor and steady voice, Obama defused what could have come to be seen as negative associations with controversial figures.

To gain credibility, politicians like to associate themselves with such popular people as public figures, sports heroes, astronauts, or Hollywood celebrities. These individuals come from outside the political world and often have a great deal of mainstream influence and respect. By associating with them and winning their endorsements, politicians attempt to piggyback onto the high credibility these individuals have among voters in general.[15]

Demonization is the process of turning an opponent into an evil being or satanic figure. Wartime enemies are condemned as murderers, terrorists, or barbarians. Political opponents are portrayed as extremists out of touch with the mainstream or guilty of immoral behavior. Adversaries are identified with policy actions that are widely condemned or seen as socially destructive.

For example, an entry in an anti-Bush ad contest sponsored by the MoveOn.org Voter Fund intermingled pictures of Adolf Hitler and George W. Bush making speeches. In a clear effort to demonize the sitting president, the spot concluded with the tagline, "What were war crimes in 1945 is foreign policy in 2003."[16]

Meanwhile, commercials sponsored by the Progress for America Voter Fund, a conservative political action committee, attacked Kerry by showing pictures of Osama bin Laden and September 11 hijacker Mohamed Atta. The unmistakable message in these spots was that Kerry was not to be trusted with defending America's security.[17]

As with the other principles, demonizing the opposition is a tactic that must be used carefully. There must be some believability in the specific appeal for an ad to have credibility. One cannot simply make charges that are unsubstantiated or so far out of bounds as to exceed voters' ability to internalize them. Demonization must bear some resemblance to the facts for this tactic to influence citizens.

Code words are shorthand communication devices that play on common stereotypes and connotations associated with particular kinds of language. Even in the limited space of thirty seconds, campaigns can use short messages to communicate broader messages to the public. Many people feel that thirty seconds is too brief a period to convey much in the way of substantive themes, but during election campaigns, single words or expressions can take on enormous importance.

For example, in the 1960s and 1970s, Republicans used the phrase "law and order" to play to voter conceptions that Democrats were permissive on crime, race, and morality, whereas Republicans could be counted on to protect the social order. Democrats were paired with images and voice-overs of urban riots and social protests to convey complex political messages.

Democrats, meanwhile, have used a similar tactic in regard to the code word of *right wing.* Following the surprise GOP takeover of the House and Senate in 1994 and Newt Gingrich's ascension to the Speakership, Democrats played to voter stereotypes about Republicans being uncaring and insensitive. Using examples of extreme rhetoric and policy proposals that sought to slow the rate of increase in spending on various federal programs, Democrats associated GOP candidates with unsympathetic and extremist images. Throughout the country in 2000, House Democrats used the phrase *right-wing extremists* to refer to their Republican counterparts.[18]

Code words are powerful communication devices because they allow voters to associate a particular message with a specific code word. One of the most frequently used code words has been *liberal* by Republicans. In 1988, George Bush Sr. called Democratic candidate Dukakis a liberal thirty-one times in his speeches. The message got through to voters. Whereas 31 percent in May 1988 believed Dukakis was liberal, the figure rose to 46 percent by September 1988.

In 1992, Bush's use of the term *liberal* rose to sixty-two times. Similar to 1988, the word took on a number of negative meanings, such as being fiscally irresponsible, soft on crime, and dangerously out of touch with the American public. This approach allowed Bush to condemn Clinton with the single word liberal without having to voice more detailed descriptions of his opponent's position[19]

By 1996, the country's airwaves were filled with ads using the *L*-word. Dole ran ads condemning Clinton as a tax-and-spend liberal and as someone whose failed policies were liberal. In one speech in September 1996, Dole used the word fourteen times. Republican congressional candidates used the same appeal all across the country. Ads financed by the Republican National Committee criticized Democratic House and Senate candidates as "liberals," "ultra-liberals," "super-liberals," "unbelievably liberal," "embarrassingly liberal," "foolishly liberal," and "taxingly liberal." Because of the country's changed political climate after the abortive Republican Revolution to downsize government, though, the use of the word liberal as an epithet did not resonate with voters. As one voter in a focus group put it, the term liberal meant helping people. Others felt that "liberal is having an open mind."

This view was supported in a 1996 CBS News/*New York Times* survey asking people what they thought of when they heard someone described as liberal or conservative, respectively. The most common responses for liberal were open minded (14 percent), free spending (8 percent), high degree of government involvement (7 percent), helps people (5 percent), and pro-handouts (5 percent). The most common responses for conservative were fiscally responsible (17 percent), closed minded (10 percent), careful (8 percent), against change (7 percent), and low degree of government involvement (6 percent).[20]

In the 2004 campaign, however, use of the *liberal* epithet returned to the campaign trail. President George W. Bush criticized Kerry for advocating a return to "massive new government agencies" with power over health care. Through an ad showing a map of a complex federal bureaucracy, Bush charged that Kerry's health care program would cause "rationing" and that "Washington bureaucrats, not your doctor, [would] make final decisions on your health."[21] In addition, the Republican National Committee sent a mass mailing to voters in Arkansas and West Virginia accusing "liberals" of seeking to ban the Bible in order to promote policies on gay marriage.[22]

With conservative disgust over the decision of the French government not to support the war in Iraq, the 2004 election introduced the code word *French* to political discourse. Not only did some lawmakers seek to rename French fries "freedom fries," Bush's Commerce secretary, Don Evans, accused Kerry of looking "French" because he spoke the language, was cosmopolitan, and had French relatives.[23] The National Rifle Association also associated Kerry with France by using a mailing with a French poodle wearing a Kerry campaign sweater and having a bow in its hair to condemn the Democrat's record.[24]

As explained by Françoise Meltzer, a humanities professor at the University of Chicago, in the 2004 electoral context, "French really means un-American." It was a striking contrast to earlier periods, when France was viewed favorably in the United States because it had aided the thirteen colonies during the American Revolution and given America the gift of the Statue of Liberty.[25]

The 2008 presidential election was a code word bonanza. Democrats argued that McCain was an "out of touch" politician who didn't even use a computer or e-mail. Meanwhile, Republicans complained that Obama was a liberal or even a socialist, and that he associated with domestic terrorists. Obama sought to disarm these attacks by joking at the end of the campaign that some people thought he was a secret communist because he'd "shared [his] toys in kindergarten."[26]

How Ads Are Put Together

Production techniques for commercials have improved dramatically since the 1950s. Early ads were rudimentary by contemporary standards. Political spots often took the form of footage from press conferences or testimonials from prominent citizens. Many were of the "talking head" variety in which the candidate (or his or her supporter) looked straight into the camera and spoke for thirty or sixty seconds without any editing.

Contemporary ads, in contrast, are visually enticing. Technological advances in television and on the Internet allow ad producers to use colorful images and sophisticated editing techniques to make spots more compelling. Images can be spliced together, and animated images visually transpose one person into another in a split second using a technique called "morphing." As we see in the next sections, catchy visuals, music, and color capture viewer attention and convey particular political messages in a variety of ways.

Visual Images

The visual aspect of advertising is the most important part of commercials. According to the old adage, a picture is worth a thousand words. Contemporary ads use graphic imagery to grab the public's attention and convey messages. Whereas traditional research focused on the spoken content of ads to determine ways of conveying messages, modern analysts study both audio and visual aspects of advertising.

Candidates often attempt to undermine political opponents by associating them with unfavorable visuals. A 1990 campaign ad by Sen. Bennett Johnston, D-La., against his opponent, state representative David Duke, showed pictures of Duke addressing a Ku Klux Klan rally in the presence of a burning cross to make his point that Duke was an extremist who should not be elected to a seat in the U.S. Senate.

A similar phenomenon happened in 1996. Taking advantage of House Speaker Newt Gingrich's unpopularity, Democrats across the

United States broadcast ads showing pictures of Gingrich side by side with Bob Dole and House and Senate Republican candidates. The message was clear: A vote for the Republican Dole was a vote for Gingrich.

In 2000, George W. Bush positioned himself as a "compassionate conservative" and frequently appeared at election rallies with retired general Colin Powell, a popular African American leader who later became Bush's secretary of state. Bush surrounded himself in photo opportunities and ads with women, minorities, and children to convey the idea he was a different kind of Republican than Gingrich. For his part, Gore relied on pictures of himself with his wife, Mary Elizabeth (Tipper) Gore, to communicate the idea that he was a candidate with firm values and a strong marriage. It was a way to distinguish himself from the personal scandals of the Clinton era.

In 2004, terrorism was mentioned in 13 percent of all the ads run after Labor Day.[27] Some advertisements mentioned Osama bin Laden by name or showed pictures of him. One Republican Senate candidate in Wisconsin even invoked the visual image of a burning World Trade Center on September 11, 2001, to charge that "Russ Feingold voted against the Patriot Act and the Department of Homeland Security."[28]

However, by 2008, public fear over domestic terrorism had faded. In his campaign for the Republican presidential nomination, former New York City mayor Rudy Giuliani attempted to play to citizen concerns by broadcasting ads reminding people of 9/11. But unlike 2004, when these fears helped Bush win reelection, visual images of past terrorist attacks did not resonate with voters; the electorate was much more worried about the economy.

Indeed, the powerful imagery in the fall general election centered on the economy. With the startling meltdown of major financial institutions in the weeks leading up to the November election, voters saw major companies failing or merging and an extraordinary amount of taxpayer dollars infused into banks and insurance companies. Images of unemployed workers, people losing health benefits, and senior citizens forced to scrimp on needed prescription drugs were commonplace. Through these and other devices, Obama effectively tied McCain to Bush and negative perceptions about the Republican Party's economic policies.

The visual aspect of campaign advertising is important because it is the one that has the most impact on viewers. The reason is simple— people remember visuals longer than they do spoken words. Images also have the advantage of creating an emotional response much more powerful than that which results from hearing the spoken word.

CBS news reporter Lesley Stahl tells the story of a hard-hitting evening news piece broadcast on Reagan's presidency in 1984. The story claimed that Reagan had done certain things, such as cut the budget for the elderly, that were contrary to what he said he had done. Accompanying the story was a series of pleasant visual images of Reagan "basking in a sea of flag-waving supporters, beaming beneath red-white-and-blue balloons floating skyward, sharing concerns with farmers in a field." After the story aired, Stahl was surprised by a favorable telephone call from a top Reagan assistant. Asked why he liked the story, given her harsh words, the Reagan adviser explained she had given the White House four and a half minutes of positive pictures of President Reagan: "They don't hear what you are saying if the pictures are saying something different."[29]

Visual Text

Visual text is a print message appearing onscreen, generally in big, bold letters. Printed messages grab viewers' attention and tell them to pay attention to an ad. As an example, Ross Perot's 1992 ads used visual text scrolling up the screen to persuade the American public to vote for him (see Appendix for texts of memorable ads in recent elections). Spots for Clinton in 1996 used big, splashy text onscreen to make the political point that Republicans wanted to "CUT MEDICARE." Dole sought to characterize Clinton as "LIBERAL" and "UNTRUSTWORTHY." In 2000, Democratic ads often noted that Texas ranked "50TH" in family health care, and Republican ads complained that Gore was guilty of "EXAGGERATIONS." Republican ads against Obama in 2008 superimposed text such as "INEXPERIENCED" or "NOT READY" to argue that the Democrat lacked the necessary credentials for the chief executive position. Obama countered by saying that McCain was "More of the Same." Advertisers have found that memory of a message is greatly enhanced by combining visual text with spoken words and descriptive images.

Music and Sounds

Music sets the tone for an ad. Just as party hosts use upbeat music to accompany festivities or an educational institution plays "Pomp and Circumstance" to set the scene for a graduation ceremony, campaign ads use music to convey the mood of a particular commercial.

Uplifting ads use cheery music to make people feel good about a candidate. For example, the 1984 campaign featured an independently produced ad called "I'm Proud To Be an American" that used music from country singer Lee Greenwood's song by that same name. The music played over scenes of Reagan, the American flag, and cheerful scenes of happy Americans. It conveyed the message that things were good in America and people should vote for Reagan.

Conversely, somber or ominous music in an ad seeks subliminally to undermine support for the opponent. In George H. W. Bush's "Revolving Door" ad in 1988, dark and threatening music accompanied scenes of prisoners walking through a revolving door while an announcer attacked Dukakis's record on crime. The sounds of drums, the footsteps of guards on metal stairs, and threatening voices were integral to the ad's message that voters should reject Dukakis in the November election because he was soft on crime.

Color

Color communicates vivid messages in ads. Media consultants use bright colors to associate their candidates with a positive image and grayish or black and white to associate opponents with a negative image. In 2000, for example, the NAACP-sponsored spot about the dragging death of James Byrd was broadcast in black and white to make the point that something dramatically different and calamitous had taken place and viewers should pay close attention.

The 1992 Bush campaign developed an ad called "Arkansas Record" that featured a vulture looking out over a dark and barren landscape to make its point that Clinton had poorly governed Arkansas. That year, Bush also used a low-quality, grayish photographic negative of Clinton from an April 20, 1992, *Time* magazine cover to exhort voters to defeat the Arkansas governor in November. The cover with the photographic negative of Clinton was entitled, "Why Voters Don't Trust Clinton." Bush's ad juxtaposed a nice color image of himself to reinforce the message that voters should not vote for Clinton.

A 1996 Dole commercial took a color videotape clip in which Clinton said if he had it to do over again, he would inhale marijuana, and rebroadcast the image in black and white to make Clinton look sinister. The opposite technique (going from black and white to color) was used by Gore in his 2000 ad called "Veteran." It opened with a black and white photo of a youthful Gore in Vietnam, then shifted to color frames of Gore with Tipper.

Editing

Editing determines the sequencing and pacing of an ad. The *sequencing* of ad images refers to how images in one scene are related to following scenes. For example, the 1984 Reagan ad "Morning in America" showed images of Reagan interspersed with scenes of Americans at work and a country at peace. The sequencing linked the president with the popular themes of peace and prosperity. These images were accompanied by music that enhanced the emotional impact of the ad.

An Obama attack ad in 2008 showed a shifty-eyed McCain grimacing, raising his eyebrows, and smiling awkwardly to suggest he was not the right man for the presidency. At a time of domestic crisis, according to the spot, the United States needed someone better equipped to handle economic and foreign policy issues.

The *pacing* of an ad refers to whether the images flow smoothly or abruptly from scene to scene. Abrupt cuts from image to image create a jarring effect that tells viewers something bad is appearing before them. Such cuts are commonly used to convey negative feelings in attack ads.

Voice-Overs

Through an off-screen announcer, a voice-over provides a road map that knits together visual scenes. A campaign ad is composed of different pictures that convey particular points. The announcer guides viewers through these scenes to clearly communicate the message of the ad.

Typically, attack ads use male announcers to deliver blistering criticisms, but Dole made history in 1996 by using a female announcer to condemn Clinton's "failed liberal drug policies." The use of a woman for the voice-over was designed to soften any potential backlash from going on the attack and to appeal to women concerned about drug use and moral permissiveness in American society.

However, in 2000, both George W. Bush and Gore reverted to the historical pattern and relied more frequently on male announcers for the audio components of their ads. One exception was a Bush ad called "Compare," which used a female announcer to criticize Gore's prescription drug plan. Female narrators are used for health care ads because market research reveals that women make the preponderance of health care decisions in U.S. households. Another exception took place in 2004 during a Bush ad known as "Wolves."

This spot used the image of a pack of wolves to argue that the United States was surrounded by dangerous enemies. It used a female announcer to take the edge off what was a hard-hitting attack on the opposition.

How Ads Are Financed

The financing of campaign ads has changed dramatically in recent decades. In the post-Watergate reforms of the 1970s, candidates generally paid for the bulk of their advertisements out of so-called hard money contributions. These were gifts given directly to candidate organizations for voter persuasion. Campaigners would use these funds to produce and broadcast ads that were put out on the airwaves under a candidate's direct sponsorship. Both the Republican and Democrat nominees broadcast ads designed to frame the contest and set the agenda of political dialogue.

Over time, though, a series of loopholes appeared that transformed campaign ad financing. Interest groups and party organizations began to exploit a loophole that allowed unlimited amounts of money (so-called soft money gifts) to be spent on voter education and get-out-the-vote efforts. Originally created by the 1976 *Buckley v. Valeo* Supreme Court case on the post-Watergate reforms, this loophole was designed to strengthen political parties and outside groups and allow them to mobilize and educate supporters. Donors could give whatever money they desired without being limited to the $1,000 per individual and $5,000 per organization rules for hard money contributions.

This loophole reached its zenith in the 1990s when President Bill Clinton used large amounts of soft money contributions to the Democratic National Committee (DNC) to run ads extolling his virtues and lambasting those of the Republican opposition. Rather than using the money for get-out-the-vote or party-building activities, the DNC ran commercials that were virtually indistinguishable from hard money–financed candidate spots. Republicans did the same thing through the Republican National Committee to criticize Clinton and campaign against Democratic House and Senate candidates.[30]

The ensuing controversy over these funding practices (and a post-election investigation into Clinton's campaign spending) eventually led to enactment of the 2002 Bipartisan Campaign Reform Act (BCRA) sponsored by John McCain and Democrat Russell Feingold. Among its key principles were the outlawing of soft money gifts at the national party level (although state party organizations still could accept these contributions), an increase in individual contributions to $2,000 per candidate per election cycle, and a requirement that candidates personally appear in ads saying they paid for their commercials and took responsibility for their contents.

Groups still could run issue ads that talked about specific policies. For example, they could say that Republicans were harming poor people or that Democrats loved to raise taxes. But ads broadcast by these organizations in the sixty days before a general election could not engage in electoral advocacy. Groups could not criticize the policy stances of a specific federal candidate without registering as a political action committee and being subject to disclosure requirements.

The result of this legislation is a hodgepodge of rules concerning ad financing. Candidates can use hard money gifts to run advertisements, as can national party organizations. State party groups can rely on soft money contributions for political advertisements. Interest groups can spend unlimited amounts of money on issue ads without any disclosure of spending or contributors, except in the last sixty days before a general election. At that point in the campaign, they can run ads criticizing federal candidates, but they have to disclose who paid for the spots.

Unaffected by the 2002 reform legislation are radio ads, direct mail, phone calls, and Internet advertisements. Officials had focused on television ads because they form the bulk of political communications and are the technology that critics most worry about in terms of misleading voters. By restraining the most worrisome television maladies, the hope is that this reform will improve the content and tone of civic discourse. However, as discussed later in this volume, there is little evidence from 2004 or 2008 that the new rules made candidate appeals any more civil.

The 2004 and 2008 elections saw the rise of ad financing through Internet contributions. Howard Dean in 2004 and Obama in 2008 democratized fund-raising by using Web sites to raise large amounts of money from many small donors. With the Democratic base upset at President George W. Bush and alarmed at the Iraq War, these anti-war candidates raised huge amounts of money. Obama's total contributions exceeded $600 million, an all-time record for an American presidential candidate. This allowed him to fund a wide variety of television commercials, radio spots, Internet advertisements, a thirty-minute infomercial the week before the election, and get-out-the-vote efforts on Election Day.

The Impact of Ads on Voters

Ads are fascinating not only because of the manner in which they are put together but also because of their ability to influence voters. People are not equally susceptible to the media, and political observers have long tried to find out how media power actually operates.[31]

Consultants judge the effectiveness of ads by the ultimate results—who wins. This type of test, however, is never possible to complete until after the election. It leads invariably to the immutable law of advertising: Winners have great ads and losers do not.

As an alternative, journalists evaluate ads by asking voters to indicate whether commercials influenced them. When asked directly whether television commercials helped them decide how to vote, most voters say they did not. For example, the results of a Media Studies Center survey placed ads at the bottom of the heap in terms of possible information sources. Whereas 45 percent of voters felt they learned a lot from debates, 32 percent cited newspaper stories, and 30 percent pointed to television news stories, just 5 percent believed they learned a lot from political ads. When asked directly about ads in a CBS News/*New York Times* survey, only 11 percent reported that any presidential candidate's ads had helped them decide how to vote.[32]

But this is not a meaningful way of looking at advertising. Such responses undoubtedly reflect an unwillingness to admit that external agents have any effect on individual voting behavior. Many people firmly believe that they make up their minds independently of the campaign. Much in the same way teenagers do not like to concede parental influence, few voters are willing to admit they are influenced by television.

In studying campaign ads, one needs to emphasize the overall context in which people make decisions. The same ad can have very different consequences depending on the manner in which an opponent responds, the way a journalist reports the ad, the number of times the spot is broadcast, or the predispositions of the viewer.

A vivid example is found in Kathleen Hall Jamieson's study of the 1988 presidential campaign.[33] The effectiveness of Bush's "Revolving Door" ad on Dukakis's crime record was enhanced by the majority culture's fears about black men raping white women and by earlier news stories that had sensationalized Horton's crime spree. Bush did not have to mention Horton in his ad for viewers to make the connection between Dukakis and heinous crimes.

This idea is central to understanding campaign advertisements. Commercials cannot be explored in isolation from candidate behavior and the general flow of media information. An analysis of thirty-second spots requires a keen awareness of the structure of electoral competition, strategic candidate behavior, media coverage, and public opinion. A variety of long- and short-term factors go into voter decision-making. In terms of long-term forces, things such as party loyalties, ideological predispositions, the rules of the game, and socioeconomic status linked to education, income, sex, race, and region affect how people interpret ads and judge candidates. Meanwhile, there are a variety of short-term factors during a campaign that affect people. These include how the media cover ads, what reporters say about the candidates, candidate strategies, and debate performance.

Generally, the better known candidates are, the less ads are able to sway voter impressions. In a situation in which voters have firm feelings about campaigners based on long-term forces such as party and ideology, it is difficult for any of the short-term forces to make a difference. However, if the candidate is not well known or there is volatility in the political climate, news, ads, and debates can make a substantial difference in the election outcome.

The Structure of Electoral Competition

The structure of the electoral process defines the general opportunities available to candidates. The most important development at the presidential level has been the dramatic change in how convention delegates are selected. Once controlled by party leaders in small-scale caucus settings thought to be immune from media influence, nominations have become open and lengthy affairs significantly shaped by the mass media. The percentage of delegates to national nominating conventions selected through primaries increased significantly after 1968. From the 1920s to the 1960s, about 40 percent of delegates were selected in primaries, with the remainder chosen in caucus settings dominated by party leaders. However, after rule changes set in motion by the Democratic Party's McGovern-Fraser Commission following the 1968 election, about 70 percent of convention delegates in each party now are chosen directly by voters in presidential primaries.

Nominating reforms have required candidates to appeal directly to voters for support and in the eyes of many observers have altered the character of the electoral system.[34] No longer are candidates dependent on negotiations with a handful of party leaders. Instead, they must demonstrate public appeal and run campaigns that win media attention. Campaigns have become longer and have come to depend increasingly on television as a means of attracting public support.[35]

Some campaigns get far more attention than others. Citizens are more interested in and knowledgeable about presidential general election campaigns than nominating contests. Although variation exists among individual contests depending on the candidates involved, nomination races typically generate less citizen interest and less media coverage. Of course, the 2008 Democratic nominating contest sparked unusual interest because of the clash of superstar candidates Obama and Clinton.

These differences in the visibility of the candidates and the extent of media coverage are important for the study of television advertisements. Because less visible races feature candidates who are not well known, ad effects on citizens' opinions of the candidates often are significant. Past research has demonstrated that television's impact is strongest when viewers have weakly formulated views.[36] It is easier to run ads against a candidate who is not well known because there is no preexisting attitudinal profile to shield that individual against critical claims.

In addition, candidate behavior is conditioned by the rules of the game. Presidential elections in the United States are determined by the state-based Electoral College. Candidates seek to assemble a majority of Electoral College votes by winning targeted states. This electoral structure has enormous implications for advertising strategies. Most candidates do not run a fifty-state campaign. Instead, because many states tend to vote consistently over time, they focus on the fifteen to twenty states that swing back and forth between the two major parties.

Daron Shaw has undertaken an innovative study of Electoral College strategies and found that candidates apportion their time and advertising dollars in systematic ways. According to his study, strategies center on five categories: base Republican, marginal Republican, battleground state, marginal Democratic, and base Democratic.[37] Factors such as electoral history, size of the state's electoral vote, and current competitiveness dictate how campaigners allocate their resources. These decisions tend to be stable across presidential elections. This demonstrates the way in which electoral rules affect candidate strategies.

Advertising and Strategic Politicians

Early research downplayed the power of ads to mold the public images of candidates. The pioneering study in this area was Thomas Patterson and Robert McClure's innovative effort, *The Unseeing Eye*.[38] Looking at both content and effects, they sought to dispel the concerns of the public and journalists regarding political commercials. Using a model of psychological reasoning based on voters' knowledge about candidates, these researchers examined whether television ads enabled voters to learn more about the policy views or about the personal qualities of campaigners. They found that voters learned more about the issues from ads than from the news, because the ads addressed issues whereas the news was dominated by coverage of the "horse race"—who is ahead at a given time. Popular concerns about the strategic dangers of ads affecting how viewers thought of candidates were minimized as uninformed hand-wringing.

The study's results fit with the general view among election experts of the 1960s and 1970s that political strategies were not very decisive in determining election results. Researchers in the era following the 1960 publication of Campbell et al.'s classic work on voting behavior, *The American Voter*, proclaimed such long-term forces as party identification as the most important. Few scholars disputed this interpretation, even as many argued that short-term factors related to media coverage, candidates' advertisements, and campaign spending simply were not crucial to vote choice. For example, Harold Mendelsohn and Irving Crespi claimed in 1970 that the "injection of high doses of political information during the frenetic periods of national campaigns does very little to alter the deeply rooted, tightly held political attitudes of most voters."[39] Even the later emergence of models based on pocketbook considerations did little to change this interpretation. Paid ads were thought to have limited capacity to shape citizens' impressions of economic performance.

Recent decades, though, have begun to see changes in previous viewpoints. Candidates have started to use commercials more aggressively, reporters have devoted more attention to paid advertising, and ad techniques have grown more sophisticated. It now is thought that voters' assessments can change based on short-term information and that candidates have the power to sway undecided voters who wait until the closing weeks of the campaign to make up their minds. Evidence from elections across the United States suggests that ads are successful in helping candidates develop impressions of themselves.[40]

This is particularly true when campaigners are unknown or in multicandidate nominating contests. The more strategic options that are available with the larger number of candidates involved, the more potential there is for the campaign to affect citizen judgments. One study of the New Hampshire primary by Lynn Vavreck, Constantine Spiliotes, and Linda Fowler, for example, found that a variety of campaign activities affected voters' recognition of and favorability toward specific candidates.[41]

Furthermore, candidates no longer hold a monopoly on advertising. Political parties, interest groups, and even private individuals run commercials around election time. In fact, there are discernible differences in the percentage of attack ads run by different sources. The most negative messages involve issue ads run by interest groups. Fifty-six percent of those ads were attack oriented in recent elections, compared with 20 percent of candidate-sponsored advertisements.[42]

Because paid ads are so important in contemporary campaigns, candidates take the development of advertising strategies quite seriously. Commercials often are pretested through focus groups or public opinion surveys.[43] Themes as well as styles of presentation are tried out before likely voters. What messages are most appealing? When and how often should particular ads be aired? Who should be targeted? How should ads best convey information?

The number of times an ad is broadcast is one of the most important strategic decisions made during the campaign. Professional ad buyers specialize in picking time slots and television shows advantageous for particular candidates. Whereas a candidate interested in appealing to senior citizens may air ads repeatedly during television shows catering to the elderly, youth-oriented politicians may run spots on Fox Network or MTV, and minority candidates may advertise on Black Entertainment Television. Obama, for example, advertised extensively on minority stations, whereas McCain broadcast ads on television shows with large older audiences, such as *NCIS*.

The content and timing of ads are crucial for candidates because of their link to overall success. Campaigns have become a blitz of competing ads, quick responses, and counter-responses. Ads have become serial in nature, with each ad building thematically on previous spots. Election campaigns feature strategic interactions as important as the individual ads themselves.

In the fast-changing dynamics of election campaigns, decisions to advance or delay particular messages can be quite important. Quick-response strategies require candidates to respond immediately when negative ads appear or political conditions are favorable. Candidates often play off each other's ads in an effort to gain the advantage with voters.

Advertising and the News Media

One of the developments of the contemporary period has been coverage of political advertising by reporters. Network news executive William Small described this as the most important news trend of recent years: "Commercials are now expected as part of news stories."[44] Many news outlets have even launched "ad watch" features. These segments, aired during the news and discussed in newspaper articles, present the ad, along with commentary on its accuracy and effectiveness. The most effective ads are those whose basic messages are reinforced by the news media.

Scholars traditionally distinguished the free from the paid media. Free media meant reports from newspapers, magazines, radio, and television that were not billed to candidates. The paid media encompassed commercials purchased by the candidate on behalf of the campaign effort. The two avenues of communications were thought to be independent in terms of effects on viewers because of the way viewers saw them.

But the increase in news coverage of advertising has blurred or even eliminated this earlier division between free and paid media. People who separate the effects of these communications channels need to recognize how intertwined the free and paid media have become. It is now quite common for network news programs to rebroadcast entertaining, provocative, or controversial ads. Even entertainment shows are filled with references to contemporary politics. Journalists and entertainers have begun to evaluate the effects of campaign commercials, and it has become clear that the free media provide significant audiences for television ads.

Ads broadcast for free during the news or discussed in major newspapers have several advantages over those aired purely as commercials. One strength is that viewers traditionally have trusted the news media—at least in comparison with paid ads—for fairness and objectivity. William McGuire has shown that the credibility of the source is one determinant of whether the message is believed.[45] The high credibility of the media gives ads aired during the news an important advantage over those seen as plain ads. Roger Ailes explained it this way: "You get a 30 or 40 percent bump out of [an ad] by getting it on the news. You get more viewers, you get credibility, you get it in a framework."[46]

The 2004 presidential election introduced a new category of advertisements—*phantom,* or *vapor, ads.* These are commercials produced and distributed to journalists but barely broadcast. Journalists complained that Kerry released half a dozen spots on topics such as health care, taxes, and the Iraq War that were never aired to the general public. This made the ads "video news releases purporting to be substantial paid advertising," according to reporters.[47]

In 2008, McCain and Obama did the same thing. One vapor ad by McCain attracted considerable media attention. Although it aired infrequently, it accused Obama of supporting comprehensive sex education for kindergarten children because of a law he had cosponsored while in the Illinois Senate. The ad was misleading because the intent of the legislation was to protect young kids from sexual predators, not to indoctrinate them with sexual content.

Commercials in the news guarantee campaigners a large audience and free air time. Opinion polls have documented that nearly two-thirds of Americans cite television as their primary source of news. This is particularly true for what is referred to as the "inadvertent audience"—those who are least interested in politics and among the most volatile in their opinions.[48]

But there can be disadvantages to having an ad aired during a newscast. When an ad is described as unfair to the opposition, media coverage undermines the sponsor's message. The advantages of airing an ad during the news can also be lost if reporters challenge the ad's factual accuracy.

During recent elections, though, journalists have tried in vain to keep up with the onslaught of negative and misleading appeals.[49] Both candidates in 2004 pushed the envelope of factual inaccuracy. For example, Kerry accused the Bush White House of having a secret plan to reintroduce a military draft and of wanting to privatize Social Security. Bush, meanwhile, complained that Kerry's health care program would create new federal bureaucracies and that Kerry thought terrorism was a nuisance like prostitution and gambling. In 2008, McCain broadcast a number of misleading ads, such as the sex education spot described above, and commercials saying Obama would raise taxes on middle-class families. This led to considerable media criticism alleging that these claims were misleading at best or downright inaccurate.[50]

Reporters write stories criticizing the candidates for misleading and inaccurate claims, but the sheer volume of ad expenditures and campaign trail rhetoric overwhelms press oversight.[51] Journalists simply cannot compete with the hundreds of times ads are broadcast by the candidates. Campaigners are very adroit at communicating directly with the public and ignoring critical press stories about their advertisements.

Changes in Public Opinion

Public opinion and voting behavior have undergone significant changes that are relevant to advertising. Voters are less trusting of government officials today than they were in the past. Whereas 23 percent of voters in 1958 agreed that you cannot trust the government to do what is right most of the time, 84 percent were untrusting at the turn of the twenty-first century. A significant bloc of voters does not identify with either one of the major parties.[52] These citizens are often the kind of voters who swing back and forth between the parties.

The independence of American voters and the volatility in American politics unleashed by corporate downsizing and the end of the Cold War have uprooted some parts of citizen attitudes. People's impressions of short-term political events can be fluid, and the issues or leadership qualities seen as most important at any given time can change.[53]

Each of these developments has altered the tenor of electoral campaigns and led to extensive efforts to appeal to undecided voters. Writing in the 1830s, Alexis de Tocqueville worried that the great masses would make "hasty judgments" based on the "charlatans of every sort [who] so well understand the secret of pleasing them."[54] The prominence today of an open electoral system filled with mistrusting voters and fast-paced ads has done nothing to alleviate this concern.

Conclusion

In short, there are many different things that affect the use, interpretation, and impact of campaign ads. No single perspective can explain why an ad works well at a particular time but may backfire in a different context. One must look at the political environment, the nature of public opinion, how reporters cover the ads, the way in which ads are edited and financed, and the strategies of stereotyping, association, demonization, and code words used by campaigners.

Chapter 2

Buying Air Time

The heart of a candidate's advertising strategy concerns decisions on when, where, and how often to broadcast ads. Candidates do not air all commercials with the same frequency. Some spots are aired repeatedly, whereas others are broadcast infrequently or targeted toward more narrowly defined areas. The choices of when and where to place commercials as well as how frequently particular spots are run influence how candidates are seen by the viewing public. These strategic determinations, called *ad buys,* have a profound effect on the outcome of elections. Few political actions have greater importance than these communications decisions.

The Case of John Connally

The importance of ad strategy is illustrated by the ill-fated presidential campaign of John Connally. Connally's 1980 race for the Republican nomination was one of the biggest flops in recent memory. He spent nearly $10 million on a campaign that netted just one delegate.[1] Connally was the Democratic governor of Texas from 1963 to 1969. On November 22, 1963, he was catapulted into national prominence for riding in the same car as President John F. Kennedy on the day Kennedy was fatally shot in Dallas. Connally sustained gunshot wounds himself, but he recovered and went on to build a successful political career.

Unhappy with the liberal drift of the Democratic Party, Connally switched parties in 1973 and was named secretary of the Treasury by Richard Nixon. Firmly ensconced in the Republican Party, Connally decided to make his own run for the presidency in 1980. Because he had high name recognition and the ability to raise large sums of money, Connally chose a national strategy for the nomination. Unlike George Herbert Walker Bush, then a little-known Republican who put nearly all his resources into Iowa and New Hampshire, Connally spread his financial resources across the country. In terms of advertising buys, Connally ran print ads in national news magazines and bought time on national television. His goal was to boost his name recognition nationwide and create an overwhelming clamor for his nomination.

But in following this strategy, Connally ignored the fundamentals of ad buys. As with any resource decision, candidates have to buy air time based on the dictates of the election calendar. The nominating process is sequential in nature, and reporters give disproportionate attention to early contests in Iowa and New Hampshire; therefore, candidates need to orient their ad buys to those locales. Connally violated this dictum and suffered a costly political defeat.

The Strategies of Ad Buying

Ad buys center primarily on ratings points, defined by Marilyn Roberts as "the percentage of individuals or households exposed to a particular television program at a specific time."[2] Each ratings point nationally represents around one million households. The goal of campaigners is to maximize gross ratings points, which is the rating for each spot times the number of times each spot has aired, for the least amount of money.

Candidates face four key choices in their ad buys. First, they must decide on how many issues to emphasize. The basic dilemma centers on the trade-off between many messages and few messages. The advantage of putting out many messages is that it allows a candidate to appeal to different types of voters and experiment with various alternatives until successful messages are found. The disadvantage lies in the risk that voters and news reporters will be confused by the diverse messages being run and not be able to get a clear view of where the candidate is coming from.

Such a potentially negative outcome leads some aspirants to follow the few-messages model instead. Under this approach, a relatively small number of themes are presented to voters through commercials, and these themes are repeated over and over. The strength of this strategy is clarity of the themes being presented, but the risk is that candidates will choose the wrong themes and have nothing to fall back on if their choices do not connect with likely voters.

Second, in keeping with recent emphasis on attack politics, candidates face decisions on when (and if) to air attack ads. Early attacks may enable a candidate to define an opponent before the opponent's own message is put out. But as Democrats Howard Dean and Richard Gephardt discovered in the 2004 Iowa caucuses, these attacks can backfire if the press or the public conclude the attacker is being unduly negative. Late attacks shield against backlash but may occur too late to define the campaign dialogue.

Third, candidates must choose how often to broadcast certain messages. Unlike other areas of human endeavor, repetition is a virtue in the advertising world. Because people do not pay close attention to politics, messages must be repeated frequently to be heard and internalized by viewers. Campaigners must decide which of the messages are most crucial and therefore most important to repeat during the race.

Fourth, decisions about the proper mix of national and local ad buys must be made in presidential races. This is not much of a dilemma during the nominating process. The state-centered nature of presidential primaries means that, Connally's national strategy to the contrary, almost all nomination buys are local.

In the general election, though, this strategic decision is quite important. Because the election takes place simultaneously in all fifty states plus the District of Columbia, and the Electoral College is guided by a winner-take-all system in every state except Maine and Nebraska, presidential aspirants must decide on an appropriate mix of national and local ad buys. National buys reach a wider audience, but they are very expensive. They also have the disadvantage of hitting all areas equally, regardless of political competitiveness. For these reasons, presidential candidates have begun to bypass national networks in their ad buys and purchase time directly from selected local stations. This allows candidates to target messages to particular audiences and emphasize geographic areas central to their election strategies.

How Ad Buys Go Wrong

Connally's case clearly represents bad judgment in ad buys, but it also demonstrates how easily such ill-fated decisions can be made. Ad buys are risky because air time must be purchased weeks before an election in order to get the most desirable broadcast slots. Television stations are required by law to sell federal candidates air time at the cheapest rate available, but federal regulations do not guarantee desirable slots unless the money is paid upfront. And candidates for state offices have no guarantee that stations will sell them time at any point. In the rapidly changing world of campaign politics, ad-buy choices that look good several months before an election may turn out poorly once the active campaign gets under way.

It is not enough to be on television with ads; instead, spots need to be placed around shows whose viewers are likely to be persuaded to vote for the candidate. Candidates must target the demographics of particular shows to build their electoral coalitions. Television shows vary dramatically in the numbers of senior citizens, African Americans, and women watching, and candidates must match their ad buys to time slots that make political sense for them.

In addition, there are turnout considerations. Candidates want to target citizens who are sympathetic and likely to vote. For this reason, political ads often appear around the evening news. The time before and after the news is most desirable because this is when the largest number of viewers interested in public affairs is watching. Because these are the individuals most likely to vote, this is an ideal time slot for election advertisements.

Ad-buy decisions are tricky because campaigns are not one-player games. Rather, they are contests in which each candidate's ads are assessed in light of what rival candidates are broadcasting. These strategic interactions, not just individual ads, determine how voters see the respective candidates. Campaigners may make ad buys that miss the mark before they see where and how often their opponents are running ads.

The Study of Ad Buys

It has been difficult in the past to study ad buys because of problems in getting adequate information. Material had to be compiled directly from candidates, the national networks, local television affiliates, or ad-buying services. Early efforts required researchers to collect ad-buy information directly from local stations and ad buyers.[3] Detailed logs had to be assembled based on how often specific ads aired in particular television markets. This was a tedious and time-consuming process that made it difficult to collect systematic data.

However, improved technology now allows researchers to track ad buys across the country. Unlike previous systems that depended on checking in personally with ad buyers or local station managers, a media buying firm, National Media, Inc., developed the Political Advertising, Reporting and Intelligence System (POLARIS). This technology uses "sound pattern recognition technology originally developed by the Pentagon to monitor, track, and report client schedules of buys, as well as those of the opponent."[4]

Under this system, computers monitor satellite transmissions by broadcast and cable networks and record commercials aired in each of the nation's top seventy-five media outlets. The system covers about 80 percent of the country as well as twenty-five major cable networks. Researchers then can use this information to see which spots are running in each market and how frequently.

Entering this material into a database allows analysis of how candidates are using their campaign advertisements. As discussed in the following sections, scholars can examine how often particular spots are broadcast, which geographic markets are targeted, what the mix of nationally and locally aired spots is, how opponents' ads affect ad-buy decisions, whether candidates spend their ad dollars early or late in the campaign cycle, and what the impact of these advertising decisions is on voters.

Ad Frequency and Diversification

The most important ad-buy decisions are how often to run ads and how many different spots to run. In 1992, independent candidate Ross Perot ran the largest number of different spots (twenty-nine in all). This was much greater than the seventeen different commercials Clinton broadcast in the fall and the nine ads Bush used. Of the three candidates, Bush used the fewest ads to convey the same message over and over again. In his mind, repetition was more of a virtue than diversification.

Bush's most widely used national ad was called "Agenda." This spot started running October 22, two weeks before the election. It ran sixty-four times nationally and featured Bush discussing his agenda for American renewal. The ad was notable because of its positive thrust. However, Bush's second and third most frequently aired ads ("Gray Dot" and "Federal Taxes") were negative spots that ran often in early and mid-October, when Bush was trying to regain the offensive by criticizing Clinton. The "Gray Dot" commercial ran forty times on network television and asserted that Clinton could not be trusted because he didn't believe in anything. According to the commercial, one candidate was in favor of term limits, and the other opposed them. The ad closed with a gray dot obliterating a picture of Clinton as a tagline said, "Too bad they're both Clinton." The "Federal Taxes" spot was broadcast twenty-five times nationally and claimed that if Clinton were elected, he would raise federal taxes.

Clinton's most frequently aired national ads included "Remember" (run forty-one times) and "Even" (broadcast twenty-three times). "Remember" built on Pat Buchanan's critique of Bush's economic record during the Republican primaries. It tied the poor economic performance under the Bush administration directly to the sitting president's 1990 tax flip-flop and the perception of his general insensitivity to the plight of the average person. "Even" was a positive ad listing a number of prominent economists who had endorsed Clinton's economic program.

In the 1996 presidential campaign, there were 57 million commercials aired in the top 75 American media markets from April 1 to November 4; 752,891 of these were political spots from the nomination and general election campaigns. Clinton and the Democratic National Committee (DNC) broadcast ads 93,167 times; Dole and the Republican National Committee (RNC) ran spots 72,861 times.[5] Twenty percent of the total ads aired (150,578 ads) were broadcast during the presidential general election campaign by the two major candidates and their respective national parties.

In 2000, Bush, Gore, and the two parties' national committees spent $127 million on television advertising between June 1 and Election Day. According to figures collected by Kenneth Goldstein of the University of Wisconsin and the Brennan Center for Justice at New York University, Republicans spent $65 million ($28.3 million by Bush, $36.3 million by the Republican Party, and $400,000 by outside groups) and Democrats spent $61.6 million ($21.2 million by Gore, $31 million by the Democratic Party, and $9.4 million by outside groups).[6]

For the first time in American electoral history, political parties outspent the candidates on television advertising. Typically, candidates broadcast the bulk of election spots because of their desire to control the content and timing of the message. However, in the wake of various court rulings that allowed party organizations to use large soft-money contributions to finance ads touting specific candidates, more of the ad sponsorship moved to the party committees.

Meanwhile, interest groups became more aggressive at contesting elections. In the presidential campaign, around $10 million was spent in independent expenditures by groups, the bulk of it on behalf of Democrats. Groups such as Planned Parenthood, the Sierra Club, Handgun Control, and various labor unions devoted millions to ads designed to influence voters in the presidential campaign. In addition, according to reports filed with the Internal Revenue Service, groups spent another $130 million on issue advocacy. Democratic activist Jane Fonda single-handedly contributed $11.7 million in gifts to tax-exempt groups designed to protect abortion rights.[7]

In 2004, George W. Bush spent a record $188 million on advertising, compared to the approximately $160 million that John Kerry devoted to campaign ads.[8] Overall, there were about four million ad airings at all levels of the campaign. Ohio and Florida represented the top ad targets, but the campaigns also spent considerable funds in Wisconsin, Pennsylvania, Nevada, Colorado, Iowa, Michigan, and Minnesota.

Interestingly, despite all the media attention to anti-Kerry advertising sponsored by the Swift Boat Veterans for Truth in August 2004, the group only paid for 739 airings in a small number of media markets (Charleston, Dayton, Green Bay, LaCrosse, Toledo, Wassau, and Youngstown). According to the Wisconsin Advertising Project, only 2.1 percent of the American population resided in those markets.

This made that ad purchase one of the most successful small ad buys in the history of American campaigns. According to a CBS News/*New York Times* national public opinion survey in mid-September, nearly two-thirds of voters said they had heard of the Swift Boat ads. Of voters familiar with the commercials, 33 percent indicated the ad charges against Kerry were true, while 47 percent said they were false.[9] This demonstrates the extent to which these ads were able to raise doubts about Kerry among one-third of the electorate.

The most dramatic feature of the 2008 television air wars was Obama's tremendous fund-raising advantage over McCain. Fueled by grassroots antagonism toward the Bush administration and innovative use of digital outreach, Obama raised more than $645 million in his presidential campaign, compared to $372 million for McCain. Of this amount, Obama spent around $170 million on political advertisements, while McCain devoted $110 million. This disparity allowed Obama to outspend McCain by a two-to-one or three-to-one margin in major battleground states. It also funded a thirty-minute prime-time presentation on seven national television networks the week before the election, a major ground game in key states emphasizing voter identification and get-out-the-vote efforts, and lots of old-fashioned door-to-door canvassing.

The two major political parties also made expenditures on behalf of their nominees. The RNC spent more than $10 million on ads promoting McCain, and the DNC spent a more modest half million dollars. In some cases, the party apparatus played the "bad cop" to the candidate's "good cop": Ads run by the parties generally took a tougher tone and employed more questionable claims regarding political vision and personal background. They sometimes said things that would have been politically difficult for the candidates to say. Interest groups were not as visible in 2008 as they had been in prior elections. There were lots of ads from Planned Parenthood, the National Rifle Association, Sierra Club, Freedom Defense Fund, Vote Vets, and MoveOn.org, but none attracted the prominence of the Swift Boat ads from 2004 and none had a discernible impact on the electoral result.

The National-Local Mix and Targeting Strategies

It used to be that candidates would buy time on national television networks and broadcast commercials to the entire nation. There was no targeting, and whoever happened to be watching television in various states would see the spots. The disadvantage of this approach was that it carried ads to all states regardless of whether they were leaning Republican or Democrat or swung between the two.

Now candidates either mix national and local television station ad buys or place all their ads on local stations so they can target particular areas. With satellite hookups, candidates have the technological means to beam spots to local stations across the country.

In the 1992 general election, both Bush and Perot spent most of their money on national ad buys. Perot made the most buys (205) in the fall, compared with Bush (189) and Clinton (143). Clinton's limited national ad-time buys were in keeping with his organization's decision to target eighteen states in the fall campaign. He and his staff consciously decided to run no ads in the remaining states either because his lead was secure in those areas or because the states had a clear history of going Republican in presidential elections.

In 1996, Clinton focused all his advertising on medium-sized markets in twenty-four swing states. In the Northeast, his campaign emphasized Maine and Connecticut. In the South, ads were broadcast in Florida, Georgia, North Carolina, Tennessee, Kentucky, Arkansas, and Louisiana. In the Midwest, spots appeared in Ohio, Pennsylvania, Michigan, Wisconsin, Illinois, Minnesota, Iowa, Kansas, and Missouri. Targeted Western states were California, Washington, Oregon, Nevada, New Mexico, and Colorado.

One DNC ad opened with Bob Dole proclaiming, "We sent him the first balanced budget in a generation. He vetoed it. We're going to veto Bill Clinton." An announcer then replied: "The facts? The president proposes a balanced budget protecting Medicare, education, the environment. But Dole is voting no. The president cuts taxes for forty million Americans. Dole votes no. The president bans assault weapons; demands work for welfare while protecting kids. Dole says no to the Clinton plans. It's time to say yes to the Clinton plans—yes to America's families."

Dole went through a three-stage strategy against Clinton. The first stage, starting at the Republican convention and continuing through the early part of September, emphasized an economic message based on Dole's 15-percent income tax cut proposal and Clinton's signature on what the Dole camp claimed, using numbers not adjusted for inflation, was the largest tax increase in U.S. history. The ad claimed that federal taxes had risen $1,500 for the typical American family and that was "a big price to pay for his broken promise." The next day, Clinton's team responded with an ad showing a 1984 Newt Gingrich quote saying Dole was the "tax collector for the welfare state," and a man responsible for "thirty-five years of higher taxes."

In mid-September, Dole shifted to a "drugs and crime" phase in which he criticized the president for rising drug use and crime rates during his presidency. By early October, Dole went to his end game, focusing attention on character issues and scandals, such as Whitewater, Travelgate, and the acceptance of campaign funds from foreign sources.

The Dole ad that talked about Clinton's MTV admission of wanting to inhale marijuana and having liberal drug policies aired 7,300 times on local television stations from September 16 to September 25, with 949 airings (13 percent) in Florida alone. The Dole campaign targeted shows aimed at women and senior citizens on the grounds that these people would be most upset about rising teenage drug usage. The ad buys were heavily concentrated in fourteen states: Florida, Arizona, Nebraska, Ohio, Michigan, Kentucky, Tennessee, Georgia, Iowa, Pennsylvania, Connecticut, New Mexico, Colorado, and California.

Clinton's response ad on this issue ran 4,600 times from September 16 to September 25, which represented double the ad-buy time of earlier ads. Clinton's ad buyers also paired their drug response ad with another ad claiming Dole was against Medicare, student loans, and a higher minimum wage.

By the end of this time period, the CNN/*USA Today* daily tracking poll showed Dole had closed the margin to ten points (49 percent for Clinton and 39 percent for Dole), which was the smallest Clinton lead that fall. Before this ad volley began, Clinton had held a seventeen-point lead with 53 percent of the vote, compared with Dole's 36 percent.[10] But this tightening did not hold up. By the following week, all of Dole's gains had proved to be short term.

Overall, there were interesting differences in the geographic areas targeted by Clinton and Dole. Clinton's top areas for ad buys from April 1 to November 4, 1996, were Albuquerque, New Mexico (3,079 spots aired); followed by Lexington, Kentucky (2,681 spots); and Sacramento, California (2,535 spots). Dole's top areas were Los Angeles (3,543 spots), Denver (2,727 spots), and Sacramento (2,635 spots).

In 2000, virtually no money was spent on national television network buys. Unlike in 1992, when the candidates spent $72 million on network advertising—fueled in part by Perot's spending spree, and 1996, when $34 million was devoted to national network ad buys, neither candidate spent much on the networks. In an era of highly targeted campaign appeals, both candidates preferred to buy time on local television stations in specific markets so that they could reach the desired voters.[11] It was a way to target messages to specific audiences in particular states.

Bush targeted twenty-one states for ads, whereas Gore focused on seventeen. The four states that featured only Republican commercials were North Carolina, Georgia, Nevada, and New Hampshire. Both sides spent heavily in the big battleground states: Michigan, Pennsylvania, Florida, Missouri, Washington, Wisconsin, Ohio, and Illinois. Neither devoted any effort in the first round of ad buys to California, although Republicans budgeted $8 million in ad spending there for the fall.[12] Both sides broadcast ads in Spanish in Florida, California, and New Mexico to court Hispanic voters. Republicans devoted $2 million to Spanish ads, whereas Democrats spent $1.75 million.[13]

In terms of targeted states, Bush's top areas for advertising included Pennsylvania, Florida, and Ohio, whereas Gore's top states were Pennsylvania, Ohio, and Michigan. Gore's top media markets based on number of ads aired included Philadelphia (4,762); Detroit (4,344); Portland, Oregon (4,248); and Seattle-Tacoma (4,085). Meanwhile, Bush's top markets were Seattle-Tacoma (3,490); Cleveland (3,026); Grand Rapids, Michigan (3,011); and Portland, Oregon (2,921). Bush spent around $5.5 million on California, and Gore spent nothing, but the Democrat still won the state comfortably.[14]

Similar patterns were found in 2004. With the exception of money spent on national cable news shows, nearly all the ad money was devoted to local buys in nineteen key states. These were the so-called *battleground states,* where the election was very competitive. Most other states were solid Democrat or Republican areas, so there was little reason to spend precious ad money in those locales.

The 2008 presidential election featured a different dynamic because more "swing" states were in electoral play. At the beginning of the general election campaign, nearly two dozen states were the objects of electoral jockeying. The nomination of a maverick Republican and an African American Democrat put such states as Virginia, Indiana, and Montana into play as never before. Of course, as the campaign wore on, ad expenditures targeted an increasingly small set of states, including Ohio, Pennsylvania, Florida, Wisconsin, Virginia, and Nevada.

As was the case in previous years, the vast bulk of the ad buys were targeted on key local markets in the most competitive states. Some of these were large, competitive states in the Midwest; others were Rocky Mountain states and a few southern states that had experienced demographic inflows from more Democratic locales. There were some interesting exceptions to this local ad-buy strategy. During the Olympics, both Obama and McCain ran commercials on national broadcast channels in order to reach the widest possible audience. Furthermore, each spent more than $4 million on national cable television ad buys.

In addition, the week before Election Day, Obama spent between $4 and $5 million on a minidocumentary outlining his vision for the future of the United States. With its emphasis on glistening wheat fields and personal vignettes from families harmed by Bush policies, the infomercial was Reaganesque in its approach to cinematography. More than thirty-three million people watched the piece, a record for this type of broadcast.

Strategic Interactions with the Opposition

Ever since Michael Dukakis reacted slowly to George Bush Sr.'s attacks on him in 1988, candidates have been advised to respond immediately to campaign attacks. Taking this lesson to heart, presidential candidates now pay close attention to opposition activities and adjust their own strategies in light of moves by their opponents. This is true both in terms of overall ad buys as well as responses to negative attacks. For example, in 1992, Clinton and Bush's daily national buys mirrored one another until the last two weeks, when Clinton began broadcasting twice as many spots as Bush.

The rapidity of these strategic interactions was partly a result of technological advances in production that allowed media consultants to develop new ads almost instantly and beam them via satellite to television stations across the country. But after the election, Clinton media adviser Frank Greer confessed that his campaign staff had been so fast in its counter-responses because members had intercepted Bush satellite transmissions of ads to local television affiliates and thereby had copies of the Bush ads *before* they were broadcast.[15]

In 2000, the two sides also adjusted rapidly to one another. The RNC aired an ad on behalf of Bush called "Priority MD" about prescription drug benefits. According to the announcer, "George Bush has a plan: Add a prescription drug benefit to Medicare. . . . And Al Gore? Gore opposed bipartisan reform. He's pushing a big-government plan that lets Washington bureaucrats interfere with what your doctors prescribe." The next day, the DNC responded with a spot criticizing Bush's prescription drug plan. An announcer said, "George Bush's approach leaves millions of seniors with no prescription drug coverage. . . . Al Gore is taking on the big drug companies to pass a real prescription drug benefit that covers all seniors."[16]

Democrats attacked Bush's Texas record as well. Whenever a governor runs for president (such as Carter in 1976, Reagan in 1980, Dukakis in 1988, Clinton in 1992, and Bush in 2000), the classic strategy is to criticize the level of performance within the state and blame the sitting chief executive. The DNC advertisement pointed out that "Texas ranks forty-ninth out of fifty in providing health coverage to kids. It's so bad a federal judge just ruled Texas must take immediate corrective action."[17] Never mind that these attacks on state performance rarely stuck. Of the five governors subject to this kind of criticism, four won.

At this point in the campaign, Republicans made a crucial strategic adjustment. Gore's unexpectedly strong showing in Florida required Bush to rethink his ad allocations. According to election handicapper Charles Cook at the time, "Bush is lightening up on California and going heavy in Florida. Gore is potentially lightening up on Pennsylvania and Illinois and going heavy in Florida and Ohio." Republicans had not expected Florida to be in play. They also thought Bush would be doing better in New Jersey, Pennsylvania, and Illinois than he was. Gore's lead in several large industrial states led Bush to shift toward smaller states, such as Arkansas (the home of Clinton), Tennessee (Gore's residence), New Hampshire, and West Virginia, all of which Bush ultimately won.[18]

With Gore ahead by a few percentage points in national tracking polls, the RNC attacked his personal credibility. In an ad targeted on Michigan and Pennsylvania, a female announcer intoned, "Al Gore is promising campaign finance reform. Can I believe him? Because of Gore's last fund-raising campaign, twenty-two people have been indicted, twelve convicted, seventy took the Fifth Amendment, and eighteen witnesses fled the country. Now Al Gore is promising more accountability in our schools. . . . Just more politics from Al Gore."[19]

In late October, Bush continued to question Gore's credibility. His ad stated, "Remember when Al Gore said his mother-in-law's prescription cost more than his dog's? His own aides said the story was made up. Now Al Gore is bending the truth again [on Social Security]." With the race locked in a dead heat, Gore launched the toughest ad of the campaign on Bush's readiness to lead. "As governor, George W. Bush gave Big Oil a tax break while opposing health care for 220,000 kids. Texas now ranks fifth in family health care. He's left the minimum wage at $3.35 an hour, let polluters police themselves. Today, Texas ranks last in air quality. Now Bush promises the same $1 trillion for Social Security to two different groups. He squanders the surplus on a tax cut for those making over $300,000. Is he ready to lead America?"[20]

At that point, Bush unleashed retired Gen. Norman Schwarzkopf, a hero of the Persian Gulf War, who made a series of automated phone calls and mailings to battleground states on the Social Security issue. Financed by $15 million in Bush expenditures, the general said, "I can promise you that George W. Bush will never do anything to hurt seniors or threaten Social Security. Don't be fooled by the scare tactics."[21]

According to a *Washington Post* tracking survey, voter sentiment turned in favor of Bush on October 24, and the GOP nominee retained a two- to three-point advantage for the duration of the campaign. By the end of the campaign, Bush led in every major tracking poll, except for a last-minute Zogby poll that gave Gore a narrow margin. That survey suggested some last-minute deciders might have been influenced by the late campaign disclosure that twenty-four years earlier, Bush had been arrested for driving under the influence of alcohol. Ultimately, Bush lost the popular total by a half million votes but after a lengthy court battle over the Florida results, he captured a majority in the Electoral College.

In 2004, both major candidates jockeyed for advantage amidst a political climate buffeted by the domestic economy, the September 11 attacks on the World Trade Center and the Pentagon, and the Iraq War. Throughout the campaign, polls indicated a very close race. During the spring and summer, Bush's advertisements characterized Kerry as a flip-flopper who changed his position on key issues to suit his political needs. In conjunction with ads sponsored by the Swift Boat Veterans for Truth, Republicans attacked Kerry's service record and argued he was not to be trusted.

Initially, Kerry's campaign was slow to respond to these charges. Rather than pointing out that Bush also had changed his position on important issues (such as the creation of a homeland security department), Kerry chose silence, hoping the charges would go away. However, extensive media coverage accompanied Bush's criticisms, and in the fall, Kerry brought several old Clinton hands into the campaign and shifted to an attack strategy. From that point on, Democrats challenged Bush's record on job creation, the Iraq War, protecting Social Security, and providing flu shots for needy citizens.

In 2008, the political climate had shifted from concern over international terrorism to a major financial meltdown of leading companies and a weak domestic economy. Similar to 1992, the election theme became "It's the Economy, Stupid." McCain's efforts to attack Obama as a celebrity comparable to Paris Hilton or as a tax-and-spend liberal did not resonate with voters. Instead, they saw McCain as someone not likely to bring real change to Washington and someone too close to President George W. Bush.

Early Advertising

The conventional wisdom in political campaigns is to save the bulk of your advertising expenditures for the end of the race, when undecided voters are tuning in and the campaign is therefore in the strongest position to influence them. This was Clinton's strategy in 1992 against Bush. Unlike the sitting president who suffered electorally from a dismal economy, Clinton had the luxury as the front-runner in pre-election polls of saving his most frequently aired ads for the last two weeks of the campaign. Whereas Bush started big national buys in late September, Clinton's biggest buys began on October 22, two weeks before Election Day. His most prominent ad at this time was the attack spot "Remember." Clinton's "Even" spot started October 28 and ran each day for the rest of the campaign. On October 29, Clinton also started buying national time for his "Senator Nunn" ad discussing how he and Al Gore represented new-style Democrats who supported capital punishment and a new way of thinking about social problems.

However, in 1996, Clinton shifted to an early advertising strategy. Two years earlier, Republicans had surprised the experts by winning control of Congress. Led by Speaker Newt Gingrich, the GOP embarked on a bold policy restructuring called the "Contract with America." This contract proposed downsizing government, cutting taxes, and getting tougher on criminals.

Sensing that Republicans had overreached and taking advantage of the fact that the GOP nominee was Dole, who also had served with Gingrich in Congress as the Senate majority leader, Clinton started his presidential advertising campaign in 1995, a year and a half before the general election. While Republicans were attacking one another, Clinton had an uncontested renomination. Through soft money ads financed by the DNC, Clinton spent $15 million in 1995 alone on ads promoting his candidacy and attacking the GOP. These spots argued that Clinton was the remaining safeguard against Republican extremism in the areas of Medicare, Medicaid, and the environment.

As Republicans settled their nomination on Dole, the DNC launched another torrent of attack ads for Clinton in mid-March against a Dole campaign that was literally out of money due to the competitive primaries. From March 7 to March 18, Democrats made 2,500 ad buys in forty-two cities—two and a half times the number of ad buys for Dole during this period.[22] From March 1 to June 14, the DNC and Clinton's reelection committee ran more than 17,000 ads. The ads targeted shows from *CBS Sunday Morning* to daytime talk shows such as *Live with Regis and Kathie Lee*.[23]

The 1996 presidential contest demonstrates the value of early ad spending to set the agenda of a campaign. Political communications experts long have argued that such expenditures were wasted money, believing that no one pays attention to campaigns fifteen months before the election and that the only people who decide how they are going to vote that early are strong partisans with well-defined political views. These are not the type of voters one would predict to be very susceptible to advertising. But through early spending and a clear Democratic advantage in ad expenditures throughout the winter of 1995 and the spring and summer of 1996,

Clinton framed the election as a referendum on the "Republican Revolution" of downsizing government and coasted to an easy reelection. According to a Clinton summary of 1995 Democratic polls designed to measure the impact of early advertising, "In these areas where we have shown these ads, we are basically doing 10 to 15 points better than in the areas where we are not showing them, and these areas include areas not all of them friendly to me."[24]

In 2004, President George W. Bush sought an early knockout against John Kerry. On March 4, right after Kerry had accumulated enough delegates for his party's nomination, Bush began broadcasting $60 million in ads in nineteen states questioning Kerry's background, character, and leadership abilities. One commercial claimed Kerry would "raise taxes by at least $900 billion" and "weaken the Patriot Act used to arrest terrorists and protect America." The spot ended with the tagline: "John Kerry: Wrong on taxes. Wrong on defense."

According to an analysis of Bush's 2004 ad buys undertaken by Ken Goldstein of the Wisconsin Advertising Project, around 60 percent of the Bush buys were for negative attacks on Kerry. The most negative months for Bush's commercials were July (100 percent negative), October (90 percent negative), and April (80 percent negative). His least negative months were June (0 percent negative), September (15 percent negative), and March (35 percent negative).[25]

Reeling from a bruising primary battle with Howard Dean, Richard Gephardt, and John Edwards, it took Kerry nearly two months to raise enough money to respond to Bush. By early May, he had the funding to purchase $25 million in air time. Rather than criticizing Bush directly, Kerry followed the classic advertising strategy of introducing himself to voters. Taking advantage of his personal life story, Kerry discussed his background as a soldier in the Vietnam War and his twenty years of service in the U.S. Senate, where he had fought for children's health care and supported a balanced budget amendment.

In contrast to Bush, only 5 percent of Kerry's advertisements were negative. Kerry was more likely to use contrast ads that showed differences between him and Bush. His most negative month for advertising was October, during which 10 percent of his ad buys were in attack mode; most other months had very small percentages of attack ads.[26] Because of their large campaign war chests, both Bush and Kerry had sufficient funds to communicate with voters throughout the campaign and avoid the classic trade-off between early and late advertisements.

TABLE 2-1
*Ad Spending by Obama and Clinton in 2008
Primaries and Caucuses (in millions)*

States	Obama	Clinton
Iowa	9.7	7.5
New Hampshire	7.0	6.4
Nevada	1.3	.862
South Carolina	1.6	1.5
Super Tuesday states*	13.2	10.2
Louisiana, Nebraska, Washington	.664	.203
Maryland, Virginia, D.C.	2.0	.573
Wisconsin, Hawaii	1.5	.328
Ohio, Texas, Rhode Island	14.5	7.8
Mississippi	.433	.07
Pennsylvania	10.7	4.9

Source: Jim Rutenberg, "Its Candidates Otherwise Engaged, Democratic Party Goes after McCain," *New York Times*, April 29, 2008, A16.

*The Super Tuesday states are Alabama, Arizona, Arkansas, California, Connecticut, and Georgia.

The long 2008 Democratic nominating battle between Obama and Clinton produced record expenditures on campaign advertising. One noteworthy aspect of this battle was that Obama outspent Clinton on ads in virtually every primary and caucus state. Table 2-1 shows the differences in ad spending between the candidates throughout the country during the primary campaigns.[27]

According to the Wisconsin Advertising Project analysis of TNS Media Intelligence/Campaign Media Analysis Group ad-buy data, nearly $200 million was spent on campaign advertising by the leading presidential contenders, $135 million by Democrats and $57 million by Republicans. This included $75 million by Barack Obama, $46 million by Hillary Clinton, $32 million by Mitt Romney, and $11 million by John McCain.

Overall, there were 301 different candidate-produced advertisements, 195 by Democratic candidates and 106 by Republican aspirants. This included seventy-nine ads by Hillary Clinton, forty-nine by Barack Obama, thirty-two by John Edwards, eleven by Bill Richardson, thirteen by Chris Dodd, seven by Joe Biden, two by Dennis Kucinich, and two by Mike Gravel. On the Republican side, Mitt Romney aired forty-two different ads, compared to twenty-three by John McCain, seventeen by Rudy Giuliani, six by

Mike Huckabee, six by Fred Thompson, nine by Ron Paul, and one each by Duncan Hunter, Sam Brownback, and Tom Tancredo.

However, the candidate who spends the most on advertising does not always triumph. On the Republican side, Mitt Romney outspent McCain by a huge margin, yet still lost the nomination. In Iowa, Romney purchased 8,059 ad buys, compared to 1,371 for Mike Huckabee and 1,164 for Fred Thompson. In New Hampshire, Romney broadcast 6,790 ads, compared to 2,675 for Rudy Giuliani, 2,525 for John McCain, and 90 by Huckabee (based on Campaign Media Analysis Group data). From January to November 2007, Romney ran 17,173 television spots nationwide, compared to 945 for McCain. Overall, in the 2007–2008 campaign cycle, Romney broadcast ads around 35,000 times, about half of all the ads aired by Republican candidates.[28]

The extended conflict between Democrats in the nominating process gave GOP candidate John McCain extra months to go after his Democratic opponents. While the two Democrats were sniping at one another, Republican Party operatives in North Carolina ran an ad called "Extreme" in which they used video footage of Obama's hometown minister, the Rev. Jeremiah Wright, making inflammatory racial statements to argue of Obama that "he's just too extreme for North Carolina."[29] McCain denounced this controversial ad and asked the GOP to pull it from the airwaves.

In the fall, the candidates devoted the majority of their ad dollars to key battleground states and local markets. The top states for advertising dollars are summarized in Table 2-2, and the local markets in which Obama and McCain bought the most ads are displayed in Table 2-3. In the general election, Obama broadcast eighty-five different ads, compared to sixty-three for McCain, but it was the sheer size of Obama's ad spending advantage over the Arizona senator, combined with a public opinion climate centering on domestic economic issues, that helped him secure his victory.

The Impact on Voters: The Two Cases of Ross Perot

Ad buys can make an enormous difference in how voters see the candidates. This is illustrated by Perot's great success in 1992 and subsequent dismal failure in 1996. In 1992, Perot started his national ad campaign on October 10 with his "Kids" ad noting the build-up of national debt being left to the country's children. He added the "Storm" spot on October 14 and broadcast it heavily

TABLE 2-2
Top States for Advertising Expenditures, Fall 2008 (in millions)

	Obama	McCain
Florida	4.615	1.441
Pennsylvania	2.742	1.388
Virginia	2.45	.637
Ohio	1.984	.753
Missouri	1.105	.437
North Carolina	1.094	.537

Source: Ken Goldstein, "Obama Outspending McCain 3 to 1 on TV," unpublished press release, October 31, 2008.

TABLE 2-3
Top Local Markets for Ad Buys, 2008 Presidential Campaign

Obama	McCain
Philadelphia, Pa. (978)	Tampa, Fla. (519)
Tampa, Fla. (685)	Orlando, Fla. (506)
Washington, D.C. (661)	Des Moines, Iowa (447)
Las Vegas, Nev. (628)	Reno, Nev. (410)
LaCrosse, Wisc. (601)	Albuquerque, N.M. (396)

Source: Ken Goldstein, "Obama Outspending McCain 3 to 1 on TV," unpublished press release, October 31, 2008.

until October 26. Beginning on October 28 and for the rest of the race, Perot emphasized his "We Can Win" and "How to Vote" spots. His ads rarely mentioned his opponents by name but rather emphasized the need for action to solve pressing national problems.

Perot's top ads were "Storm" (run twenty-three times), "Purple Heart" (run sixteen times), and "We Can Win" and "How to Vote" (each run fourteen times). "Storm" was an emotional spot that showed storm clouds approaching while an announcer talked about the country's problems being unaddressed. "Purple Heart" also was an emotional ad that told the story of a Vietnam veteran who had lent a purple heart to Perot for the campaign as a sign of his trust and confidence in the candidate. "We Can Win" appeared late in the campaign and talked about how Perot could win the race and take action as president to break the logjam in Washington.

Perot's ad buys played a key role in his strong finish of 19 percent of the 1992 vote. Because he reentered the race in early October, he was able to spend nearly all his advertising dollars in the last three weeks of the campaign, thereby far outspending either Bush or Clinton during that crucial period. This saturation of the airwaves made his commercials unusually memorable for viewers and helped create positive impressions of his leadership abilities.

However, Perot was not able to replicate this success in 1996. Shut out of the debates and unable to make electoral inroads, Perot was a non-factor in the campaign. Unwilling to spend as much of his own money as he had in 1992, Perot had to save about 75 percent of his $29 million in public monies for the last three weeks of the campaign. This meant that he was buying around $1.1 million of ads and infomercials each day. The night before the election, Perot bought thirty-minute infomercials on CBS and NBC and an hour on ABC, at a total cost of $2 million. However, in the end, he was able to garner only 8 percent of the vote.[30]

Conclusion

Ad buys form the strategic heart of presidential candidates' advertising strategies. Through decisions on when, where, and how often to broadcast ads, candidates present positive images of themselves and attack the opposition. These decisions help campaigners frame an election and set the political agenda. Ultimately, ad buys determine who wins the campaign.

Although ads are the major vehicle for candidate communication, neither party relies solely on the air war. Instead, party organizers and sympathetic groups supplement television advertising with a highly targeted ground war using such communication tactics as phone calls and direct mail. In the 2000 election, Bush campaign manager Karl Rove estimated that in the ten days leading up to the national election, the GOP made 70 million phone calls, mailed 110 million letters, and organized an army of 243,000 volunteers.[31] On the Democratic side, unions, environmentalists, and pro-choice activists devoted a similar effort on behalf of favored candidates. Increasingly, the air war is being joined by a ground war of highly targeted communications.

Chapter 3

Ad Messages

Candidates do not choose their advertising messages lightly. Most campaigners develop commercials based on game plans that outline the desired targets of the campaign as well as the themes and issues to be addressed. Candidates often test basic messages through polls and focus groups.

Ronald Reagan's campaign manager Ed Rollins said in reference to the 1984 campaign against Walter Mondale: "We made some fundamental decisions . . . to take [Mondale] on the tax issue . . . to try to drive [his] negatives back up. . . . The decision was to go with two negative commercials for every one positive commercial. . . . Let me say the commercials clearly worked, we drove [Mondale's] negatives back up again, the tax thing became the dominant issue at least in our polling, and it helped us get ready for the final week of the campaign."[1]

As campaigns have opened up and nominating battles have become common, the strategic aspect of electoral appeals has emerged as a major determinant. Candidates face more choices than at any previous point in American history. A system of presidential selection based on popular support places a premium on these decisions. Campaigners who pursue the wrong constituencies, go on the attack prematurely, or address noncrucial issues end up in political oblivion.

For these reasons, it is instructive to look at ad content and style of presentation with an eye toward strategic behavior. Do ad messages vary by party? How have candidates' presentations changed over time? Are there differences in electronic appeals at different stages of a campaign? What messages are communicated via Internet ads and candidate Web sites?

Ad Content

The classic criticism of American ads was written by Joe McGinniss following Richard Nixon's 1968 presidential campaign. Nixon entered that race with a serious image problem. His previous loss in 1960 and public impressions of him during a long career in public service led many to believe he was a sour, nasty, and mean-spirited politician. His advisers therefore devised an advertising strategy meant to create a "new" Nixon. McGinniss, who had unlimited access to the inner workings of Nixon's advertising campaign, described the strategy: "America still saw him as the 1960 Nixon. If he were to come at the people again, as [a] candidate, it would have to be as something new; not this scarred, discarded figure from their past. . . . This would be Richard Nixon, the leader, returning from exile. Perhaps not beloved, but respected. Firm but not harsh; just but compassionate. With flashes of warmth spaced evenly throughout."[2]

The power of this portrait and the anecdotes McGinniss was able to gather during the course of the campaign helped create a negative impression of political ads that has endured to this day. (The American electorate felt betrayed by this recasting of Nixon as a "good guy" after the Watergate scandal came to light and he resigned from office, feeling that initial impressions of him had been correct.) For example, Robert Spero describes the "duping" of the American voter in his book analyzing "dishonesty and deception in presidential television advertising."[3] Others have criticized ads for being intentionally vague and overly personalistic in their appeals.

Political commercials do not have a great reputation among voters either. A CBS News/*New York Times* survey during the 1988 presidential general election asked those exposed to ads how truthful they considered commercials for each candidate. The George H. W. Bush ads and Michael Dukakis ads scored the same: Only 37 percent felt they were mostly truthful. The remainder believed that campaign commercials were either generally false or had some element of falsehood. Even more interesting were overall beliefs about the impact of television ads. People believed that ads were most effective in influencing general feelings about the candidates and least effective in the communication of substantive information. Fifty percent said ads made them feel good about their candidate, whereas only 25 percent said ads had given them new information about the candidates during the fall campaign.[4]

Studies of the effects of ads have rarely paid much attention to the dimensions of evaluation. Many criticisms of commercials have failed to define the elusive notion of substance or distinguish it from image-oriented considerations. This problem notwithstanding, several efforts have been made to investigate the content of ads and assess the quality of the information presented to viewers.[5] In keeping with the interest in issue-based voting and recognizing the centrality of policy matters to democratic elections, much of the work on ad content has focused on the treatment of issues. Given popular beliefs about the subject, it is surprising to note that most of the research has found that ads present more substantive information than viewers and journalists generally believe.

Richard Joslyn wrote a study of television spot ads aired during contested general election campaigns. He measured whether political issues were mentioned during the ads. His research revealed that 79.6 percent of presidential ads mentioned issues. Based on this work, he argued that "political spot ads may not be as poor a source of information as many observers have claimed."[6]

Others have reached similar conclusions. Richard Hofstetter and Cliff Zukin discovered in their analysis of the 1972 presidential race that about 85 percent of the candidates' ads included some reference to issues. In comparison, only 59 percent of the news coverage of George McGovern and 76 percent of the news coverage of Nixon had issue content. Likewise, Thomas Patterson and Robert McClure demonstrated in a content analysis of the 1972 race that issues received more frequent coverage in commercials than in network news coverage. Michael Robinson and Margaret Sheehan reported in regard to 1980 CBS news coverage that 41 percent of the lines of news transcript contained at least one issue mention, which was lower than what appeared in ads.[7]

These projects have attracted considerable attention because they run contrary to much of the popular thinking and press criticism about media and politics. The findings are reassuring because they challenge conventional wisdom warning of the dangers of commercials. Rather than accepting the common view, which emphasizes the noneducational nature of ads, these researchers claim that commercials offer relevant information to voters.

But it remains to be seen whether the results stand up over time. In addition, past research has ignored the variety of ways in which substantive messages can be delivered, beyond direct policy mentions.[8] For example, character and personal qualities are increasingly seen as vital to presidential performance. It is therefore important to assess the full range of ad content to reach more general conclusions about the rhetoric of candidates.

Prominent Ads

The study of ad content is complicated because not all ads are equally important. A random sample has the unfortunate tendency to weight important, frequently aired ads the same as less important ads. The failure to distinguish prominent from less important commercials is troubling, because in each presidential year certain ads attract more viewer and media attention than others. In addition to being aired more frequently, prominent ads are discussed and rebroadcast by the media. Owing to the general noteworthiness of these ads and their heightened exposure through the free media, they are the most likely to influence voters. It makes sense to more closely investigate commercials generally regarded as the crucial ones in particular campaigns.[9]

For this text, I studied prominent ads as defined by Kathleen Hall Jamieson, the leading historian of political advertisements. For every presidential campaign since 1952, Jamieson, on an election-by-election basis, has described the presidential campaign ads that were newsworthy, entertaining, flamboyant, or effective. I used her detailed histories to compile a list of prominent spot ads from 1952 to 1988. For 1992 to 2008, I defined prominent ads as those broadcast in *CBS Evening News* stories.[10]

My list is a complete enumeration of the most prominent spots cited by Jamieson, and for the last five presidential elections, aired during the *CBS Evening News*.[11] A perusal of *New York Times* and *Washington Post* coverage of political ads reveals that Jamieson was generally successful in identifying the commercials that attracted media attention. The commercials included in this analysis come from both the presidential nominating process and the presidential general election.

For these ads, codes were compiled for each commercial based on election year, type of election (presidential general election or nominating stage), sponsoring party (Republican, Democrat, or other), and ad content. Ad messages were classified into the areas of domestic concerns, international affairs, personal qualities of the candidates, specific policy statements, party appeals, and campaign process. Specific policy appeals involved clear declarations of past positions or expectations about future actions. General categories were subdivided into more detailed types of appeals. Domestic concerns included the economy; social welfare; social issues; crime, violence, and drugs; race and civil rights; taxes and budgets; corruption and government performance; and energy and the environment. International affairs consisted of war and peace, foreign relations, national security and defense, and trade matters. Personal qualities included leadership, trustworthiness and honesty, experience and competence, compassion, independence, and extremism. Party appeals were based on explicit partisan messages (such as the need to elect more Republicans) and references to party labels. Campaign appeals included references to strategies, personnel matters within the campaign, electoral prospects, and organizational dynamics.

The Paucity of Policy Appeals

Issue information in advertising can be assessed either as *action statements* or as *policy mentions.* The former refers to specific policy statements—that is, clear statements of past positions or expectations about future actions. For example, Reagan's 1980 ad promising a "30 percent federal tax cut" that would benefit every group and offer the government a gain in revenue was an action statement. Lyndon Johnson's criticism of Barry Goldwater for past statements proposing that Social Security become a voluntary retirement option was a specific policy mention, although Johnson never made clear whether Goldwater still supported this proposal. (One of the ads supplied the dates of Goldwater's statements.)

Few discussions of domestic or international matters reach this level of detail, however. The more common approach is the policy mention, in which general problems within the economy, foreign relations, or government performance are discussed, but no specific proposals to deal with the matter are made. For example, a Dwight Eisenhower ad about the economy in 1952 showed a woman holding a bag of groceries and complaining, "I paid $24 for these groceries—look, for this little." Eisenhower then said, "A few years ago, those same groceries cost you $10, now $24, next year $30. That's what will happen unless we have a change." [12] This commercial obviously does not suggest a plan for combating inflation, although it does portray the painfulness of price increases.

As seen in Table 3-1, prominent ads were more likely to emphasize personal qualities (34 percent), domestic performance (26 percent), and

TABLE 3-1
Content of Prominent Ads, 1952–2008

Appeal	Overall	Republican	Democrat	Other
Personal qualities	34%	32%	40%	15%
Domestic performance	26	26	24	33
Specific domestic policy	24	27	19	39
Specific foreign policy	4	2	5	3
International affairs	6	9	3	3
Campaign	5	3	8	6
Party	1	2	1	0
N	(544)	(268)	(238)	(33)

Sources: Kathleen Jamieson, *Packaging the Presidency,* 2nd ed. (New York: Oxford University Press, 1992) for 1952–1988 campaigns, and *CBS Evening News* tapes for 1992–2008 campaigns.

Note: Entries indicate the percentage of ads devoted to each type of appeal.

specific domestic policy appeals (24 percent). Ads for Republicans included more specific pledges (29 percent) than did ads for Democrats (24 percent). Those for Republicans were more likely to emphasize international affairs (9 percent) than were those for Democrats (3 percent). In contrast, ads for Democrats were much more likely to emphasize personal qualities (40 percent) than were those for Republicans (32 percent). Ads sponsored by third parties and interest groups were the most substantive, with 42 percent of them featuring specific domestic or foreign policy appeals.

These differences reflect interests within each party and have consequences for how the parties are viewed by the public. The greater attention paid by Republicans to international affairs and by Democrats to domestic areas is consistent with each party's general platform. It helps to explain why Democrats are viewed as weak on foreign policy and Republicans are seen as inattentive to domestic matters. Outside groups and third parties, such as the Green, Libertarian, and Reform Parties, tend to be substantive because their political mobilization is based at least in part on discontent with the status quo and advocacy of a particular policy stance.[13]

Shifts over Time

There is little reason to treat all elections the same or assume that every contest engenders the same types of advertising appeals. Based on obvious differences in strategic goals among presidential aspirants

Figure 3-1   Prominent Ad Content by Election Year, 1952–2008

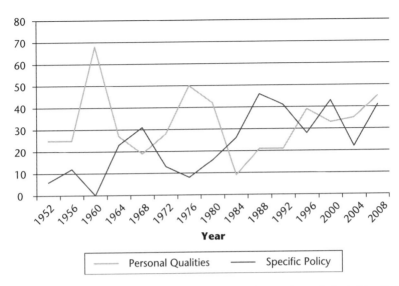

Sources: For 1952–1988, Kathleen Jamieson, *Packaging the Presidency,* 2nd ed. (New York: Oxford University Press, 1992), and for 1992–2008, *CBS Evening News* tapes.

and shifts in voters' priorities over the years, one would expect extensive fluctuations in commercials from election to election. To see exactly how advertising messages have changed, it is necessary to study ads from a series of elections.

Some analysts believe that ads have become less policy oriented and more personality based in recent years. When one looks at changes in policy appeals, it is obvious that prominent ads run during specific campaigns were more substantive than those run during others (Figure 3-1). For example, 26 percent of commercials in 1984, 46 percent in 1988, and 41 percent in 1992 included specific statements about public policy. In 2000, 43 percent of ads featured policy-specific statements, up from the preceding two elections. This dropped to 22 percent in 2004, but rose back to 41 percent in 2008.

The only other elections during which specific policy messages were common were 1964 (23 percent) and 1968 (31 percent). However, as has been found in other areas of research, the 1960s were an anomaly in terms of specific policy mentions. The more common pattern in earlier historical periods was a relatively low level of specificity.

Ads based on personal qualities reached their high point in 1960 (68 percent of all appeals), 1976 (50 percent), and 1980 (42 percent) but dropped back to lower levels of 9 percent in 1984 and 21 percent in 1988 and 1992. In 1996, however, nearly twice as many appeals were based on personal qualities (39 percent) than in 1988 or 1992. This change reflects attacks during the nominating process on experience and qualifications and, in the case of Bill Clinton in 1996, honesty and integrity. In 2000, with George W. Bush's attacks on Al Gore's integrity and Gore's criticisms of Bush's inexperience, 33 percent of ad appeals centered on personal qualities. In 2004, 35 percent of the pitches were based on personal characteristics, and in 2008, 45 percent focused on personal dimensions. In that election, McCain devoted extensive attention to attacks on Obama's inexperience.

Races placing the greatest emphasis on personal qualities involved challengers who were either unknown or inexperienced. For example, in 1960 many questions were raised about the qualifications and experience of John F. Kennedy. Similarly, ads during the Gerald Ford–Jimmy Carter contest in 1976, the Reagan–Carter–John Anderson campaign in 1980, the George H. W. Bush–Clinton–Ross Perot race of 1992, and the George W. Bush–Gore contest of 2000 devoted a great deal of attention to personal characteristics, such as leadership, trustworthiness, and experience. The same thing happened in 2008 when the Senate veteran John McCain faced the relatively inexperienced Barack Obama. McCain sought to highlight Obama's inexperience by saying the Democrat was not ready for presidential leadership and was likely to be tested in foreign crises he was not prepared to face.

It is interesting to examine variations in ad categories over time. Table 3-2 presents the breakdowns of prominent ads for the broad categories of domestic matters (specific domestic policy appeals combined with general domestic performance), international affairs (both specific and general mentions), personal qualities, party appeals, and campaign-related messages. Party appeals were stronger in the 1950s than in any period since then. Twelve percent of prominent ads in 1956 emphasized appeals to party, the highest level of any election in this study. In fact, for many elections from 1960 through 2008, no prominent ads featured direct party pitches.

The 1956 election may have been a high point in terms of the strength of party appeals in the post–World War II era. The classic study of voting behavior, *The American Voter*, argued that party identification was the dominant structuring principle of public opinion.[14] In the 1950s, it made sense for candidates to incorporate partisan pitches in their television advertising: Partisanship allowed

TABLE 3-2

Detailed Breakdowns of Prominent Ads, 1952–2008

	1952	1956	1960	1964	1968	1972	1976	1980	1984	1988	1992	1996	2000	2004	2008
Domestic Matters	62%	62%	24%	39%	30%	46%	38%	44%	68%	58%	68%	59%	60%	30%	44%
Economy	50	25	12	0	0	8	17	31	30	7	8	4	0	9	16
Social welfare	6	25	12	31	12	18	3	6	4	3	11	9	30	17	4
Social issues	0	0	0	0	6	0	0	2	4	0	19	4	4	0	9
Crime, violence, drugs	0	0	0	4	12	3	6	0	0	41	11	16	4	0	1
Race, civil rights	0	0	0	0	0	0	0	0	0	0	0	4	0	4	0
Taxes, budgets	0	0	0	0	0	12	6	5	26	0	17	20	7	0	12
Corruption, government performance	6	12	0	4	0	5	6	0	0	0	2	2	4	0	0
Energy, environment	0	0	0	0	0	0	0	0	4	7	0	0	11	0	2
International Affairs	6	0	6	19	37	21	3	11	17	10	6	0	0	31	6
War and peace	6	0	0	15	25	8	3	3	4	0	2	0	0	22	4
Foreign relations	0	0	6	4	12	5	0	2	4	3	2	0	0	0	1
National security, defense	0	0	0	0	0	8	0	6	9	7	0	0	0	9	1
Trade matters	0	0	0	0	0	0	0	0	0	0	2	0	0	0	0
Personal Qualities	24	24	69	27	18	29	50	41	8	20	21	39	31	34	45
Leadership	6	0	25	0	0	5	3	8	0	0	2	13	9	4	14
Trustworthiness, honesty	6	0	0	0	6	0	31	6	0	10	11	6	15	13	6
Experience, competence	0	12	25	4	6	8	8	18	0	3	2	7	7	9	11
Compassion	0	12	0	0	0	13	8	6	4	7	6	2	0	0	8
Independence	12	0	19	0	0	0	0	0	4	0	0	7	0	4	0
Extremism	0	0	0	23	6	3	0	3	0	0	0	4	0	4	6
Party	6	12	0	0	0	3	3	3	0	0	6	0	0	0	0
Campaign	0	0	0	16	12	3	9	0	4	10	6	3	4	4	5
N	(16)	(8)	(16)	(26)	(16)	(39)	(36)	(62)	(23)	(29)	(53)	(55)	(54)	(23)	(91)

Sources: Kathleen Jamieson, Packaging the Presidency, 2nd ed. (New York: Oxford University Press, 1992) for 1952–1988 campaigns, and CBS Evening News tapes for 1992–2008 campaigns.

them to win votes from the electorate. Hence, we see Republican Eisenhower and other members of his cabinet exhorting viewers to give them a "Republican Congress" and making other explicit appeals based on party leanings.[15]

However, after the 1950s, party loyalties in the American public began to decline. In their research, reported in *The Changing American Voter,* Norman Nie, Sidney Verba, and John Petrocik show how party identification and party-based voting ebbed in strength.[16] Independents began to rise as a percentage of the overall electorate, and candidates rarely made advertising appeals based on party. Candidates' messages were designed to appeal to the party base (such as GOP attacks on tax-and-spend Democrats and Democratic spots characterizing Republicans as uncaring and insensitive), but these messages were not framed explicitly in party terms.

Instead, advertising shifted toward other topics. Not surprisingly, given the nature of the times, war and peace issues rose during the Vietnam period. Fifteen percent of ads in 1964 and 25 percent in 1968 discussed war and peace topics. For example, in 1964, some of Johnson's advertising effort against Goldwater emphasized the dangers of war and Johnson's record of preserving the peace.

In the 1968 Democratic nominating race, print ads for Eugene McCarthy attacked Robert Kennedy for John Kennedy's decision to send troops to Vietnam: "There is only one candidate who has no obligations to the present policies in Vietnam and who is under no pressure to defend old mistakes there." Another noted that "Kennedy was part of the original commitment. . . . He must bear part of the responsibility for our original—and fundamentally erroneous—decision to interfere in Vietnam." In the general election, both Nixon and Hubert Humphrey ran spots emphasizing Vietnam. For example, Nixon tried to tie his Democratic opponent to the unpopular war. In contrast, a voice-over in a Humphrey ad criticized Nixon's refusal to discuss Vietnam: "Mr. Nixon's silence on the issue of Vietnam has become an issue in itself. He talks of an honorable peace but says nothing about how he would attain it. He says the war must be waged more effectively but says nothing about how he would wage it."[17]

Meanwhile, domestic economy and tax and budget matters attracted considerable attention in the late 1970s and the 1980s. In 1976, 17 percent of ads addressed economic concerns, whereas 31 percent in 1980 and 30 percent in 1984 touched on the economy. One has to harken back to the 1950s to find elections with as much emphasis on the economy. Tax and budget matters were also particularly popular. Republicans have repeatedly run ads challenging past Democratic performance, and Democrats have criticized Republican failures to deal with federal deficits.

There have been some interesting nonissues on the advertising front. Until 1992, advertisements on social issues, such as abortion, busing, and the Equal Rights Amendment, were not common.[18] With the exception of a George Wallace ad against school busing in 1968 and a 1980 Carter commercial in which actress Mary Tyler Moore told viewers Carter had "been consistently in favor of any legislation that would give women equal rights,"[19] political spots generally avoided these subjects because they were seen by candidates as divisive.

But a change of tactics in 1992 altered this situation, at least temporarily. Along with other challengers across the country, Indiana Republican congressional candidate Michael Bailey used graphic anti-abortion footage during his attempt to unseat pro-choice Democratic representative Lee Hamilton. The goal obviously was to attract media attention and raise public awareness. Yet there is little evidence in overall results that this effort worked. Of the thirteen congressional candidates in 1992 who relied on this tactic during the nominating process, only two won their primaries and none won in the general elections.[20]

In 1996, television advertising on the issue of abortion was used more extensively. Johnny Isakson, the leading Republican candidate for the U.S. Senate in Georgia, highlighted his support for abortion rights through an ad to distinguish himself from the other five Republicans in the primary. With his wife, Dianne, and their nineteen-year-old daughter, Julie, by his side, Isakson's spot took the unusual step of using a female announcer to attack his Republican opponents on the grounds that they would "vote to ban abortions, making criminals out of women and their doctors." But this appeal was not successful. Isakson lost the Republican primary.[21]

In 2000, 60 percent of ad appeals focused on domestic matters (especially health care and education) and 0 percent were devoted to international affairs. These results reflect the end of the Cold War and the fact that the country was at peace. Thirty-one percent of prominent commercials that year emphasized personal qualities.

During the 2004 contest, appeals were equally divided among personal qualities (34 percent), international affairs (31 percent), and domestic matters (30 percent). These percentages reflect an era in which the agenda was bifurcated between domestic and foreign policy controversies.

In 2008, ad pitches focused on leadership (14 percent), taxes and budget problems (12 percent), and personal experience (11 percent). Attention to domestic matters (44 percent) far exceeded time devoted to international affairs (6 percent). Even though the United States was involved in two wars in Iraq and Afghanistan, the country's financial meltdown during the fall of that year highlighted problems related to domestic economic and budget challenges.

The Impact of Campaign Stage

Television ads used to be the near-exclusive purview of presidential general elections. As noted in chapter 1, the nominating process was an elite-based activity in which party leaders exercised dominant control over delegate selection. Because voters were not central to the process, candidates made little use of television advertising. Much greater emphasis was placed on personal bargaining and negotiations with political leaders.

However, in recent years, advertising has become a prominent part of presidential nominating campaigns. Candidates spend a considerable amount of their overall campaign budget on advertising. Commercials have become a major strategic tool in the nominating process. Candidates use ads to convey major themes, make comments about the opposition, and discuss each other's personal qualities.

As pointed out previously, substantial differences exist between various stages of the campaign, and one might expect to find different appeals in the nominating and general election campaigns. In nominating contests, candidates of the same party compete for their party's nomination. There are often a number of candidates on the ballot. In contrast, general elections typically are two-person battles between major-party nominees. One can expect political commercials to emphasize different points at different stages.

Table 3-3 lists the distribution of prominent ad appeals from 1952 to 2008 by campaign stage. Personal qualities were used more often in the nominating campaign (43 percent) than in the general election (31 percent), although personalistic appeals were common in 2008, which is discussed in more detail in other parts of this text. For example, in 1980 Carter used so-called character ads to highlight the contrast between his own family life and that of his Democratic opponent, Massachusetts senator Edward Kennedy: "I don't

TABLE 3-3

Ad Content by Campaign Stage, 1952–2008

Appeal	General Election	Nominating
Personal qualities	31%	43%
Domestic performance	31	18
Specific domestic policy	20	28
Specific foreign policy	3	5
International affairs	8	3
Campaign	5	4
Party	2	0
N	(340)	(178)

Sources: Kathleen Jamieson, *Packaging the Presidency,* 2nd ed. (New York: Oxford University Press, 1992) for 1952–1988 campaigns, and *CBS Evening News* tapes for 1992–2008 campaigns.

Note: Entries indicate the percentage of ads devoted to each type of appeal.

think there's any way you can separate the responsibilities of a husband and father and a basic human being from that of the president. What I do in the White House is to maintain a good family life, which I consider to be crucial to being a good president." Personal qualities also played a major role in Carter's 1976 nominating campaign effort. Taking advantage of public mistrust and skepticism following Watergate disclosures, Carter pledged he would never lie to the public: "If I ever do any of those things, don't support me."[22]

Structural and strategic differences between the nominating and general election stages of a campaign help to explain the use of personal appeals in the primary season. The nominating stage often generates more personal appeals because, by the nature of intraparty battles, personality and background divide candidates more often than substantive matters. With Democrats competing against Democrats and Republicans against Republicans, there are at this time usually as many agreements as disagreements on policy issues and general political philosophies. Politicians, therefore, use personal qualities to distinguish themselves from the field and point out the limitations of their fellow candidates.

Domestic performance appeals in prominent ads were less common in the nominating process than in the general election campaign. One standard appeal concerned credit claiming on economic matters. A 1976 Ford ad showed a woman with bags of groceries meeting a friend who was working for the Ford campaign. The Ford supporter asked the shopper whether she knew that President Ford had cut inflation in half. "In half?" responded the shopper. "Wow!" A 1980 ad for Democratic contender Edward Kennedy had actor Carroll O'Connor say that Carter may "give us a depression, which may make Hoover's look like prosperity."[23] By using a prominent personality, ad makers hoped to enhance the credibility of their message.

The attention devoted to domestic matters is important, and several articles have addressed issue-based voting by primary voters.[24] But few of these projects examined the role of candidates in providing substantive cues. For there to be extensive issue-based voting, candidates must emphasize substantive matters and provide issue-based cues. Although a fair amount of attention is paid to domestic affairs in the nominating process (the percentage of specific domestic policies issues is actually higher than for the general election), for prominent ads these types of appeals occupy a smaller percentage of ad time in the spring than in the fall.

Perhaps not surprisingly, international relations receive more emphasis in prominent ads during the general election than during the nominating stage, but far less attention is paid to it than domestic performance in general. Trying to capitalize on a United Nations vote seen as harmful to Israel, Edward Kennedy in 1980 ran an ad saying Carter "betrayed Israel at the UN, his latest foreign policy blunder." Meanwhile, on the Republican side, a Reagan ad noted, "Our foreign policy has been based on the fear of not being liked. Well, it's nice to be liked. But it's more important to be respected." A 1976 Ford ad aimed at Reagan said, "Last Wednesday, Ronald Reagan said he would send American troops to Rhodesia. On Thursday he clarified that. He said they would be observers or advisers. What does he think happened in Vietnam?" The ad then concluded with the tagline "Governor Reagan couldn't start a war. President Reagan could."[25]

Internet Sites and Ads

The 1996 elections were historic for introducing a new type of political communication: information and ads delivered via candidate Web sites. Interested browsers could read full-text speeches, detailed biographies, discussions of policy positions, and copies of press releases online.

Almost all of the material on the Web sites that year presented positive portrayals of each candidate's positions, organization, or background. Except for the occasional press release buried several screens into a respective Web site, there were no attacks on the opposition. Instead, Internet users could browse Steve Forbes's family pictures and read his announcement speech. Pat Buchanan's Web site was filled with speeches and position papers on everything from immigration to trade policy. Bob Dole's site featured video snippets of the Kansan discussing his beliefs.

The most novel feature of any of the Web sites was Forbes's Flat Tax Calculator. Visitors entered their wage and salary income, checked a box for their personal exemption ($25,600 for joint married returns), and their number of dependents. After clicking the "calculate" box, the Web site automatically calculated the viewer's income tax under Forbes's 17-percent flat tax proposal. The site also would produce a table showing the tax savings, between the current and the flat tax rates, for five different income levels. The demonstration concluded with the tagline "It's simple. It's honest. And that's a big change for Washington."

In the general election, candidates also made extensive use of the Internet. Clinton, Dole, and Perot each had Web sites emphasizing their general themes: "Building a Bridge to the 21st Century" for Clinton, "More opportunities. Smaller government. Stronger and safer families" for Dole, and "For Our Children and Our Grandchildren" for Perot. Their sites contained sections outlining the candidates' policy positions, speeches, biographies, and press releases, among other things. Perot was alone in not featuring a picture of his running mate, Pat Choate, on his Web site.

Dole offered an interactive feature on his fall general election page clearly modeled after Forbes's Flat Tax Calculator. This was the Dole-Kemp Interactive Tax Calculator, which gave visitors the opportunity to estimate the "value and magnitude of the Dole-Kemp tax cuts for a person or family at your income level." After entering marital status, number of dependent children under the age of eighteen, and income level in 1996, the visitor could have the Web site automatically calculate his or her current tax costs, what the person's tax would be under Dole-Kemp tax cuts, and the value of the estimated savings.

By 2000, the Internet had become more vital to the electoral process. The number of Americans online rose nearly tenfold from 7.5 million in 1996 to 67 million in 2000, roughly 40 percent of the adult population.[26] With hits on candidate Web sites more plentiful, all of the presidential aspirants sought to harness the Internet for voter outreach, financial contributions, news and ad delivery, and volunteer mobilization.

Both Republican and Democratic candidates used their Web sites during the nominating process to communicate with volunteers. By utilizing e-mail, the Bill Bradley campaign mobilized five thousand volunteers throughout the Northeast to help with voter canvassing in New Hampshire. Forbes organized his volunteers into five thousand e-precincts based on e-mail addresses. Both John McCain and Bradley became masters of fund-raising over the Internet. Following his surprise win over George W. Bush in New Hampshire, McCain raised 40 percent of his subsequent $10 million from his Web site. Bradley generated several million from his site between October and December 1999. Both Gore's and Bush's sites had press releases, speeches, policy position statements, and a place where visitors could get information on how to volunteer in individual states. Gore also had a place where constituents such as Asian Americans, gays, environmentalists, women, students, senior citizens, and African Americans could receive appeals tailored to their particular interests.

In contrast to 1996, several candidates began to take advantage of interactive features of the Internet for the 2000 race. In addition to e-mail, search, and volunteering capabilities, Bush had two interactive features on his site. Following on the heels of Forbes and Dole in 1996, he developed the Bush Tax Calculator that allowed visitors to plug in their filing status, number of children, income level, and income percentage from a second earner to see what their income tax cut would be with both the current code and the Bush plan. Around tax day, Bush placed ads for the tax calculator on the Yahoo.com Internet portal. However, Democrats criticized the calculator because it covered income levels only through $100,000, even though much of the tax cut would go to higher-income earners. To publicize this omission, Democrats set up their own Web site—MillionairesForBush.com—that showed how the super-rich would benefit disproportionately from Bush's tax reductions.[27] Bush also posted the names and amounts for all his campaign contributors on his Web site and made the database searchable so that people could look up who had given what amounts of money to his campaign. Gore's site had places where visitors could apply for internships, sign up for automatic e-mail updates, and make campaign contributions.

All of the candidates used video streaming technology that posted television spots on their Web sites and allowed viewers with video players and sound cards to watch ads that were broadcast over the airwaves. Many of the candidates even placed video from speeches and Webcasts onto their Web sites for later viewing by voters. Candidates tended not to advertise on sites other than their own because viewership levels, even on major Web sites, during the nominating process were not very large.

In the general election, Bush and Gore made extensive use of the Internet. Unlike in 1996, the presidential candidates used their Web sites for democratic outreach. Citizens could contribute money, volunteer, register to vote, and develop their own Web sites to aid the candidates. One novel feature of Gore's site was GoreNet, which provided interactive town meetings and a chance for Gore supporters to talk with one another. Both Gore and Bush provided language translation for Spanish-speaking voters and easy access to audio and video clips. On Gore's site, citizens could register for automatic e-mail updates and could personalize the site to their own particular interests. The same was true for Bush's site, which had a feature called Daily Trivia (on August 24, 2000, the question was "Which hand does Governor Bush write with?"). It also offered a contest to name an airplane and a store featuring George W. merchandise. One problem with the site, however, was that it used a small type size that made it more difficult to read.

In terms of content, the candidates in the 2000 campaign set up sites that had more of a news-casting quality than those in 1996. Bush's site, for example, included news items that made him look good or his opponent look bad. When the Rand Corporation issued a study of Texas schools that indicated little progress had been made, GeorgeWBush.com quickly posted another Rand study that showed better results for the state's education system. It also listed an e-government study that ranked Texas first among the fifty states in using the Internet to bring services and information to the general public. Gore's site, in contrast, had fewer "newsy" items and more features that publicized his initiatives, speeches, and town meetings.

Unlike in 1996, when candidate Web sites featured mostly positive material, in 2000, Web sites started to emphasize a blend of positive and negative appeals. Bush's site attacked what the Republican said was a pledge "to create or expand more than 250 federal programs" and said that "Gore's 'small government' rhetoric doesn't match his 'big government' plan." Gore's Web site tended to emphasize more positive appeals, but it occasionally took a shot at Bush over various policy proposals. Both candidates relied on alternative sites to deliver the more hard-hitting attacks. The Republican National Committee (RNC) operated the site GoreWillSayAnything.com, whereas the Democratic National Committee (DNC) ran a site called IKnowWhatYouDidinTexas.com.

By 2004, candidates were using their Web sites in the same way they did television spots: to present a blend of attacks on the opposition along with positive statements of their own programs. The biggest shift from earlier years was in the large number of attack ads featured on the Bush and Kerry sites. Both candidates used the Internet to publicize hard-hitting attacks on the opposition.

Similar to television advertising, though, the organizations running the most negative Web sites were the political parties and outside groups. For example, the RNC had a game known as "Kerryopoly" on its site in which players moved pieces around a board showing Kerry's five homes and various luxury possessions.[28] Meanwhile, the DNC had a feature called "Bush Record Exposed" on its Web site that listed his "Top 10 Lies," "Top 10 Flip-Flops," and "Top 5 Scandals."

In terms of overall themes, Bush's site had the early slogan "Steady Leadership in Times of Change." Later, this shifted to "Building a Safer World and a More Hopeful America." The site explained how to become a Bush volunteer, make a contribution, register to vote, write a supporting letter to a newspaper, and host a party for the president. At the same time, it attacked Kerry's "raw deal" and complained that Kerry "plays politics and makes empty promises." Every week new television ads were presented on the site for people who lived in states not targeted for ad expenditures.

In a twist on past elections, Bush's site presented a "Kerry Gas Tax Calculator" that estimated how much more money people would pay if Kerry's 50-cent-per-gallon proposal was enacted into law. This calculator asked people in which state they lived and how many miles they drove in an average week and then computed how much a gas tax increase would cost them. Not only could people calculate their own cost, they could forward the link to someone else via e-mail so that individual could determine his or her own increase.

The site also had an animation game called "John Kerry's Flip-Flop Olympics," in which players were asked to name Kerry's positions on improving education, whether he owned an SUV, tax relief, and Iraq. After allowing visitors to indicate how Kerry had voted and what statements he had made on these issues, the game listed what it said were Kerry's contradictory positions over the years.

Kerry's Web site emphasized "A Fresh Start for America." It explained how to volunteer, recruit fellow voters, and organize local campaign events. Visitors could contribute to campaign blogs and learn about a variety of issue positions. There also was a Rapid Response Center on the site that provided answers to GOP criticisms and attacks on Kerry. Another section featured a link titled "Bush-Cheney: Wrong for America," which accused Bush of leading one of the most negative campaigns in history.

Although there were no animated games or tax cut calculators, the site presented ads that were airing across the country. These included both ads explaining Kerry's vision for the future as well as commercials attacking the Bush-Cheney record. The site also featured longer videos explaining Kerry's background and why he was well suited to lead the country.

Neither candidate in the 2004 campaign devoted much money to running ads on commercial Web sites. According to a study by the Pew Internet and American Life Project, Kerry and Bush spent less than $2 million on Internet advertising, a small proportion of each campaign's overall expenditures. Of this, Kerry spent around $1.5 million and Bush expended around $500,000.[29]

The 2008 presidential contest became the first truly digital campaign in the United States, much as 1960 represented the country's first television election. Digital communications came into their own in this race, in both good ways and bad ways. On the positive side, the candidates (especially Obama) used the Internet to raise record amounts of money and to place speeches, ads, and video "Q and A"s on YouTube, MySpace, and Facebook. Both nominees also placed nearly all their advertisements on their Web sites, allowing voters to see the spots either on television or over the Internet. This helped free campaign communications from television stations and gave candidates much greater freedom over paid advertising. It also nationalized campaign advertising, because rather than forcing voters to be dependent on local television stations for candidate commercials, people could see ads at a candidate's Web site as well as a variety of news and entertainment outlets.

However, befitting the multifaceted nature of digital communications, e-mail and Internet sites also illustrated the downside of the digital age. Early in the presidential campaign, anonymous opponents of Barack Obama engaged in a "viral" advertising campaign against him by circulating an e-mail characterizing him as "Barack Hussein Obama" and suggested that he "joined the United Church of Christ in an attempt to downplay his Muslim background." According to the widely publicized communiqué, "the Muslims have said they plan on destroying the U.S. from the inside out; what better way to start than at the highest level?"

Indeed, the false idea that Obama was Muslim, not Christian, spread throughout the country. National surveys found that more than 10 percent of Americans erroneously believed that Obama was a secret Muslim, despite his professed beliefs to the contrary. A *New York Times* investigation traced the source of this rumor to sixty-two-year-old Andy Martin. A man with a checkered history of imprisonment, anti-Jewish comments, and litigiousness, Martin put out his first anti-Obama press release in 2004, when Obama first ran for the U.S. Senate.[30]

Obama critic Ted Sampley used Martin's comments in 2006 to claim that Obama had attended "Jakarta's Muslim Wahjhabi schools. Wahjhabism is the radical teaching that created the Muslim terrorists who are now waging jihad on the rest of the world." According to Obama's autobiography, Obama had lived in Indonesia during his childhood, but had attended a Catholic not a Muslim school. Later, a right-wing Israeli activist named Ruth Matar sent a widely distributed e-mail claiming Obama would be America's "first Arab-American president" if elected.[31] Through these and other digital communications, critics sought to portray Obama in a manner later picked up by McCain—Obama was too radical, did not reflect basic American values, and was not like most Americans.

Another charge that arose in regard to Obama was that he was a tax-and-spend liberal who would raise taxes for the middle class. In the closing weeks of the general election, McCain repeated this complaint repeatedly in ads and debates and on the campaign trail. One ad, for example, called "Tax Cutter," showed footage of Obama claiming "I'm a tax cutter." The subsequent voice-over rejected that characterization and claimed that Obama voted ninety-four times for higher taxes. The spot then showed newspaper headlines describing higher taxes and spending by Democrats. It closed by saying: "Congressional liberals. The truth hurts . . . (long pause) you."

Similar to candidates before him, Obama defended himself from the higher taxes argument by setting up a Web site with a tax cut calculator. On this site, he asked people to enter their income, marital status, and number of children, and then click on a button that compared what their taxes would be under his plan versus under McCain's. This site, TaxCutFacts.org, generated thousands of hits during the closing days of the campaign and helped Obama rebut the tax increase claim. By the end of the campaign, national polls showed that Obama successfully had reduced the confidence spread between him and McCain on the tax issue.

The Rise of Negative Advertising

Critics have widely condemned the advertising style of recent elections, but few have defined what they mean by *negativity*. Observers often define it as anything they do not like about campaigns. Defined in this way, the term is so all-encompassing it becomes almost meaningless. The broadness of this definition brings to mind former justice Potter Stewart's famous line in a concurring opinion concerning pornographic material. When asked how he identified pornography, Stewart conceded that he could not define it. But, the justice asserted, "I know it when I see it."[32]

Others, such as Jamieson, have proposed drawing a distinction between three types of advertisements: attack (spots criticizing the opposition), advocacy (spots presenting a positive presentation), and contrast (those criticizing the opposition and presenting a candidate's own perspective). One study at the University of Pennsylvania Annenberg Public Policy Center demonstrated the differences in voter reactions to attack and contrast commercials. According to the research, "People are more upset by one-sided attack ads than two-sided contrast ads that include both an attack and a defense of the candidate's position. When shown an attack ad on Social Security reform, just over a third said it was responsible. But two-thirds said they viewed a contrast ad on the same issue as responsible."[33]

In his research of the constitutional ratification campaign of 1787–1788, William Riker distinguished direct criticism; charges of threats to civil liberties, governmental structure, and state power; and other types of appeals. Relying on contemporaneous documents used by each side in the ratification campaign, Riker was able to define negativity more clearly as unflattering or pejorative comments and show that the modern period has no monopoly on negative campaigning.[34]

For my study, I examined prominent ads from 1952 to 2008 to determine the tone and object of attack. I included as negative any ad that challenged an opposing campaigner in terms of policy positions or personal qualities in at least 50 percent of its presentation. This category therefore subsumes the categories of both attack and contrast spots. If an ad included unflattering or pejorative comments made about an opponent's domestic performance, it was labeled negative. Overall, negative comments were classified into the categories of discussions about personal qualities, domestic performance, specific policy statements, international affairs, the campaign, and the political party affiliation in general. Fifty-six percent of prominent ads during the period I studied were negative, with ads at the general election stage being more negative (58 percent) than those in the nominating stage (51 percent). Republicans (61 percent) were more negative in their prominent ads than were Democrats (51 percent).[35]

As seen in Figure 3-2, campaigns through 1960 were not particularly negative in their advertising. Twenty-five percent of prominent ads in 1952 were negative, and 38 percent were negative in 1956. In 1960, only 12 percent of the prominent ads featured critical statements. However, starting in the Johnson-Goldwater race of 1964, advertising turned more negative. Fifty percent of the prominent ads in 1964 and 69 percent of the prominent ads in 1968 were negative. The 1964 campaign produced a successful effort on Johnson's part to portray his opponent as a political extremist and threat to world peace. This race, as mentioned in chapter 1, featured the "Daisy" ad and others that damaged Goldwater's political prospects. One of the most visible ads of that campaign showed someone cutting off the eastern seaboard of the United States with a saw to make the point that Goldwater was extreme in his perspective. An ad that never aired linked Goldwater to the Ku Klux Klan. Although the ad was produced and given the go-ahead for regional airing, it was pulled at the last minute, according to one Johnson aide, because it "strained the available evidence, it was going too far."[36]

The effectiveness of Johnson's television ad campaign undoubtedly encouraged candidates in 1968 to use negative advertising. The race that year, among Nixon, Humphrey, and Wallace, was quite negative. The presence of Wallace in the race threatened both Nixon and Humphrey, and each responded with ads attacking the Alabama governor. Humphrey ran an ad showing a large picture of Wallace while actor E.G. Marshall explained, "When I see this man, I think of feelings of my own which I don't like but I have anyway. They're called prejudices. . . . Wallace is devoted now to his single strongest prejudice. He would take that prejudice and make it into national law."[37] Democrats also sought to take advantage of popular displeasure over the vice-presidential qualifications of Spiro Agnew. One of their ads opened with a poster of "Spiro Agnew for Vice

Figure 3-2   Negative Ads as a Percentage of Total, 1952–2008

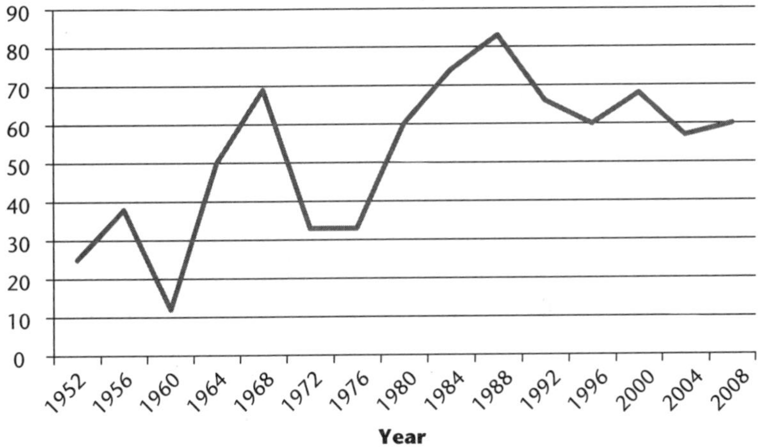

Sources: For 1952–1988, Kathleen Jamieson, *Packaging the Presidency*, 2nd ed. (New York: Oxford University Press, 1992), and for 1992–2008, *CBS Evening News* tapes.

President," while in the background a man looking at the picture gradually collapsed in laughter.[38]

Republicans sought to capitalize on the bloody riots that occurred during the 1968 Democratic convention in Chicago by running an ad linking the street disorder with Humphrey. In one of the campaign's most controversial ads, Nixon contrasted footage of the bloody riots with pictures of a smiling Humphrey accepting the nomination. With music from the song "Hot Time in the Old Town Tonight" playing in the background, the ad ended with the tagline, "This time vote like your whole world depended on it."[39]

The elections of 1972 and 1976 were not nearly as negative in tone. In both races only about one-third of prominent ads were negative. Campaigners may have become more reluctant to air negative commercials because of the backlash that followed the highly emotional ads of the 1964 and 1968 races. McGinniss's exposé of the electronic merchandising of Nixon in the 1968 campaign created a climate of skepticism among reporters that increased the risks of negative campaigning. Moral outrage against attack ads dominated the 1976 elections, which followed the "dirty tricks" associated with Watergate.

These sentiments, though, dissipated with time. As the memory of Watergate receded, the outrage associated with it also began to decline. Voters no longer associated attacks on the opposition with unfair dirty tricks. The result was that presidential contests in the 1980s reached extraordinarily high levels of negativity. In 1980, 60 percent of prominent ads were negative; 74 percent were negative in 1984; and 83 percent were negative in 1988. For example, the 1980 campaign featured efforts, albeit ultimately unsuccessful, to portray Reagan as a dangerous extremist in the mold of Goldwater. Carter used "person-in-the-street" ads in an effort to portray Reagan as dangerous: "I just don't think he's well enough informed. . . . We really have to keep our heads cool, and I don't think that Reagan is cool. . . . That scares me about Ronald Reagan."[40] Another ad sought to characterize the Californian as trigger happy by listing cases in which Reagan had backed military force, including the time he said a destroyer should be sent to Ecuador to resolve a fishing controversy.

Mondale used a similar strategy in 1984 when he ran an anti-Reagan ad showing missiles shooting from underground silos, accompanied by the musical track of Crosby, Stills, Nash, and Young singing from their song "Teach Your Children."[41] Mondale also sought to play on concerns about Gary Hart's leadership ability during the nominating process by running an ad featuring a ringing red phone to raise doubts about Hart's readiness to assume the duties of commander in chief.

The 1988 campaign attracted great attention because of numerous negative ads, such as George Bush Sr.'s "Revolving Door." This commercial sought to portray Dukakis as soft on crime by saying the Massachusetts governor had vetoed the death penalty and given weekend furloughs to first-degree murderers not eligible for parole. Although Willie Horton was never mentioned in this ad, the not-so-veiled reference to him generated considerable coverage from the news media, with numerous stories reviewing the details of Horton's crime of kidnapping and rape while on furlough from a Massachusetts prison. The Bush team, headed by Roger Ailes, also hammered Dukakis for his failure to clean up Boston Harbor. Dukakis, meanwhile, ran ads that reminded viewers of concern about Bush's most important personnel decision, the choice of Dan Quayle as the Republican vice-presidential nominee. Widespread doubts about Quayle's ability gave Dukakis a perfect opportunity to run an ad criticizing this selection. The ad closed with the line, "Hopefully, we will never know how great a lapse of judgment that really was."[42]

The 1992 race featured sharp attacks from Clinton and Perot on Bush's economic performance and from Bush on Clinton's past record and trustworthiness, but throughout there was a lower level of negativity than in 1988. Overall, 66 percent of prominent ads were negative. One memorable spot for Clinton tabulated the number of people who had lost jobs during Bush's administration. Bush, meanwhile, portrayed Clinton as just another tax-and-spend liberal who had a weak record as governor of Arkansas and was shifty in his political stances. Perot ran a generally positive campaign, with commercials and infomercials that addressed the national debt, job creation, and the need for change. However, in the closing days of the campaign, Perot ran the infomercial titled "Deep Voodoo, Chicken Feathers, and the American Dream," which attacked both Bush and Clinton. One of the most memorable segments of this program featured a map of Arkansas with a big chicken in the middle to convey the message that job growth during Clinton's governorship had occurred mainly through low-paying jobs in the chicken industry.

The 1996 campaign showed a slight drop in the level of negativity, as 60 percent of the ads attacked an opponent. In the nominating process, Forbes ran a series of attacks first on Dole and then on Buchanan and Lamar Alexander. In the general election, Dole attacked Clinton's character, his record on fighting drugs, and his overall liberalism. Meanwhile, the Clinton campaign linked Dole with unpopular House Speaker Newt Gingrich and accused the duo of slashing popular programs in the areas of Medicare, education, and the environment.[43]

In 2000, 50 percent of prominent ads during the primaries were negative, which was the lowest level since 1976. With many media stories about Forbes's 1996 onslaught and with memories of George Bush's attack campaign against Dukakis in 1988 still on the minds of political professionals, candidates toned down the negativity of their spots to avoid a backlash from voters turned off by attack politics. However, this cease-fire lasted only as long as the primaries. In the general election, ads featured a preponderance of heavy-hitting attacks on the opposition. An average of 84 percent of the prominent fall ads were negative in tone (91 percent of Bush's, 100 percent of Gore's, and 60 percent of ads aired by outside groups). Both major candidates hammered at what were seen as weak personal qualities in the opponent: trust and integrity for Gore and knowledge and experience for Bush.

In 2004, 33 percent of primary ads were negative, which was far lower than in preceding years. Howard Dean and Richard Gephardt incurred the wrath of Iowa voters when they attacked opponents.

Their poor finish in those caucuses dissuaded other candidates from going negative for the rest of the nominating stage. But as in the 2000 campaign, this cease-fire proved temporary; the general election between Bush and Kerry featured an extraordinary number of negative attacks. Eighty-two percent of the fall advertisements were negative in tone, making it the second most negative presidential general election in the post–World War II period (1988 was the most negative at 83 percent). Bush complained that Kerry was not trustworthy on terrorism and too willing to raise taxes, whereas Kerry faulted Bush's policies in Iraq and complained about job losses during the Republican administration.

Efforts during the 2008 campaign matched the negativity of past prominent advertisements. Overall, 60 percent of the prominent primary and general election spots were negative. During the general election, McCain ran a very negative campaign because public opinion on the major issues such as the economy and Iraq War tended to favor Democrats. Around 88 percent of McCain's prominent spots in the general election were negative, compared to 62 percent for Obama. McCain complained that Obama was a tax-and-spend liberal, out of touch with American values, and too inexperienced to be president. Obama had a lower percentage of negative ads, but because he was able to outspend McCain, he broadcast a large number of attack spots. His fund-raising advantage, though, allowed Obama to balance his negative attacks with positive messages in the battleground states. This helped voters see his overall advertising as less negative than McCain's (see chapter 8 for a discussion of the blame game). The University of Wisconsin Advertising Project's independent assessment of all campaign ads (not just prominent ones) found that 63 percent of Obama's commercials and 79 percent of McCain's were negative in tone, demonstrating one of the reasons voters ended up blaming the Arizona senator for having a negative style of discourse.

The Objects of Negativity

Attack ads are viewed by many people as the electronic equivalent of the plague. Few aspects of contemporary politics are as widely despised. Many observers complain that negative campaign spots are among the least constructive developments in politics of recent years. Furthermore, they are thought to contribute little to the education of voters.

But in reviewing the objects of attack ads, it is somewhat surprising to discover that the most substantive appeals actually came in negative spots. For example, the most critical prominent commercials from 1952 to 2008 appeared on specific foreign policy claims (79 percent of which were negative) and specific domestic policy (64 percent), followed by international affairs (61 percent), domestic performance (54 percent), personal qualities (53 percent), campaign appeals (44 percent), and mentions of political party (17 percent).

Candidates often use attack ads to challenge the government's performance or to question the handling of particular policy problems. Despite the obvious emotional qualities of the commercial, Bush's infamous "Revolving Door" ad was quite specific in attacking Dukakis's record: "As governor, Michael Dukakis vetoed mandatory sentences for drug dealers. He vetoed the death penalty. His revolving-door prison policy gave weekend furloughs to first-degree murderers not eligible for parole."[44]

Negative commercials are more likely to have policy-oriented content because campaigners need a clear reason to attack the opponent. Specificity helps focus viewers' attention on the message being delivered. Issue-oriented ads often attract public attention and are likely to be remembered. Political strategists need to be clear about the facts in case of challenges from the media as reporters often dissect negative ads and demand evidence to support specific claims.

In addition, campaigners are reluctant to criticize candidates personally for fear that they would make themselves look mean spirited. In 1980, Carter ran ads challenging Reagan's experience and qualifications, and he was roundly criticized for being nasty. Results of research by Karen Johnson-Cartee and Gary Copeland demonstrate that voters are more likely to tolerate negative commercials that focus on policy than on personality. Voters' reactions help to reinforce the patterns noted previously.[45]

Critics often condemn attack ads for disrupting democratic elections and polarizing the electorate. Based on experimental research, Stephen Ansolabehere and Shanto Iyengar argue that attack ads lower turnout.[46] However, recent experience does not bear this out. Despite a Republican primary battle in 1996 that was the nastiest in modern history and the complete absence of a Democratic primary contest, turnout in 1996 was higher than in 1988 and 1992 in every state primary or caucus except five.[47] And in the 1996 general election, the percentage of attack ads dropped from 1992, but the number of nonvoters rose, which is contrary to the prediction of

Ansolabehere and Iyengar. In 2008, there was a high level of negative attacks during the general election, but record voter turnout.

Indeed, most other scholars have found little association between ad negativity and drops in voter turnout. Martin Wattenberg and Craig Brians find "no evidence of a turnout disadvantage for those who recollected negative presidential campaign advertising." Steven Finkel and John Geer suggest that campaign negativity actually may enhance turnout by heightening the perceived stakes of the race. Kim Kahn and Patrick Kenney argue that negativity per se does not reduce turnout, but that "mudslinging," meaning harsh and strident attacks on the opposition, does. Using ad-buy data on the frequency of negative attacks, Paul Freedman and Ken Goldstein conclude there is "no evidence that exposure to negative advertising depresses turnout. Instead exposure to negative ads appears to increase the likelihood of voting." Richard Lau and his collaborators find that negative political ads "do not seem to have especially detrimental effects on the political system."[48]

There is little reason to expect a clear-cut relationship between ads and turnout. The most powerful predictor of turnout is mistrust and the general sense of political efficacy—in other words, whether people feel their vote will make a difference. Negative ads are as likely as positive ones to make individuals feel their vote matters and that they should care about the electoral outcome. Attack ads can convince viewers that a race is competitive, that there are differences between the candidates, and that the substantive stakes are high. In this situation, attacks are as likely to stimulate as depress voter turnout.

In researching the effectiveness of negative advertising, Richard Lau and Gerald Pomper conclude that "negative campaigning is relatively effective for challengers" because it helps them become known to voters and draw differences with the opposition. However, positive strategies work better for incumbents because they already are well known.[49]

From the standpoint of substantive content, therefore, negative ads contribute to public education when they are accurate. They do not necessarily lower voter interest. Observers interested in increasing the amount of substantive information in commercials should realize that negative ads are more informative than is commonly believed. Rather than focus on ad negativity, more attention should be devoted to the problems of ad accuracy and distortion. Commercials that convey distorted information are more problematic from the standpoint of democratic elections than attack ads per se.

Conclusion

Campaign communications have come a long way since printed pamphlets were the primary means of dialogue. Radio and television and the recent rise of e-mail and the Internet have offered candidates a variety of means to communicate with the general public. As is made clear in this chapter, political aspirants appeal to voters based on the matters that are on the public mind. In a time of war, matters of foreign policy move to the forefront. During recessions, economic issues predominate. When there have been scandals or national crises, personal qualities rise in importance.

There also are natural variations in the cycle of negativity. After a series of vituperative campaigns in the 1980s, negativity subsided in the 1990s, then re-emerged in the 2004 and 2008 general elections. Policy discussions are not very detailed in any time period, yet ads still provide a sense of the values and priorities of the various contestants. Ironically, some of the most specific policy appeals are those broadcast in negative ads. As long as voters see the criticisms as focusing on substantive matters, they are more tolerant of negativity. However, when charges are unsubstantiated or center on personal background or character, they become more of a risk for the attacking politician.

Chapter 4

Media Coverage of Ads

Reporters used to be governed by the norms of old-style journalism—the "who, what, where, when, and how" approach to news gathering. Candidates' statements were reported more or less at face value; behind-the-scenes machinations fell outside the news; and, by implicit agreement, the private behavior of political leaders was pretty much ignored. However, Lyndon Johnson's deception in the Vietnam War and Richard Nixon's lying in the face of the deepening Watergate scandal led reporters to take more interpretive and investigative approaches to news gathering. Rather than sticking to hard news, journalists today see a responsibility to put "the facts" in broader context.

This style of journalism also led reporters to a different approach to campaign coverage. Once content to cover candidates' speeches and travel, reporters began to emphasize behind-the-scenes activities. What strategies were candidates pursuing? What blocs of voters were seen as most critical to electoral success? What clues did campaigns provide about candidates' underlying beliefs and preferences? Following the lead of Theodore White, who revolutionized coverage of presidential campaigns, reporters began to devote greater attention to analysis.[1]

Changes in the nature of presidential selection following the 1968 election created new opportunities for reporters.[2] The decline in the power of party leaders, rise in the number of primaries, and extension of races over a number of months made it dramatically easier for reporters to explore behind-the-scenes maneuvering. In fact, the entry of little-known candidates into open nominating contests made it important for reporters to cover the backgrounds and goals of candidates.

But according to observers, the media have not fulfilled their responsibility. Research generally has found that the media devote little space to policy matters. A thorough study, by Henry Brady and Richard Johnston, of every United Press International story on the Democratic candidates from January 1 through July 31, 1984, revealed that only 16 percent of lines of press coverage were devoted to policy positions. The more common topics included discussions of the campaign (50 percent overall, with 21 percent devoted to prospects of election, 20 percent devoted to campaign appearances, and 9 percent devoted to sources of support), personal qualities of the candidates (23 percent), and comments about the opposition (11 percent). These figures are comparable to what Doris Graber found in her study of *Chicago Tribune* coverage of the 1983 mayoral election. In that race, 42 percent of the lines dealt with the campaign, 20 percent were devoted to policy matters, 19 percent dealt with personal qualities, and 20 percent involved other matters, such as ethics or party affairs.[3]

These findings are disappointing to those who believe the media should play a central role in educating the electorate. Rather than devoting space to matters that would facilitate public education, the press focuses most often on who is ahead and who is behind. Michael Robinson and Margaret Sheehan show in their study of the 1980 presidential campaign that once the nominating season gets under way, this so-called horse-race coverage far outpaces coverage of issues and candidates.[4] Just at the point when voters start to pay attention to politics, reporters devote relatively little coverage to the candidates' stances on issues and devote substantial attention to the contest.

This pattern of reporting has affected voters. In their path-breaking survey research on the 1948 presidential campaign, Bernard Berelson, Paul Lazarsfeld, and William McPhee discovered that 67 percent of voters' conversations with one another dealt with the policy positions and personal qualifications of candidates, whereas about 25 percent involved questions of "winnability."[5] But by 1976, these numbers had reversed in public opinion surveys. According to Thomas Patterson, the "game was the major topic of conversation in 1976."[6] In June of that year, near the end of the nominating cycle, 69 percent of conversations involved the game and only 18 percent dealt with substantive matters.

The horse race has become a popular object of press attention because it often involves drama and suspense. Nothing attracts media attention like a surprise showing that surpasses their expectations. Candidates who come out of nowhere and do well in early caucuses and primaries attract a disproportionate share of media coverage.[7]

Jimmy Carter's nominating campaign was the classic case of momentum fueled by media coverage. In the months before the 1976 Iowa caucuses, the Georgia governor was a virtual unknown. Public opinion polls a year before the election had put him on the list of "asterisk" candidates, those individuals who fell in the "others" category because their public preference ratings were less than 5 percent. When Carter did better than expected in Iowa, he received an extraordinary amount of news coverage, much of which dealt with his success in the horse race. He then skyrocketed in the polls, was able to raise much more money, and eventually became the Democratic Party nominee.

The Increasing Coverage of Ads

To see how advertising is covered by reporters, I tabulated the number of *New York Times* articles from 1952 to 2008, *Washington Post* articles from 1972 to 2008, and *CBS Evening News* stories from 1972 to 2008 that covered political advertising.[8] There were some differences among the news outlets, but the general trend was a substantial increase in coverage of advertisements since the 1980s.[9]

For both nominating and general election contests, the 1970s did not generate many television stories about political spot ads (see Figures 4-1 and 4-2, respectively, for the stages). For example, in 1972 only seven CBS stories about ads appeared during the nominating process in the spring and four during the general election campaign in the fall. In 1976, CBS ran fourteen ad stories in the spring and five in the fall.

However, the numbers started to rise in 1980 and continued to rise throughout that decade. The 1988 race produced approximately twice the number of ad stories in the nominating campaign (twenty-nine) and approximately five times the number in the general election campaign (twenty-one) as did the elections of the 1970s. Similarly, the 1992 contest generated twenty-nine nomination and twenty-four general election campaign ad stories. Since then, though, campaign ads have generated less news coverage. For example, the 1996 campaign had fewer stories (twenty-one in the nomination stage and fourteen in the general election stage) than 1988 or 1992, and 2000 and 2004 saw a continuing decline in the number of television and newspaper stories about campaign ads. This trend, though, reversed again in 2008. The historic nature of that campaign stimulated considerable public interest, and the massive amount of money spent in that election led the press to cover the campaign with greater frequency than in the past. Major news

Figure 4-1 Media Coverage of Nomination Campaign Ads, 1952–2008

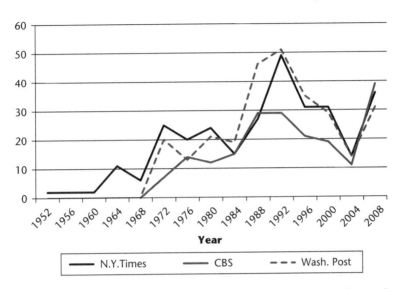

Sources: *New York Times,* 1952–2008; *CBS Evening News,* 1972–2008; *Washington Post,* 1972–2008.

Figure 4-2 Media Coverage of General Election Campaign Ads, 1952–2008

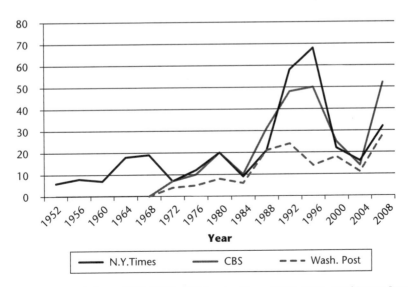

Sources: *New York Times,* 1952–2008; *CBS Evening News,* 1972–2008; *Washington Post,* 1972–2008.

outlets ran more than twice as many stories as in 2004, both during the primaries and the general election.

In regard to the *New York Times,* the critical turning point in ad coverage for the nominating process occurred in 1972. Before then, there were few stories about political advertising. In 1952, 1956, and 1960, there were two *New York Times* articles about ads each year in the presidential nominating period from January to June. A March 26, 1960, article, for example, described Stuart Symington's decision not to launch a pre-convention television drive against Nixon. In 1968, for the same period, six stories appeared. An article on May 8 recounted Robert Kennedy's decision to spend heavily on television in Indiana because of Gov. Roger Branigan's control of the party organization. Most of the other articles dealt with the content of or strategies behind ads.

However, after Democratic reforms and the rise in the number of primaries, the number of stories on ads during the nominating process rose dramatically. The 1972 campaign was the first election conducted under the new nomination reforms, which added more primaries and therefore gave citizens a more direct voice in delegate selection. It is not surprising that press coverage of ads during the nominating period increased considerably. Twenty stories appeared in the *Washington Post* in 1972, compared with thirty-one in 2008. Twenty-five articles about campaign commercials appeared in the *New York Times* between January and June of 1972, whereas thirty-six appeared in 2008.

Newspaper coverage of general election advertising has changed as well. In general, the number of stories has fluctuated considerably, depending on the closeness of the race. Campaigns that were seen as competitive (1968, 1976, 1980, 1988, 1992, 2000, and 2008) generated many more stories than did those with a clear front-runner (1972, 1984, and 1996). This was particularly true in 1992, as the three-way battle between George Bush, Bill Clinton, and Ross Perot prompted a dramatic increase in the number of news stories. In close elections, the media devote more coverage to campaign phenomena, such as television advertising, that are thought to make a difference in voters' choices.[10]

Horse-Race Coverage of Ads

The increase in the coverage of ads highlights the blurring of free and paid media, but the raw figures do not reveal what reporters

TABLE 4-1
Content and Tone of CBS News Coverage, 1972–2008

Appeal	Descriptions of Ads	News Stories about Ads
Personal qualities	32%	13%
Domestic performance	22	9
Specific policy statements	34	15
International affairs	5	1
Campaign	6	62
Party	1	0
N	(337)	(337)
Negativity level	66%	54%

Sources: Vanderbilt Television News Index and Abstracts for 1972–1988 campaigns, and *CBS Evening News* tapes for 1992–2008 campaigns.

Note: Entries indicate the percentage of *CBS Evening News* stories devoted to each type of appeal.

actually said. There has been widespread criticism about media attention to horse-race considerations and the limited time spent on policy matters. Because television is the major news source for most Americans, I examined in detail all the stories about campaign advertising that appeared on the *CBS Evening News* from 1972 through 2008. I analyzed two features: the content of the ad reference and the general topic of the news story in which the ad was discussed. I then developed several categories to assess the quality of coverage and to facilitate comparison with the results for ads themselves.

There were interesting differences between the descriptions of ads in news stories and the content of the news stories. As shown in Table 4-1, the major contrast concerned the tendency of reporters fascinated with the horse race to convert substantive ad messages into news stories about campaign prospects or strategies. More ads reported on in the news were specific (34 percent) than the news stories themselves (15 percent).

CBS often rebroadcast ad segments that were particularly pointed in their charges about opponents' policy positions. For example, a Nixon ad featured on the *CBS Evening News* on October 30, 1972, lambasted George McGovern's defense posture and noted which specific weapons programs the Democrat would oppose. In the same vein, on January 19, 1988, CBS showed a Jack Kemp ad that attacked George Bush and Bob Dole for being willing to reduce Social Security benefits. Nominating campaign coverage tended to be more specific about policy than was coverage of the general election campaign.

In contrast, most of the news stories about ads dealt with the campaign (62 percent).[11] Many of these stories included discussions of how particular ads fit strategic goals of the campaign (35 percent), how they affected the candidate's electoral prospects (19 percent), or how they were produced and financed within the campaign organization (8 percent).

For example, on January 29, 1980, CBS broadcast a story describing an Edward Kennedy ad that addressed the Chappaquiddick incident. The ad itself dealt with personal qualities, such as Kennedy's honesty, but the story emphasized the change in the campaign's strategy, which had been designed to reassure voters about the senator's conduct. Another example appeared February 12, 1988, when a Michael Dukakis ad on the economy was analyzed in terms of its contribution to the candidate's campaign strategy.

In general, however, news reports placed much less emphasis on personal qualities, domestic performance, or specific policy statements than did the ads themselves. Reporters often blame candidates for not discussing the issues, but it appears that fascination with the horse race leads journalists to turn substantive messages into campaign stories.

In addition, ads broadcast as part of news stories tended to be more negative than the news stories were. Sixty-six percent of ads described in the news were negative in orientation, compared with 54 percent of the news stories themselves. Negative ads have become more common. Negative commercials tend to be more controversial, which produces greater coverage than otherwise would be the case. But the media devote considerable time to rebroadcasting negative ads, which reinforces the widespread public view about the negativity of television ads. In fact, it is well known in political circles that one of the easiest ways to attract press coverage is to run negative commercials. Media adviser Roger Ailes explained it this way: "There are three things that the media are interested in: pictures, mistakes, and attacks. . . . If you need coverage, you attack, and you will get coverage."[12]

Shifts in Ad Coverage over Time

An intensive study of *New York Times* ad coverage since 1952 shows exactly how press coverage of commercials has shifted over time. In the 1950s, consistent with the old-style journalism practiced at that time, considerable attention was devoted to the use of celebrity endorsements in the presidential campaign. For example,

Eleanor Roosevelt filmed an endorsement of Adlai Stevenson that generated press attention simply because of her celebrity status. In 1960, an April 20 story discussed a New York telethon plan to raise money for fall advertising time, and a March 26 article recounted Symington's decision not to spend $400,000 in a pre-convention television drive against Nixon.

Both of the 1960 articles are noteworthy because of their emphasis on factual events. Hard facts were emphasized, and announcements from campaign officials were taken at face value. There was little discussion of how the decisions fit broader strategic goals. There was no analysis of campaign maneuvering or how candidates actually reached particular decisions. Furthermore, no attention was paid to the motivations of campaign decision makers. Reporters did not examine the true motives or goals of Symington or the telethon planners to determine what they really were trying to accomplish or who was winning organizational battles.

However, the *New York Times* began to cover political advertising differently during the 1970s and 1980s. A January 14, 1972, article describing Maine senator Edmund Muskie's use of television in his bid for the Democratic nomination illustrates the new tendency to put the campaign in context and tell the story behind the event. The article noted that television would be the dominant element in Muskie's campaign. His strategy was described as contrasting himself to Nixon's weak credibility. The newspaper's approach was clearly a departure. The story emphasized strategic considerations—how advertising furthered vote-getting—and illustrated the effort to report the behind-the-scenes story. The attention to the candidate's motivations and goals reflected the new direction in the coverage of political ads.

This discussion is not meant to imply that strategic considerations were the reporters' only focus. Journalists also devoted attention to the substance of television ads. A March 21, 1984, article covering Democratic Party ads focused on the "ethical and moral" violations of the Reagan administration. Rep. Tony Coelho, D-Calif., was quoted as criticizing President Reagan's willingness to blast welfare cheats but not those who violate the public trust. There were stories in 1988 that discussed Rep. Richard Gephardt's trade ads in Iowa. The Democratic representative from Missouri used highly effective commercials blasting Far East trading partners for closing their markets to American products while flooding the United States with cheaper imports. But even this type of coverage often incorporated considerations of candidates' strategic thinking. A number of stories describing the content of ads showed how particular messages were designed to appeal to particular constituencies.

"Daisy," "Daisy II," and the "Revolving Door"

Nothing illustrates the controversy over how the media cover political commercials better than Johnson's "Daisy" spot in 1964, the Republican remake of that ad ("Daisy II") by a group of Texans in 2000, and George Bush Sr.'s "Revolving Door" ad in 1988. The "Daisy" commercial is probably the most infamous ad in television history. It opens with a young girl standing in a meadow plucking petals from a daisy. After she counts "1, 2, 3, 4, 5, 6, 7, 8, 9," a solemn voice begins its own countdown: "10, 9, 8, 7, 6, 5, 4, 3, 2, 1, 0." At zero, the picture of the child dissolves, and a mushroom cloud fills the screen. Johnson closes the ad by warning, "These are the stakes. To make a world in which all of God's children can live, or to go into the dark. We must either love each other or we must die."[13]

This ad aired only once, during NBC's *Monday Night at the Movies* showing of *David and Bathsheba* on September 7, 1964. But condemnation came almost immediately. As recalled by Bill Moyers, then Johnson's press secretary, "The president called me and said, 'Holy shit. I'm getting calls from all over the country.' Most of them said that it was an effective ad. Others said they didn't like it." Press reaction was swift. According to Lloyd Wright, an advertising strategist for Johnson, "The first night it aired, it created such a media flap that the next night it was used in its entirety on the newscasts on all three networks." Johnson pulled the ad.[14] The accusation that Goldwater would use nuclear weapons was not thought by outside observers to have any factual basis and therefore did not deserve to be on the air.

In 2000, a group of Texans used a nonprofit group called Aretino Industries to sponsor a remake of the "Daisy" ad. Featuring a similar image of a young girl plucking petals off a daisy, the commercial claimed that because President Clinton and Vice President Al Gore had "sold" military intelligence "to Communist Red China in exchange for campaign contributions," China has "the ability to threaten our homes with long-range nuclear weapons." Following the disappearance of the girl and the image of a nuclear explosion, the tagline of the commercial was, "Don't take a chance. Please vote Republican."[15] Because the group claimed it was engaging in public education, it refused to identify the source of its contributors. However, because the central claim was not documented (other than GOP charges during the investigation into the Democratic National Committee's 1996 fund-raising) and the ad was so inflammatory, the George W. Bush campaign asked the group to discontinue the ad, which it agreed to do. Perhaps surprisingly, given the media's attention to ad analysis, there wasn't much press coverage of the "Daisy II" ad.

Bush's "Revolving Door" ad in 1988 evoked a more complex set of political reactions and media coverage. Its image of prisoners flowing through a prison revolving door helped convey the idea that Dukakis was soft on crime. CBS covered this commercial in its broadcast on October 7, 1988. (News stories about Willie Horton had been broadcast September 22.) The story described the commercial as a crime ad that would highlight the prison furlough policy of Governor Dukakis. Clifford Barnes and Donna Cuomo, joint victims of an assault by a convict who had been released on a weekend furlough, were reported to be participating in a speaking tour with a pro-Bush group. Bush meanwhile was shown campaigning with police officers. This story was followed on October 20 by another, this time showing in great detail Horton's crime record and supplying background on the Bush ad. Bush was shown campaigning in New York City at a police union rally. It was not until October 24 and 25—almost three weeks after the commercial appeared—that Democratic opponents appeared on the news to claim that the "Revolving Door" ad had racist undertones.

But in keeping with the horse-race mentality of the media, a second story on October 25 also quoted media consultant Tony Schwartz as saying that Bush's ads were successful, and the "Revolving Door" spot particularly effective. Whereas the 1964 ad was immediately condemned and removed from the airwaves, reporters in 1988 treated the furlough ad as a typical advertisement. It was described as being quite effective. Criticisms came late and were never solidly addressed, and the spot was never pulled off the air.

This subdued and delayed reaction was in keeping with the general tenor of news coverage about attack ads in 1988. A number of CBS stories and *New York Times* articles during the general election campaign emphasized the overall effectiveness of negative political commercials. A September 18 *New York Times* article, for example, discussed the role of advertising in contemporary campaigns. Former California governor Jerry Brown was quoted as saying that media and professional campaign advisers think that negative commercials work better. A number of politicians and consultants were cited as saying that Bush and Dukakis would be foolish to delve deeply into policy issues. This article was followed on October 10 with another that cited campaign officials who believed the electorate had become accustomed to sharp-elbow tactics.

In addition, political professionals quoted on October 19 derided Dukakis's advertising effort. Several experts complained about the ever-shifting focus of his ad campaign and the fact that his commercials were not well timed. An October 13 story noted that 1988 was the first time candidates used more ads to criticize opponents than to promote themselves. A number of analysts even attributed Bush's lead in the polls to the success of his negative commercials and the lack of an appropriate response by Dukakis.

The grudging respect reporters had for the effectiveness of the GOP ads created a pattern of coverage that benefited Bush. Rather than condemning the "Revolving Door" ad, reporters rebroadcast it repeatedly throughout the last month of the campaign.[16] This behavior effectively erased the traditional difference between the free and paid media. It gave Bush more air time and therefore lent him more credibility than any campaign organization alone could have managed. This style of news coverage helped make Bush's 1988 advertising campaign one of the most effective in recent memory.

Swift Boat Veterans and MoveOn.org Ads

In 2004, another set of advertisements attracted considerable press attention. A group of military veterans formed an ad hoc organization called Swift Boat Veterans for Truth (later renamed Swift Vets and POWs for Truth). Upset over John Kerry's claims of courage, leadership, and bravery in Vietnam, they raised millions for commercials criticizing the Democrat. One ad claimed Kerry "is no war hero" and that he "lied to get his Bronze Star." Another took him to task for meeting with enemy leaders during the Paris peace talks and concluded "John Kerry cannot be trusted."[17]

Not to be outdone, a liberal group known as MoveOn.org challenged President George W. Bush's National Guard service during Vietnam. The group claimed Bush used family connections to avoid being sent to Vietnam and that he had not met his National Guard service duties.[18]

For weeks during the campaign, these dueling ads debated the two candidates' military records and revived controversies about the Vietnam War. Using their traditional prerogative of investigation, reporters delved into the claims of these groups. Investigative reports into the Swift Boat veterans revealed financing from individuals closely aligned with the Bush family. Journalists also noted a number of inconsistencies and factual inaccuracies in the group's claims. For example, it was found that several of the veterans criticizing Kerry's service record had praised him earlier and commended his bravery. Official military records also attested to Kerry's courage in the line of duty.[19]

Meanwhile, CBS News and others explored the MoveOn.org claims that Bush had benefited from favoritism in securing National Guard duty during Vietnam. In a highly publicized *60 Minutes* broadcast, long-lost military records were revealed that showed Bush had received preferential treatment and had not shown up for required military physicals during his National Guard duty.

The CBS broadcast touched off a firestorm of criticism, however. Documents experts claimed the military records were forgeries, citing as evidence contemporary font types not in existence in the 1970s. Eventually, after considerable embarrassment, Dan Rather and CBS News apologized for their reporting and said they could no longer verify the accuracy of documents used to question Bush's National Guard service.

The entire episode revealed the difficulty news organizations have in exercising oversight of political claims. Given the repetition of advertisements, it has proved difficult for news organizations to penalize advertisers for the use of false or misleading claims. News critiques air once while an ad is broadcast dozens of times. In addition, uncritical reporting amplifies misleading group claims.

In the end, journalists proved no match for the money and power of the candidates and their interest group allies. National public opinion polls showed that two-thirds of Americans had heard of the Swift Boat ads and one-third of those seeing the commercials believed Kerry had lied about his record, suggesting the anti-Kerry spots significantly impacted voter perceptions.[20] The declining respect people had for reporters undermined the ability of the press to act as effective oversight agents.

Media Coverage of 2008 Ads

Media coverage of advertising in the 2008 general election tended to be tougher, especially on McCain's attack strategy. The Arizona senator aired his attack spot "Celebrity" in July of that year. In it, he compared Obama to vacuous celebrities such as Paris Hilton and Britney Spears and argued that the Illinois figure was "the biggest celebrity in the world." The ad showed images of Obama's speech before adoring fans in Berlin as the crowd chanted "Obama!" the way sycophants do at rock concerts. By associating Obama with celebrity infatuation, the ad claimed that Obama lacked substance and was not ready to lead the United States.

In airing this ad and later ones questioning Obama's vision, character, and background, McCain signaled that he would run a harshly negative campaign against Obama. Subsequent ads linking Obama to convicted Chicago felons, former domestic terrorists, and his former pastor, Rev. Jeremiah Wright, revealed that 2008 would be a hard-hitting general election.

Unlike some previous years, though, the press took a tough stance on McCain's attacks, as well as some questionable claims from Obama. In regard to McCain, reporters complained that the candidate took Obama's comments out of context or used misleading or inaccurate information in spots. One positive ad aired by McCain called "Original Mavericks" said that his vice-presidential pick, Alaska governor Sarah Palin, was a true reformer who had fought such pork-barrel spending as the infamous "Bridge to Nowhere." In reality, Palin had supported the bridge until it became apparent Congress was going to kill the project, and then her state kept the highway money provided for the bridge construction. Her office also hired prominent lobbyists to try to boost Alaska's share of federal earmarks, contrary to her stated rhetoric in opposition to pork-barrel projects. When confronted with such facts, McCain ignored the new evidence and kept repeating his false claims about her record in the face of media coverage to the contrary. This undermined the candidate's credibility with reporters and increased the negative tone of their stories about him.

McCain's attack spots came under additional scrutiny when reporters questioned their accuracy. The GOP nominee repeatedly said Obama would raise taxes on the middle class even though Obama was careful to say he would raise taxes just on those individuals earning more than $250,000. This represented the top 5 percent of wage-earners in the United States and was similar to the tax stance Bill Clinton had taken during the 1992 campaign. Reporters questioned the fairness of McCain's attacks and pointed to independent analyses by tax experts that revealed that middle-class families would fare better under Obama's tax cut than McCain's.[21]

Obama, too, came under some scrutiny, although not as intense as his opponent. One newspaper story characterized his attacks on McCain's health care and Medicare positions as "inaccurate." An Obama ad claimed McCain would make $882 billion in "drastic cuts to Medicare" even though independent groups thought that was not likely. McCain said his program would leave senior citizens with exactly the same level of benefits as what they currently held.[22]

But despite these claims and counter-claims, there is little evidence that McCain's attacks on Obama were very effective; instead they backfired. Part of the problem with McCain's strategy was that he picked attacks using people and events from decades earlier. The most effective attacks involve contemporary actions, not historical ones. In addition, the unfavorable press reporting of his attacks led two-thirds of voters to blame him, not Obama, for the negative style of discourse during the campaign. Finally, McCain's attacks were less effective than in some past races, such as 1988, because many of his attacks were personal, not issue-oriented. Voters tend to feel that attacks on policy are more relevant to governing than those centering on personal character.[23]

Voluntary Efforts

Dissatisfaction with paid campaign advertisements in American elections has generated heartfelt pleas for fundamental change in the way elections are conducted. One proposal to improve civic discourse in American political life is free television time for the candidates. Put forward in its latest incarnation in 1996 by Paul Taylor of the Free TV for Straight Talk Coalition, this approach was simple. As expressed in a full-page *New York Times* ad on October 1, the coalition proposed that "from October 17 through November 1, all of the major networks carve out two and a half minutes in prime time to allow the presidential candidates to deliver mini-speeches on alternating nights."[24] This would allow office-seekers the opportunity to speak directly to the general public without mediation by journalists or interest groups.

But the problem in 1996 and 2000 was that the major networks refused to adopt a standardized format or schedule. In 1996, for example, the Fox Network agreed to broadcast ten one-minute campaign statements by Clinton and Dole during prime time in the weeks leading up to the election. Under the plan, each candidate would deliver a one-minute speech in response to each of ten questions that Fox had posed based on questions citizens had indicated were important to them in a national public opinion survey. CBS also agreed to two-minute segments by Clinton and Dole titled "Where I Stand" on each of four consecutive nights starting October 21 based on topics (education, taxes, Social Security and Medicare, and health care) defined as important by voters in a CBS News poll. However, ABC was only willing to give Dole and Clinton a single-shot, extended interview in prime time the week before the election; CNN set aside time during *Inside Politics* for candidate segments entitled "Addressing America," and NBC would only commit time during its *Dateline* news magazine program.[25] The same lack of willingness to set aside block time periods occurred in 2000, which limited the effectiveness of the free television time idea. No production assistance or voice-overs were allowed, just the candidates speaking directly into the camera. The audience for these segments was tiny as a result of the lack of press attention and the lack of a standardized schedule that could be publicized.[26]

Even more problematic was the unwillingness of television stations to provide free time for races below the presidential level. In general, television stations refused to provide free time for any candidates other than presidential contenders because of the lost revenue and concern about equal time requirements for all candidates. However, A. H. Belo Corporation, owner of seven local stations, was one of the exceptions. It offered five minutes of free broadcast time to local candidates for the Senate, House, and gubernatorial races in the seven cities in which Belo owned television stations.[27] By 2004 and 2008, though, these efforts to provide free, prime-time slots to the candidates had fizzled out, so there were no opportunities for candidates to make these kinds of appeals unless, like Obama, they purchased time for themselves.

Ad Watches

Another reform proposal centers on ad watches, newspaper columns and television segments devoted to monitoring the accuracy of political advertising. As described by Kathleen Hall Jamieson, one of the originators of the concept, ad watches provide a "grammar of evaluation."[28] In their original formulation, reporters would show an ad (or provide a transcript in the case of a newspaper story) and then critique the claims presented. Were there factual inaccuracies? Was the rhetoric overblown? Did the ad mislead the public in any way?

The 1988 presidential campaign was the first to feature ad watches. From time to time, national newspapers printed "truth boxes" in which ad claims were assessed. The television networks ran stories containing a broadcast of an ad and a critique by a reporter. However, focus groups conducted that year revealed that these ad watches did not achieve their purpose. Viewers often remembered the ad but not the media corrections.

Jamieson encountered the same problem in focus groups she conducted. When she showed a story by Richard Threlkeld of CBS debunking Bush's "Tank" ad, she was dismayed to learn that viewers internalized the ad message. In the Bush spot, a helmeted and obviously ill-at-ease Dukakis rode around in a military tank while visual text on screen claimed the Massachusetts governor opposed major weapons programs. Threlkeld ran a lengthy critique of this ad showing that Dukakis actually supported a number of weapons systems, but viewers who saw this story were more likely to believe Bush's charges against Dukakis than the news story's rebuttal.

The problem was that when Threlkeld rebroadcast the ad within his news story to critique it, the spot was shown full-screen. Reminiscent of Lesley Stahl's experience during the Reagan presidency, this approach exposed people to compelling pictures (see chapter 1). Many viewers remembered the visuals, not the audio critique.

The style of coverage in the 1988 campaign was disturbing to reporters themselves. The feeling was that by not having challenged Bush more effectively that year, candidates in subsequent elections ran deceptive ads to the detriment of campaign dialogue. Based on this experience, ad watches were changed in several ways. Instead of rebroadcasting ads full-screen, Brooks Jackson of CNN made an innovative effort on the show *Inside Politics* to review ads without hyping the candidate. The trick, according to Jackson, was to use what Jamieson called a truth box to rebroadcast a commercial in a smaller square tilted to the side so that viewers could see it was not a candidate's airing of the ad.

This shrinking of the video in an ad watch is important because it undercuts the visual impact of the advertisement. Rather than forcing news analysts to compete with powerful visual images, the CNN approach allows reporters to superimpose their own graphics, such as "misleading," "false," or "unfair" over the ad. This method puts the news story on a fairer visual footing with the ad. In the analysis of the spot, the dimensions of accuracy and fairness were separated from notions of strategic effectiveness so that viewers would realize there were several different standards of evaluation. It was hoped that this approach would overcome the tendency displayed during the 1988 presidential campaign of evaluating ads mainly on the dimension of whether they worked.

The media in 1992 devoted considerable space to ad watches. Overall, the *New York Times* ran fifteen separate reviews throughout the nominating process, and the *Washington Post* ran twenty-one. The general election campaign featured twenty-nine ad watches in the *New York Times* and twenty-four in the *Washington Post*. The television networks also incorporated ad segments into a number of stories.

Ad watches had a big impact on candidates. The 1992 campaign witnessed the rise of what I call "ads with footnotes." Reporters' scrutiny forced candidates to document their claims more carefully. This led some presidential aspirants to include factual citations directly on the screen reminiscent of footnotes in a term paper. For example, Clinton ads routinely listed the source and date of publication of a quote or fact for viewers to see. Clinton would quote a statistic and cite the Bureau of the Census or a newspaper article as the source.

This was an obvious effort to boost the credibility of the Clinton ads. Because nonpartisan sources, such as newspaper articles and government reports, have greater credibility than partisan pieces, ads with footnotes are a way of piggybacking claims onto the high credibility of more objective sources. Clinton media adviser Frank Greer said his campaign's research in 1992 "consistently found that viewers believed Bush's negative ads—such as one suggesting that Clinton would raise taxes on middle-class workers—lacked documentation. . . . They [the Bush advisers] never figured out that you needed to offer people substantiation and details. Ross Perot figured that out."[29]

Because of the close attention the media devote to ads, it is not surprising that the viewing public notices ad watches. A 1992 survey revealed that 57 percent of respondents said they had seen ad watches, 28 percent said they had not, and 15 percent did not remember. Viewers reported that they found ad watches helpful. Another survey that year asked respondents how helpful news stories analyzing ads had been.[30] Of those expressing an opinion, 21 percent indicated the stories had been very helpful, and 47 percent said they had been somewhat helpful. Only 32 percent felt the ad watch analysis had not been helpful in some way.

According to reporters, ad watches are effective oversight tools. Howard Kurtz of the *Washington Post* said they are "a great step forward for democracy because they keep candidates honest." The same sentiment was expressed by Mara Liasson of National Public Radio, who said that "candidates are more careful because they know [they] will be scrutinized."[31]

However, research by Stephen Ansolabehere and Shanto Iyengar published at the beginning of the 1996 campaign concluded that ad watches are almost completely ineffective.[32] Drawing on three simple experiments in which some viewers were shown a CNN ad watch while others were not, Ansolabehere and Iyengar obtained a surprising result. Participants developed greater support for candidates whose ads were scrutinized by reporters. This was the exact opposite of what had been intended by the ad watch. More generally, the authors raised criticism about whether it was appropriate for the press to act as self-appointed watchdogs policing the action of political candidates. Since many of the judgments of journalists are subjective and involve value-laden assessments, it would be better, Ansolabehere and Iyengar suggested, for candidates and voters to make decisions about what is unfair or misleading.

Jamieson challenged Ansolabehere and Iyengar's research on the grounds that the particular ad watches used in the experiment were not typical of the genre. Appearing on CNN's *Inside Politics* and writing later in a January 27, 1996, *New York Times* op-ed piece, Jamieson argued that the particular commercials reviewed in the study's ad watches were judged to be accurate, not inaccurate.[33] Therefore, it was a failure of the experiment, not a failure of the ad watch, when voters responded favorably.

To see how media outlets viewed ad watches, I participated in a project that conducted a telephone survey of 261 newspapers and local television stations across the country in 1996.[34] Newspaper managing editors and local television news directors were asked whether their outlets had conducted ad watches, when they had started, which election campaigns they covered, what format was used, how they evaluated the impact of the ad watches, and whether they planned to continue ad watches in the 1996 campaign.

Newspapers were much more likely (65 percent) than television stations (44 percent) to have conducted ad watches. The first ones appeared in 1988, and most television stations began to run them in 1990 and 1992. The most frequent elections covered in newspaper ad watches were gubernatorial races (54 percent of all newspapers), followed by Senate races (51 percent), House contests (47 percent), local races (36 percent), presidential campaigns (26 percent), and referenda (1 percent). Television stations were most likely to cover Senate races (21 percent), compared with presidential races (16 percent), House contests (16 percent), gubernatorial races (12 percent), local races (8 percent), and referenda (0 percent). Few editors felt that ad watches had reduced ad frequency, led candidates to withdraw ads, made campaigns less negative, or led candidates to be more careful in what they said. Yet newspaper editors expressed more support for ad watches than did news directors at television stations.

Part of the problem with ad watches concerns their format. Whereas 60 percent of newspapers used ad watches to analyze truthfulness, only 20 percent of television stations did. Only one in every ten media sources used clear language to condemn candidate ads. Most accounts leaned over backwards to be even-handed in their treatment of the major candidates. This works to the advantage of candidates willing to push the envelope and engage in deceptive appeals. Thus, some of the failures of ad watches to achieve their potential are due to an unwillingness on the part of newspapers and television stations to use them to their full effect.

The ad watches conducted in national outlets reviewed a relatively small proportion of the ads actually broadcast by candidates. Most spots were reviewed just a single time, in contrast to the dozens of times top ads aired before the viewing public.[35] Of course, media outlets have more credibility with the American public than do partisan political ads. But an imbalance exists between the frequency of ads broadcast and the frequency with which those ads are reviewed through ad watches.

Another problem was the development of different types of ad watches. Some followed the traditional model of evaluating ad accuracy. In general, based on focus groups in 1996, voters liked these segments and felt they added a valuable perspective to campaign discourse. However, other ad watches moved into the realm of strategic calculations and evaluated campaigners' goals in running particular ads. In focus groups, these segments were not as favorably received by voters. Ordinary citizens viewing these types of ad watches felt reporters were not adding much substantive information and were focusing too much on "the game."[36]

Focus groups revealed that ads have added so much visual text onscreen and that so many different candidate, party, and independent group organizations are running spots today that voters have difficulty correctly identifying the sponsors of political ads. In one focus group dealing with a Senate race, only 50 percent of participants correctly identified the sponsors of candidate and party ads they were shown. In another focus group, which dealt with the presidential campaign, only 46 percent correctly identified ad sponsors despite having just seen the ad.[37]

On average, the text identifying the sponsor of an ad is on the screen for five seconds, which is not long enough for many viewers to identify. In one case—that of an independent ad on retirement savings accounts broadcast by the American Council of Life Insurance—only 40 percent of focus group participants correctly identified its sponsor immediately after having seen the ad. Twenty percent believed it was put on by the Clinton campaign, 20 percent did not know who had broadcast the ad, and 20 percent erroneously believed it was sponsored by the Cato Institute because that organization had been listed in visual text onscreen at the beginning of the spot in a footnote for a claim made during the commercial.[38]

These observations demonstrate that in the increasingly multi-faceted world of political ads, greater attention needs to be given to disclosure of ad sponsorship. Rather than having the disclosure text shown onscreen for just five seconds, it should be shown continuously throughout the ad. This would give viewers more time to determine which organization is sponsoring the ad and put them in a stronger position to see where the ad message is coming from. The "I approve of this message" requirement from the 2002 BCRA has had no discernible impact on restraining candidate behavior or producing more positive campaigns. There is little evidence that these attributions of personal responsibility limit candidates' inclination to go negative against opponents.

The 2000 election reflected renewed interest on the part of news organizations in running ad watches. The *New York Times* printed eighteen during the nominating stage (double the 1996 rate) and fourteen during the general election. The *Washington Post* ran five during the primaries (about the same as in 1996) and six during the fall campaign. Most of the spring reviews dealt with the GOP primary, which was the more competitive of the two nominating contests. Three of the five Republican ads reviewed by the *Washington Post* involved George W. Bush or John McCain ads, whereas thirteen of the twenty ads reviewed by the *New York Times* involved

Bush, McCain, or independent groups focusing on one of the Republican candidates. In the fall, ad watches monitored the accuracy of candidates' ads and questioned the validity of attacks on Bush's Texas record and the ambiguities of competing budget claims for Bush and Gore about their health care proposals. However, with campaign spending reaching record heights, it became more and more difficult for ad watches to evaluate the endless flow of political commercials.

By 2004, ad watches had subsided again. During the nominating process, the *New York Times* ran only six ad watches; the *Washington Post* did one. In the general election, the *New York Times* carried three ad watches, compared to none for the *Post* (although the latter had stories critiquing ads). Many newspapers and television stations throughout the country dropped the practice of reviewing advertisements unless something particularly problematic took place. Bush, for example, generated a number of critical news stories when one of his early commercials referred to the September 11, 2001, attacks on the World Trade Center and the Pentagon and incorporated a few seconds of video images of firefighters carrying away victims. Critics complained that Bush was politicizing a national disaster. Yet the Bush campaign held firm and continued to talk about September 11 and the risks facing the United States.

With a literal flood of advertising expenditures in contested battleground states, the ability of journalists to oversee candidate and group claims plummeted. When commercials aired dozens of times and critical news stories appeared just once, candidates learned they could stretch the truth and engage in misleading appeals without much risk. This represents a stunning reversal of the privileged place journalists held in American politics three decades ago.

However, by 2008, media policing of the campaign airwaves became more extensive. There was a substantial increase in coverage of campaign advertising and greater efforts to evaluate factual accuracy. CBS ran a number of "Reality Checks" that examined the accuracy of candidate claims. Its national political correspondent, Jeff Greenfield, also ran a Friday feature called "the Good, the Bad, and the Ugly" that highlighted noteworthy advertisements and speeches on the part of the candidates. These features helped focus public attention on questionable claims, and brought unfavorable scrutiny to those engaging in deceptive practices.

Conclusion

The press play a vital role in policing candidate abuses. From the infamous "Daisy" ad in 1964 to deceptive and manipulative images during the 2008 campaign, journalists help set the rules of fair play and constructive discourse. Unfortunately, in recent years, journalists have relinquished that traditional role and left candidates to police themselves. This creates problems in terms of campaign behavior. Without meaningful oversight, candidates have incentives to push the envelope and engage in actions and rhetoric harmful to the democratic process. Unless journalists continue to exercise vigilance over the campaign process, it will be difficult for voters to assess candidate behavior.

Chapter 5

Learning about the Candidates

E arly efforts to study the impact of ads emphasized learning about substantive matters: Do the media provide information that increases voters' knowledge of where candidates stand on the issues? To the pleasant surprise of scholars, research from the 1970s revealed that voters who watched ads got more information than did those exposed only to television news.[1] Experimental work also supported claims about the educational virtues of commercials.[2] Ads did not help candidates create new political images based on personality; rather, political commercials allowed viewers to learn about the issues.

Notwithstanding the undeniable trend of these studies, researchers have persisted in their efforts to examine the effects of advertising. Great changes have taken place in the structure of political campaigns since earlier research was completed. New electoral arenas have arisen that do not have the stabilizing features of past settings. Furthermore, recent campaign experiences run contrary to interpretations that emphasize the educational virtues of commercials. Television is thought to have played a crucial, and not very positive, role in a number of races, a state of affairs that has renewed concern about the power of ads to alter citizens' beliefs.[3]

Indeed, recent studies have found that voters do not often cast ballots based on the issues. Citizens form many impressions during the course of election campaigns, from views about candidates' issue positions and personal characteristics to feelings about the electoral prospects of specific candidates, and those views are decisive. As ads have become more gripping emotionally, *affective models* that describe feelings are crucial to evaluations of candidates' fortunes.[4]

Favorability is an example of an affective dimension important to voter choice. Citizens often support the candidates they like and oppose those they dislike. If they dislike all, they vote for the ones they dislike the least. Anything that raises a candidate's favorability also increases the likelihood of selection.[5] Candidates devote much attention to making themselves appear more likable. Values that are widely shared, such as patriotism and pride in national accomplishments, help candidates increase their favorability ratings among voters. Conversely, hard-hitting ads are used to pinpoint the opposition's flaws.

The opening up of the electoral process has brought new factors such as electability and familiarity to the forefront. *Electability* refers to citizens' perceptions of a candidate's prospects for winning the election in November. Impressions of electability can increase voters' support of a candidate because citizens do not want to waste their votes. *Familiarity* is important as a threshold requirement. Candidates must become known to do well at election time. The development of a campaign structure that encourages less widely known candidates to run makes citizens' assessments of a candidate's prospects a potentially important area of inquiry.

Advertising and the Electoral Context

Past work on television advertising has focused on a particular kind of electoral setting—presidential general elections. For example, Thomas Patterson and Robert McClure's findings were based on the campaign that ended in Richard Nixon's landslide victory over George McGovern. The ads' apparent lack of effect on voters' assessments of the candidates is not surprising in light of the lopsided race and the fact that by the time of the initial survey in September public perceptions of the two candidates had largely been determined. In that situation, it was appropriate for Patterson and McClure to conclude that people "know too much" to be influenced by ads.[6]

However, as Patterson and McClure pointed out, other electoral settings display greater opportunities for advertising to have measurable effects. Nominating campaigns and Senate races show extensive shifts in voters' assessments of the candidates. Presidential nominations often have unfamiliar contenders vying for the votes of citizens who hold few prior beliefs about the candidates. In these settings, television commercials can play a major role in providing crucial information about the candidates.

Advertising is particularly important when news media time is scarce. In 1980, Ken Bode, then a reporter for NBC, recounted a letter written to him by Republican senator Bob Dole of Kansas following his unsuccessful nominating campaign: "Dear Ken, I would appreciate knowing how much coverage my campaign received by NBC from the date of my announcement to my final withdrawal. I've been told my total coverage by NBC amounted to fourteen seconds."[7]

Senate races also have become heavily media oriented. Candidates spend a lot of money on television advertising, and Senate contests have taken on the roller-coaster qualities of nominating affairs. Many Senate elections feature volatile races involving unknown challengers. Because some observers have speculated about the effects of advertising, it is important to study advertising in nominating and Senate campaigns to determine whether its impact varies with the electoral setting.

Citizens' Knowledge and Evaluations of Candidates

Elections in recent decades represent an interesting opportunity to study the impact of political commercials. According to electoral surveys, citizens' assessments of the candidates varied widely depending on electoral setting. Presidential general election candidates were the most well known, with a range of recognition levels from a low in 1992 for Bill Clinton (73 percent) and Ross Perot (67 percent) to a high for Gerald Ford (95 percent) in 1976. The average recognition level in presidential general elections was significantly higher than for nomination candidates or Senate contenders.

By the end of the campaign in 2004, 88 percent of respondents recognized John Kerry and 90 percent recognized George W. Bush. But it took Kerry a long time to gain this recognition level. In March, only 57 percent recognized him, and in mid-September that number was 73 percent. Kerry's relative lack of recognition gave Republicans an opportunity to use advertising to create unfavorable portraits of him. In 2008, Barack Obama started the race in January with a 70 percent recognition level, compared to 63 percent for John McCain. By the end of the general election, Obama's recognition rate had risen to 85 percent and McCain's had increased to 84 percent (see Table 5-1).

Citizens' perceptions of candidates' likability and electability have varied extensively. Of recent nominees, Ronald Reagan has been the best liked (66 percent in 1984), and George H. W. Bush (23 percent in 1992), Dole (25 percent in 1996), and Perot (18 percent in 1996) the least liked. The 2004 Republican nominee, George W. Bush, was liked by 48 percent, compared with 41 percent who liked Kerry. This

TABLE 5-1
Voter Perceptions of John McCain and Barack Obama during the 2008 Campaign

2008 Campaign	January 9–12	February 20–24	March 15–18	March 28–April 2	April 25–29	May 1–3
McCain						
Recognition	70%	68%	69%	64%	67%	67%
Favorability	57	36	38	35	33	32
Says what believes	—	—	—	—	—	51
Bring real change	—	—	—	—	—	—
Effective commander in chief	—	—	—	—	—	—
Understands needs	—	—	—	—	—	—
Obama						
Recognition	71	78	72	67	73	74
Favorability	55	45	44	43	39	44
Says what believes	—	—	—	—	—	53
Bring real change	66	—	—	—	—	—
Effective commander in chief	—	—	—	—	—	—
Understands needs	—	—	—	—	—	—

2008 Campaign	July 7–14	July 31–Aug. 5	Aug. 29–31	Sept. 5–7	Sept. 12–16	Sept. 27–30	Oct. 10–13	Oct. 19–22	Oct. 25–29
McCain									
Recognition	63	67	69	83	81	81	77	85	84
Favorability	31	33	35	46	44	39	36	39	41
Says what believes	46	49	—	—	52	—	—	—	—
Bring real change	28	—	—	46	37	—	—	—	39
Effective commander in chief	82	72	77	82	79	73	—	—	85
Understands needs	—	—	41	51	48	46	43	42	49
Obama									
Recognition	70	69	73	81	80	80	82	83	85
Favorability	39	37	39	44	45	48	50	52	51
Says what believes	43	42	—	—	51	—	—	—	—
Bring real change	58	—	—	65	65	61	—	—	64
Effective commander in chief	62	59	63	59	61	61	—	—	64
Understands needs	—	—	63	61	60	67	64	68	64

Source: CBS News/*New York Times* national surveys.
Note: Entries indicate the percentage of voters holding various impressions of the candidates.

put them around the midpoint of likability over the past few
decades. In October 2008, Obama had a 51 percent to 41 percent
favorability advantage over McCain.

In regard to electability during the fall, McGovern in 1972 was
the candidate seen as least electable (1 percent), whereas George
Bush Sr. in 1988 was seen as the most electable (85 percent), followed closely by the 83 percent of respondents in 1996 who
believed Clinton was the most electable. In 2008, Obama held an
electability advantage over McCain because voters saw it as a likely
Democratic election year.

Furthermore, voters have a sense of the policy issues and personal
traits associated with each candidate. Foreign policy considerations
were prominent in 1972 for McGovern and Nixon because of the
Vietnam War, whereas domestic matters dominated thereafter. In
terms of personal traits, this period began with candidates' experience
being the most cited and ended with leadership being the most cited.

In 2008, both Obama and McCain were seen as strong and honest leaders, but there were differences in how they were viewed.
McCain's lengthy public service gave him an experience nod over
Obama, who first had entered the Senate in 2004. By the end of the
campaign, 85 percent thought McCain would be an effective commander in chief, compared to 64 percent who felt that about
Obama. The Illinois senator, however, held advantages on change
and understanding people's needs. Sixty-four percent believed
Obama would bring real change to the United States, whereas only
39 percent thought that would be the case with McCain. Sixty-four
percent also believed Obama understood people's needs, much
higher than the 49 percent who said that about McCain.

Overall, it remains to be seen how political commercials influence
perceptions of the candidates. In general, Senate races showed the
strongest advertising effects, with exposure to campaign ads associated with high recognition of political contenders. The average difference in recognition between respondents who scored high on ad
viewing and those who scored low was twenty-seven percentage
points.[8] Senate campaigners typically are not as well known as presidential contenders, which means that political commercials can be
more influential in raising the visibility levels of those who run for
a Senate seat.

Presidential elections showed a lower association for recognition
based on advertising exposure. The largest general election difference
in recognition came during the 1988 Bush-Dukakis race. These men

were among the least known of recent party nominees. Dukakis was not known nationally, and despite having been vice president for eight years, Bush had not been particularly visible in that office.

In the nominating process, the magnitude of the difference varied according to how well known the individuals were. Candidates who were not well known used advertising to advance their name recognition. For example, in April 1976, polls from the Pennsylvania primary revealed that Jimmy Carter had a difference of twenty-one points between the high and low ends of his ad exposure scale. Michael Dukakis and Al Gore also showed substantial differences in 1988—eighteen and twenty-one percentage points, respectively. In 1992, Pat Buchanan had the greatest rating differential for visibility, whereas in 1996, Steve Forbes had the highest difference (fifteen percentage points) in recognition between those seeing and those not seeing his ads.

Ads also affected citizens' perceptions of favorability; the strongest effects were for Senate and nominating races.[9] In both the 1974 and the 1990 Senate campaigns, ad viewing produced favorability gains for the Democratic and Republican candidates. These effects were not consistent in the nominating process, but this changed for Gore and Bush in 1988. Both ran aggressive advertising campaigns, and their strategies appear to have paid off. Gore, for example, emphasized a populist image designed to win the support of white southerners. Bush ran a hard-hitting campaign designed to persuade voters that he was the logical heir to the Reagan legacy. It is interesting to note that Dukakis's ads were not associated with changes in favorability ratings. The Massachusetts governor had difficulties during the fall in overcoming public impressions that he was cool and aloof.

In 1992, Buchanan displayed the largest improvement in favorability (twelve percentage points) between the low and high ends of his ad exposure scale. He ran the spring's most prominent ad, "Read Our Lips," which painted a negative picture of Bush and questioned the president's character for breaking his promise of no new taxes. Eventually, according to Bush adviser Robert Teeter, the president was able to beat back the Buchanan challenge through attack ads that told voters, "[Our] guy's the goddamn president, and the other guy's a goddamn typewriter pusher, and the toughest thing he's had to do in his whole life is change the ribbon on his goddamn Olivetti."[10]

In terms of electability, ads were associated with significant effects for Nixon in fall 1972, Carter in spring and fall 1976, Dukakis and

Bush in spring 1988, Buchanan and Clinton in spring and fall 1992, Clinton in 1996, and George W. Bush and Gore in 2000.[11] Seeing ads for these candidates was related to believing that a candidate was politically strong. Dukakis's ads created the impression of electoral strength. Although his commercials did not make voters feel any more favorable toward him, they helped generate a sense of inevitability about his campaign. Of the races examined in this study, Bush in 1992 was the only one whose ad exposure actually hurt the perception of his electability. Frequent ad viewers were less likely to see him as electable than were infrequent viewers.

If one looks at ad impact on prominent issues and personal traits, most elections conform to the findings of Patterson and McClure, which put forth that the effects of advertising on citizens' perceptions of issues were substantially larger than the influence on assessments of personal traits.[12] However, in 1976, Carter ran an image-based campaign that produced stronger advertising effects for evaluations of personal traits than of issue positions.[13] In the 1988 nominating process, Dukakis, Gore, and George Bush had ads that produced strong effects on assessments of both issues and traits.[14]

Clinton was able to use his 1992 and 1996 campaign commercials to help viewers see him as caring and capable of handling the economy. He used ads in 1992 to tell the story of families having problems affording quality health care. His fall ads helped project an image of hopefulness and of being able to improve the economy, which was important to voters discouraged by the country's dismal economic performance.[15] Bush was the only major candidate in 1992 unable to boost impressions of himself on his positions on either issues or character.[16]

The Impact of the Campaign

When looking at how ads and the campaign affected voter perceptions of the candidates, it is clear there were important effects. Those who saw Nixon ads in 1972 were more likely to see him as wishing to uphold commitments made to other nations. The same phenomenon emerged in the 1988 nominating process. During that year, exposure to ads influenced people's perceptions of the issue positions of Dukakis (on the military), Gore (on unfair competition from Japan), and George Bush (on deficit reduction). The 1992 race helped viewers understand Buchanan's and Clinton's stances on the economy and Paul Tsongas's on competition from Japan. Each candidate ran ads that made these subjects central to his campaign.[17] During the general election, Clinton worked hard to stake out claims to particular issues to prevent Republicans from trespassing on traditionally Democratic ground, as Bush had done in 1988 when he campaigned on promises to become the environmental and education president. But Clinton's strategy also created problems for himself. One of the criticisms directed against him in spring focus groups was that he was difficult to pin down: "If you asked his favorite color he'd say 'Plaid,'" stated one focus group participant.[18]

Ads had an impact on viewers' assessments of candidates' images, likability, and electability that was at least as strong as the effect on viewers' assessments of issue positions. In terms of perceptions of likability, commercials had a significant impact in many elections. For Gore and Bush in 2000, ad exposure was related to favorability ratings; the same was true for Buchanan and Perot in 1992 and for Senate candidates in 1974 and 1990. In terms of electability, the strongest ad impact came with Dukakis in the 1988 nominating process, but effects were present for Nixon in 1972, Carter in 1976, Buchanan and Clinton in 1992, and Clinton in 1996. Conversely, people who saw Bush's ads in 1992 had a negative sense of the president's electability.

Some campaigners were able to mold public perceptions of personal traits. Those who watched Carter ads saw him as an able leader, and those who saw Gore ads in 1988 felt he was likely to care about people. Those who watched Clinton ads in the spring of 1992 believed that he was a caring individual. The ads helped create a positive view of his character, which countered the negative coverage received after Gennifer Flowers came forward to claim he had an affair with her.[19]

In the 2000 presidential general election, I looked at the connection between a viewer thinking Gore and Bush, respectively, were electable and that person seeing news and ads for the candidates. Those individuals who saw Gore's ads were more likely to report that he was electable. The same was true for Bush to an even greater extent. In 1996, those who said they saw Clinton's ads were much more likely to cite him as electable, whereas those who saw Dole's ads were significantly more likely to say he was not electable. Seeing Perot's ads or the TV news had no impact on his electability.

The weak results for Perot's ads in 1996 contrast clearly with the situation in 1992. That year, Perot's ads were the most memorable and provided a dramatic boost for the Texan in the closing weeks of the campaign. In contrast, people in 1996 who said they saw Perot's ads were not more likely to recognize him, like him, or feel that he was electable.[20] Part of the problem related to his ad-buy strategy. Unlike in 1992, when he aired $60 million in ads during the last month of the election and dramatically outspent both Clinton and Bush, he did not choose to do this in 1996.

There also were interesting relationships between viewers seeing TV news and candidates' ads and how those viewers saw candidates' personal qualities and political views. In 2000, those who saw Gore's commercials were more likely to see him as providing fiscal discipline and less likely to believe that Bush would do so. However, those who reported seeing national television news concluded the opposite: that Bush would be fiscally responsible and caring and that Gore would not likely be either.[21]

In 2004, ads were linked to changing perceptions of the candidates. Voter impressions shifted during the course of the campaign. Using national surveys undertaken by CBS News/*New York Times*, it is apparent that Kerry was far less known (57 percent recognition level in March 2004) than Bush (82 percent recognition), but became about as well known as the president by the end of October. Throughout most of the campaign, Bush held a higher favorability rating than did Kerry.

From the beginning of the general election in spring 2004, Bush attacked Kerry as a wishy-washy politician who told voters what they wanted to hear. This perception stuck with voters as the polling data revealed that Bush consistently had a huge advantage over Kerry in people's views that he says what he believes. For example, in mid-October, 59 percent portrayed Bush as saying what he believed, compared to 37 percent who felt that way about Kerry.

Bush also neutralized a traditional Democratic strength, that of being seen as caring and compassionate and understanding the needs of ordinary people. Ever since Herbert Hoover's inaction in the face of the Great Depression in the 1930s, voters have seen Democrats as caring more about ordinary folks than Republicans. However, on this key dimension, Bush was able to narrow the perception gap. Whereas in mid-October 51 percent thought Kerry understood the needs of everyday people, 44 percent felt that way about Bush. For a president whose tax cut policies had benefited wealthy Americans and who had passed billions in tax breaks for corporations, this represented a major victory. In addition, Bush tarred Kerry with the code word "liberal," similar to what his father had done to Dukakis in 1988. At the beginning of the general election, 39 percent of registered voters saw Kerry as a liberal; by mid-October, this number had risen to 56 percent.

In short, Bush used attack ads to portray Kerry unfavorably. He characterized the Massachusetts Democrat as a doctrinaire liberal who was also wishy-washy and unprincipled. These two critiques are noteworthy because in some respects, they are inconsistent: It is difficult to be simultaneously wishy-washy and a doctrinaire liberal. However, by repeating these messages over and over, Bush was able to reinforce these perceptions about Kerry.

In 2008, Obama and McCain started out with similar recognition and favorability levels. As shown in Table 5-1, 70 percent of registered voters in a January 2008 national survey recognized McCain, whereas 71 percent recognized Obama. McCain had a 57 percent favorability rating, compared to Obama's 55 percent. By the end of the general election, however, Obama held a ten-point favorability advantage over McCain. The decline of foreign policy issues such as the Iraq War and international terrorism and the rise of domestic economic issues clearly played to Obama's advantage. Public opinion surveys demonstrated that voters perceived Democrats as having a stronger capacity to handle economic issues than Republicans. Since the terrain was favorable to Democrats, the public opinion climate helped create sympathetic feelings toward the Democratic nominee.

Obama's ads played on voter anxiety about the economy by reminding people that Republicans had been in charge for eight years and that the economy had deteriorated during that time. The United States had gone from a $1 trillion budget surplus to a deficit of the same size. The combination of a weak economy and strong communications effort helped people see Obama as a caring and compassionate individual who would understand their needs. This neutralized McCain's experience advantage and offset the GOP nominee's virtue of being seen as a stronger commander in chief.

Ads and the Vote

Recent campaigns offer interesting opportunities to investigate how ads affect the vote.[22] The 1988 Democratic nominating process was a wide-open, seven-candidate affair with no well-known front-runner until Dukakis began to forge ahead at the time of the Super Tuesday primaries in March. At that point, a number of candidates were running hard-hitting ads challenging the substantive positions and personal qualifications of opponents. For example, Richard Gephardt's ads in Iowa and South Dakota criticized Dukakis for claiming naively that farmers could reverse their financial problems by planting Belgian endive. Dukakis's ads later accused Gephardt of flip-flops on policy matters.[23] Gore and Jesse Jackson also ran strong campaigns in key southern states.

Dukakis's victories on Super Tuesday were vital to the inevitability that began to surround his candidacy. Until then, he had put together a strong organization and had been successful in terms of fund-raising. But it was the support expressed at the time of Super Tuesday that began to propel him toward the nomination.[24] How did this sense of momentum develop? An analysis of the Dukakis vote during this critical period shows how decisive electability was for the Dukakis vote. The more he was seen as being electable, the more likely voters were to support him.[25]

Race, gender, and party identification were also directly linked to support for Dukakis. Race was important, owing to the presence of an African American candidate (Jackson) in the contest. Voters were clearly polarized, with Jackson receiving the vast majority of the black vote and Dukakis and Gore dividing the white vote. Gender and party identification had a strong effect on support for Dukakis, with women and strong Democrats being most likely to vote for him.[26]

Dukakis's advertising had indirect consequences for the vote by affecting perceptions regarding electability. The strongest predictor of voters' views on electability was exposure to spot commercials. More than race, gender, or partisanship, ads shown prior to Super Tuesday influenced voters to see the Massachusetts governor as the most electable Democrat.[27] The same was true when the ads of competing candidates such as Gore were included in the analysis. Seeing ads for the Massachusetts governor was associated with feeling Dukakis was the most electable Democrat, and these views about electability had a clear impact on the vote.[28]

In the 1992 Republican primaries, advertising played a different role. At the start of the race, President George Bush was on the defensive over his handling of the economy and his inattention to domestic politics in general. Buchanan ran a series of ads castigating Bush for breaking his famous "no new taxes" pledge. In part because of saturation coverage of the New Hampshire and Massachusetts markets, these commercials achieved a remarkably high level of visibility.[29]

A March survey asked viewers which ad run by a Republican presidential candidate had made the biggest impression. Of the 590 people interviewed, 92 (about 16 percent of the entire sample) were able to name a specific ad. The most frequently named commercial was Buchanan's "Read Our Lips" spot, which was cited by sixty-four people, followed by Buchanan's "Freedom Abused" spot against the National Endowment for the Arts, which was named by eleven people. Overall, eighty-five viewers cited specific ads for Buchanan, compared with six for Bush and one for David Duke.

Not only were Bush's commercials unmemorable, they also had a negative impact on views about the president. A reporter who covered the race said the president's ads about the need for change "weren't connected to reality. People smelled that. They knew he wasn't the candidate of drastic change." In contrast, Buchanan's advertisements "weren't bull. They were real. Bush had broken campaign promises." When people were exposed to ads from both candidates, they were less likely to see the president as electable or vote for him.[30] These results were surprising not only because they were negative but also because they contrasted so clearly with Bush's ad performance in 1988, when his commercials dominated those of Dukakis.

Part of the problem was that Bush's 1992 spots simply were not as catchy as Buchanan's. The challenger's ads had an air of authenticity. Bush's advertising meanwhile did not successfully use visual symbols and narrative to develop his connection with salient issues. In one ad, for example, he referred to the Persian Gulf War and attacked Congress to show how strong he was. According to Robin Roberts, Bush's ad tracker, this spot was the most frequently run in the nominating process.[31] But it did not address the main issue of concern to voters—getting the economy going again and helping the unemployed with new jobs.

President Bush suffered further because media coverage of his 1992 nominating campaign was quite negative. Reporters in New Hampshire questioned his campaigning ability, his concern about human suffering, and his disjointed speaking style (which also was mimicked by comedian Dana Carvey). This pattern of coverage undermined the president's message and made it difficult for him to impress people who saw his ads. Although he ultimately was able to win his party's nomination, Bush's spring commercials did not lay a strong foundation for the fall campaign.

In the 1996 Republican primaries, Dole's early lead produced a political situation in which other candidates, such as Forbes, went on the attack in an effort to undermine the front-runner's support. A late January and early February 1996 national survey conducted before the Iowa caucuses found that Forbes's ads had achieved a high level of visibility. Whereas 51 percent indicated they had seen ads for Dole, 40 percent said they had seen Forbes's ads, and 24 percent indicated they had seen ads for Buchanan, 20 percent had viewed Phil Gramm's ads, and 10 percent had seen ads for Lamar Alexander.[32] Of the 927 individuals interviewed in that survey, 24 percent were able to cite a commercial that had made an impression on them (higher than the 16 percent in 1992). Overall, seventy-seven individuals cited Forbes's ads, sixty-three cited Dole's, forty cited Democratic National Committee ads for Clinton, eighteen cited Gramm's, nine cited Alexander's, and eight cited Buchanan's.

Spots for Buchanan were less memorable than in 1992, but as the primary process wore on, his spots rose in memorability. They targeted emotionally provocative topics such as his views on the evils of NAFTA and the danger of immigration. Much like he had done in 1992, he was able to develop vivid ads on graphic issues. Viewers began to cite his ads more frequently and those of Forbes less frequently.

Dole's ads achieved a high degree of visibility but were not especially memorable to viewers. People remembered seeing the ads but could recall few specific details, and when asked which specific ad had made the biggest impression on them, no Dole ad got more than a single mention. But his advertising situation improved in the fall. When voters were asked which ad had made the greatest impression on them, more people named ads for Dole (sixty-four mentions) than for Clinton (fifty-six mentions) or Perot (forty-eight mentions). The most frequently cited specific ad in the general election was Dole's MTV ad (twenty-one mentions), which replayed videotape of Clinton saying he would inhale when smoking marijuana if he were doing it over again.

In 2000, a national survey asked people which television ad run by a presidential campaign during the fall had made the biggest impression on them. Overall, 23 percent mentioned some ad, and 77 percent indicated no ad had made an impression on them (about the same as in previous elections). When looking at the impact of ad exposure on electability and the vote in this election, we find interesting results. George W. Bush was the only candidate for whom there was a negative ad impact on the vote. The more people saw Gore's advertisements, the less likely they were to say they would vote for Bush. In addition, the more liberal, Democratic, and nonwhite respondents were, the less inclined they were to support Bush. These results are consistent with evidence about the memorability of particular commercials. More individuals were likely to cite Gore than Bush advertisements when asked which spot had made the biggest impression on them.

In 2004, voters started the general election showing an eight-percentage-point lead for President Bush (by a 46 to 38 percent margin). The president's advantage reflected several strengths. At that point, Kerry was not very well known. The president was also aided by voter perceptions that he was a strong leader serving in troubled times. But by the end of July, right after the Democratic convention, Kerry moved to his first lead in the race. According to the CBS News/*New York Times* national surveys, Kerry was supported by 48 percent of voters, compared to 43 percent supporting Bush. Kerry's rise reflected a well-received convention acceptance speech and the positive press coverage that accompanied this presentation.

However, August proved to be a very difficult month for Kerry. His campaign was not able to go on the air with commercials because he had exhausted his nomination funds and did not want to use his scarce general election dollars. At the same time, outside groups such as the Swift Boat Veterans for Truth (see chapter 4) were attacking Kerry's Vietnam record and alleging he was not trustworthy. Under these circumstances, he was not able to sustain his advantage. By September, Bush had regained the lead (50 to 41 percent).

Throughout the remainder of the fall, though, the two candidates were locked in a tight race. Kerry's support rose slightly during the three presidential debates; his strong performance boosted voter backing of his candidacy. But Bush maintained his own support by attacking Kerry's liberal record and inconsistent stances on terrorism. One ad entitled "Wolves" started airing October 22. It showed a pack of wolves running through woods, while a female announcer spoke of the dangers confronting the world and how "Kerry and liberals in Congress" had voted to cut spending on intelligence-gathering in the 1990s. The commercial claimed that weakness invited danger and encouraged those who wanted to harm America. By the end of the campaign, Bush's post-debate slump had disappeared: On a 51 to 48 percent popular vote, Bush beat Kerry and won reelection.

In April 2008, Obama started with a 51 to 40 percent lead over McCain. As shown in Table 5-2, he was able to maintain this lead until early September, when McCain for the first time edged to a two-point lead. Russia had invaded Georgia in August, and McCain

TABLE 5-2
Voter Preferences during the 2008 Campaign

	April 3	May 3	July 7–12	July 31– Aug. 5	Aug. 29–31	Sept. 5–7	Sept. 12–16	Sept. 27–30	Oct. 10–13	Oct. 19–22	Oct. 25–29
McCain	40%	40%	39%	39%	40%	46%	43%	40%	39%	39%	40%
Obama	51	51	45	45	48	44	48	49	53	52	51
Unsure	9	9	16	16	12	10	9	11	8	9	9

Source: CBS News/*New York Times* national surveys.

Note: Entries indicate the percentage of voter support for each candidate.

had taken a very tough foreign policy stance, calling for cutting ties to Russia and enlarging NATO to include Eastern European countries, a position strongly opposed by Russia.

However, this lead did not hold up for long. In mid-September, major financial institutions melted down, which put economic news back on the front page. In short order, the national government was forced to put public monies into major banks, and Congress enacted a landmark $700 billion financial rescue program. Between September 12 to 16, Obama surged back to a five-point lead, and soon his margin was up to double-digits. In the last survey, Obama led McCain by 51 to 40 percent, identical to the margin he had held in April.

Conclusion

To summarize, ads are one of the major ways in which citizens learn about the candidates. From advertisements, voters develop perceptions about personal qualities, values, electability, and issue positions. Not only are these perceptions important for the candidates, they affect the vote. Citizens often support those candidates they like, with whom they share values and who they feel are electable.

Ads do not operate autonomously. People bring prior beliefs such as party attachments, ideological stances, and life experiences relating to their age, gender, education, and race. For this reason, candidates undertake detailed research on voter opinions. Campaign commercials must dovetail with a person's background and political orientation for an ad to be effective. If a spot does not resonate with people, it will not inform viewers in the manner desired by candidates.

Chapter 6

Setting the Agenda

Few subjects are more central to the political system than agenda formation. It is well established that issues come and go and that at any given time only a few matters receive serious consideration by government officials.[1] *Agenda setting* refers to the process by which issues evolve from specific grievances into prominent causes worthy of government consideration. In a political system in which citizens pay only limited attention to civic affairs, it is a mechanism through which the public can influence official deliberations by conveying its sense of which problems are important.

Television is thought to play a crucial role in setting the agenda.[2] Shanto Iyengar and Donald Kinder's experimental work strongly supports a model of media agenda setting. The respondents to their study of network news regarded any problem covered by the media as "more important for the country" and "cared more about it, believed that government should do more about it, reported stronger feelings about it, and were more likely to identify it as one of the country's most important problems."[3]

However, there has been little extension of this work to political advertising. In a campaign, agenda setting is very important. Candidates use election contests to dramatize issues. They also try to de-emphasize matters that may be problematic for them. George Bush Sr.'s strategy in 1988 clearly involved a redefinition of the agenda away from certain aspects of Ronald Reagan's record and toward furloughs and flag factories (Michael Dukakis's vulnerable areas) in an effort to move the campaign debate onto terms more advantageous for Republicans. The same thing happened in 2004 when George W. Bush sought to focus the agenda on terrorism and global security and in 2008 when Democrats benefited after the agenda shifted back to the domestic economy. Candidates' advertising therefore should be assessed in terms of its ability to change citizens' perceptions of what are the most important priorities.

The Media's Role in Agenda Setting

A large number of societal problems warrant government attention. Some are domestic in nature, involving fundamental questions of poverty, justice, and social welfare, whereas others include the broad contours of macroeconomic performance or foreign policy. But not all matters of social concern get defined as political problems that deserve government attention. In the United States, many problems are considered to be outside the sphere of government. According to Stanley Feldman, it is common in the generally individualistic political culture of the United States for certain subjects to be defined as private matters related to the personal characteristics of individuals. Whereas other societies attribute responsibility for difficulties more broadly, a belief in economic individualism weakens attributions of collective responsibility in the United States.[4]

Some areas are seen as problematic but not a priority for institutional deliberations. Paul Light demonstrates convincingly in his study of presidential agenda setting how important it is for leaders to conserve their political capital and focus their attention on a limited number of issues.[5] The chief executives who are the most successful develop specific priorities and are able to communicate their preferences clearly to voters.

From the standpoint of researchers, the most interesting question is how topics move from private concerns to top priorities and what role the media play in this process. Roger Cobb and Charles Elder argue that agenda setting is a way for citizens to convey preferences to leaders in a system characterized by limited participation. They demonstrate how the characteristics of particular policy areas (such as concreteness, social significance, long-term relevance, complexity, and novelty) influence the scope and intensity of political conflicts. These authors suggest that the media—because of their crucial role in defining the nature of conflict—can "play a very important role in elevating issues to the systemic agenda and increasing their chances of receiving formal agenda consideration."[6] Their conclusions are in line with a number of public opinion studies that have found that media exposure is a major factor in how people rank policy concerns.[7] Issues that receive a lot of attention from the press generally are seen as important problems facing the country. Saturation coverage by the media, of the sort that occurred during the Watergate scandal, can have a decisive effect on the public agenda.[8]

Other scholars have been more sanguine about media influence. John Kingdon studied agenda formation using lengthy interviews with leaders as well as detailed studies of congressional hearings, presidential speeches, polling data, and media coverage. His interviews revealed that few leaders attribute much of an agenda-setting effect to the mass media. Instead, policy entrepreneurs who advocate new policy proposals are seen as very significant, and emphasis is also placed on interest groups (named as important by 84 percent) and researchers (named by 66 percent). In contrast, only 26 percent of the leaders Kingdon interviewed said the media are important.[9]

Kingdon does suggest ways in which the media can elevate particular issues. Reporters often influence agenda formation by acting as conduits of information for policymakers.[10] Because policymakers are swamped with the daily demands of governing, they sometimes use media coverage to determine which problems deserve immediate attention. The press can also act as a triggering mechanism for agenda setting by using particular styles of coverage. Through crisis reports or investigative journalism, the media can magnify particular events and turn them into catalysts for official action.

The exact magnitude of the media's impact appears to depend considerably on institutional setting. For example, Light's analysis of agenda setting in the presidency attributes more influence to the media than to much of the work conducted in Congress. Like Kingdon, Light found that the media often act as an indirect channel to the White House. Although they rarely serve as an incubator of new ideas, they are a "source of pressure."[11]

Some investigations have documented the impact of television ads on the public agenda during campaigns. For example, Charles Atkin and Gary Heald studied advertising in a 1974 open seat election to the House of Representatives.[12] Through a survey of 323 voters in the closing weeks of the campaign, they found that ad exposure altered voters' impressions of the most important policy issues in the race. Thomas Bowers meanwhile examined a number of Senate and gubernatorial races in 1970 and demonstrated that exposure to newspaper ads corresponded with survey results about most important issues.[13]

Policy and Campaign Components of the Public Agenda

In the campaign world, the agenda includes both policy and campaign components.[14] The policy agenda is rooted in the real conditions of people's everyday lives. If unemployment rises, there will be a parallel increase in concern about jobs. When oil tankers spill their cargo, worry arises regarding the environment. In contrast, campaign issues are more ephemeral and less rooted in objective realities. Questions related to momentum and mistakes often arise quickly, based on electoral developments and media coverage.[15]

Opinion polls have included a series of open-ended questions examining citizens' views about the most pressing policy concerns for the country and about the most important campaign events.[16] Since the 1970s, priorities have undergone a fundamental shift. In 1972, foreign affairs and economic matters dominated the fall general election campaign between Richard Nixon and George McGovern. By the 1974 Senate races, inflation was starting to rise nationally. At the same time, the Watergate scandal that forced the resignation of President Nixon in August of that year was renewing public concern about honesty in government. In 1976, when unemployment and inflation were cited as the most important problems, economic issues returned to the forefront. In the 1980s, foreign affairs again became a major issue, and taxes and spending also emerged as central concerns for the first time. Both Reagan and George H. W. Bush devoted great attention in their advertising and political speeches to keeping down the size of government. Bush's most famous line in the 1988 campaign occurred during his convention speech when he said, "Just read my lips—no new taxes."[17] But in the next four years, prosperity disappeared, and the economy and concern over unemployment again emerged as the top issues in 1992. The 2000 agenda emphasized education, health care, Social Security, morality, and the economy. In 2004, with an uncertain economy and controversial wars in Iraq and Afghanistan, the agenda included a number of different issues: moral values, Iraq, the war on terror, the economy, and health care. But by 2008, public attention was riveted back on "It's the Economy, Stupid."

Meanwhile, in terms of campaign-related topics, the top developments in the spring of 1976 were that Jimmy Carter and Reagan both won key primaries, whereas the presidential debates were the most notable events in the fall. The 1984 CBS News/*New York Times* survey broke down the most important campaign events for individual candidates, and 60 percent cited Reagan's mistakes in the debates. In 1988, 54 percent named George Bush's attacks on Dukakis as the most important development of the fall campaign. The 1992 primary race saw voters naming Pat Buchanan's unexpected showing in New Hampshire and Bill Clinton's scandals as the most important developments of the nominating campaign, and Ross Perot's candidacy and the debates as the most important aspects of the general election campaign. The 2000 campaign showed the debates, the Mideast crisis and the attack on the USS *Cole*, Al Gore's lies and exaggerations, and Ralph Nader's Green Party candidacy to be the most important campaign developments. In 2004, George W. Bush's lack of veracity on whether there had been weapons of mass destruction in Iraq and John Kerry's Vietnam War experiences attracted considerable attention. By 2008, the combination of the unpopular war in Iraq and the weakening national economy dominated the country's political agenda. Voters worried whether McCain's candidacy represented a third term for President George W. Bush and whether the country was ready for an African American president.

Ads and Agenda Setting

An analysis of ads and agenda setting shows that during the 1972, 1976, and 1984 campaigns, ads were not associated with voters' views on particular policies. For example, the top issue cited in 1972 was foreign affairs, and ad exposure had no significant effect on voters' opinions. There were weak ad effects in 1976 on voters' views about unemployment and inflation and in 1984 on peace and arms control as well as on taxes and spending. By contrast, in George Bush's 1988 general election campaign and Clinton's fall 1992 campaign, ad exposure did play a role in citizens' policy views.[18] Among those who did not watch ads, 21 percent cited taxes and spending as most important in 1988, whereas 46 percent of viewers who had paid attention to Bush's ads cited these issues, a whopping difference of twenty-five percentage points.

Differences were also found in citizens' assessments of campaign events. In 1976, 27 percent of those who did not watch ads cited Carter's doing well as the most important development in the campaign, compared with 36 percent of those who had paid attention to ads. In 1980, Reagan also experienced a substantial effect of twenty-six percentage points based on ad viewing among those who cited his debate performance as the most important thing he did in the campaign.

In 1988, too, there were ad effects on those campaign events cited as most important. Eight percent of respondents who had not seen ads cited Bush's campaign as his top accomplishment, compared with 14 percent of those who had paid attention to Bush's ads. There were significant differences based on ad exposure in viewers feeling that Dukakis was not responding to Bush. Among those with low attentiveness to ads, 6 percent named this problem, whereas among those with high attentiveness, 17 percent mentioned it.[19]

An analysis of the connection between ad viewing and feelings about most important problems and most notable campaign events demonstrates that advertising significantly affected voters' rating of several policy problems (honesty in government in 1974, taxes and spending in 1988, the economy and budget in 1990, and unemployment in 1992). In 1974, seeing and paying attention to ads were linked to citing honesty in government as the most important problem. Similarly, in 1992, ad exposure was related to naming unemployment as the country's top concern. In 1996, seeing Clinton's ads was associated with thinking crime and drugs were the central issues and that Medicare and Medicaid were not as important. In 2000, the top ad effect was found between seeing advertisements for Gore and believing Social Security was the most important problem.

The Influence of Individual Ads

General exposure to campaign ads is associated with citizens' assessments of the public agenda, but what about individual ads? Most past work has examined ad exposure in aggregate form with no distinction made among ads. To explore the impact of individual ads, I analyzed some of those most frequently named. In 1984 the CBS News/*New York Times* survey asked, "Both presidential candidates had a lot of television commercials during this campaign. Was there any one commercial that made a strong impression on you? (If so) Which commercial?" The top Walter Mondale ad named in the post-election survey was the "Future" commercial, whereas Reagan's top ad was the "Bear in the Woods" spot (see Appendix for descriptions of these ads). In 1988, the CBS News/*New York Times* poll again asked which ads made the biggest impression: "Tell me about the commercial for [Bush/Dukakis] that made the biggest impression on you." Viewers picked the "Revolving Door" as Bush's top ad and the "Family/Education" ad for Dukakis.

A 1992 survey asked, "Which television ad run by a presidential candidate this fall has made the biggest impression on you?" Of the people questioned, 24 percent were able to name a specific ad. Perot received by far the most mentions: 109 people cited his ads; 27 cited Clinton's, and 9 cited Bush's. Perot's most memorable ads were his infomercials, mentioned by 38 people, followed by his spot discussing job creation (19), his sixty-second spot discussing the legacy of national debt being left to the nation's children (18), and the commercial in which he discussed having received a Purple Heart in the mail from a supporter (10). Clinton's top commercials were "How're You Doing?" (7) and "Read My Lips" (5). Bush's top ad accused Clinton of wanting to raise taxes (3).

In 1996, the top ad was Dole's MTV ad in which Clinton indicated he would inhale marijuana if he were doing it over again. The second most frequently cited ad was Perot's "It's Your Country" spot, in which a series of young people talk about how important it is to make up your own mind.

To determine the effects of specific ads on citizens' views about the policy agenda, I analyzed ad exposure on those matters seen as the country's most pressing policy problems, controlling for party identification, education, age, race, gender, ideology, political interest, and media exposure.[20] In the case of Bush, Dukakis, Clinton, and Perot, the findings conformed to conventional wisdom. However, with regard to Reagan and Mondale, the common view was not supported. Mondale's "Future" ad on defense matters was very effective, at least from the standpoint of having the strongest tie to people's priorities. Among those who had not seen the ad, 20 percent cited peace and arms control as the most important problem, compared with 38 percent of those who had seen it. Mondale's ads also influenced beliefs that restoring pride in the United States had been the most important aspect of the 1984 campaign.

For all the attention devoted to Reagan's "Bear in the Woods" ad, in which the bear was seen as a symbol of the Soviet Union, this commercial had no significant effect on either of the concerns noted: peace and arms control or restoring pride in the United States. Part of the problem may have been the abstractness of the ad. Although the Reagan campaign was apparently confident of the public's ability to understand it, the spot contained abstract allusions both to dovishness—the bear may not be dangerous—and hawkishness—we need to be strong. Its complexity may have limited its effect on the agenda.

In 1988, Bush's "Revolving Door" ad was linked to mentions of crime and law and order as the most important problems facing the United States.[21] Among those who had not seen the ad, only 5 percent cited these problems, compared to 12 percent of those who had seen it. This finding fits with evidence cited by Marjorie Hershey, who found that "the proportion of respondents saying that George Bush was 'tough enough' on crime and criminals rose from 23 percent in July to a full 61 percent in late October, while the proportion saying Dukakis was not tough enough rose from 36 to 49 percent."[22] The Dukakis ad did not produce significant effects on any domestic policy dimension.[23]

In 1992, Perot's infomercials were quite effective at focusing attention on the economy, as was Clinton's "How're You Doing?" ad on unemployment. Perot's ads had a simplicity and directness that in an anti-politician year appealed to viewers. Clinton's spot was able to raise public awareness of jobs as an important problem. Focus group tests within the Clinton campaign showed that his commercial "zoomed off the charts" when played for voters.[24]

Women and the "Revolving Door" Ad

No commercial since Lyndon Johnson's "Daisy" ad has generated more discussion than George Bush's "Revolving Door." This spot was aired frequently during the evening news and discussed extensively by news commentators. In looking at the effects of this ad on agenda setting, fascinating differences arise based on the personal circumstances of viewers. Among the people most likely to cite crime as the top problem after seeing Bush's "Revolving Door" commercial were Midwesterners and young people.

But most significant were the differences between men and women in regard to Bush's 1988 ads. One of Bush's strongest agenda-setting effects from his "Revolving Door" ad, for example, was among women on the crime issue.[25] After seeing this commercial, as well as the widely publicized Horton ad produced by an independent political action committee, women became much more likely than men to cite crime as the most important issue.

The fact that the ads mentioned rape clearly accentuated their impact on women. According to Dukakis's campaign manager Susan Estrich, "The symbolism was very powerful . . . you can't find a stronger metaphor, intended or not, for racial hatred in this country than a black man raping a white woman. . . . I talked to people afterward. . . . Women said they couldn't help it, but it scared the living daylights out of them."[26]

The "Revolving Door" case demonstrates how the strategies of campaign elites and overall cultural context are important factors in mediating the significance of advertisements. The way in which this commercial was put together—in terms of both subject area and timing—was a major contributor to its impact on viewers. If Horton had assaulted a fifty-year-old black man while on furlough from a state prison, it is not likely that the "Revolving Door" ad would have affected voters' policy priorities as it did.[27]

The Strategic Dimensions of Agenda Control

Strategic interactions revolve around two key campaign decisions—what subjects to cover in advertisements and whether to attack the opposition. Matters that have attracted citizens' concerns, such as rising unemployment, oil spills, or ethics in government, are the natural subjects of television advertising.[28] The decision to "go negative" is another important part of strategic decision-making. In the 1990s, it became widely accepted that negative ads work. Attack commercials are influential because they help candidates control the agenda and drive media coverage, which enables the sponsor to set the tone of the campaign.

No case provides a better illustration of campaign strategy than the Bush-Dukakis race in 1988. Bush seized the initiative at the beginning of the fall campaign by demonizing Dukakis and tying him to unpopular issues. Recognizing that Dukakis was one of the least known nominees in recent years, Bush advisers developed a plan designed to define the terms of the campaign. When it became obvious that Dukakis was the likely Democratic nominee, Lee Atwater gave his staff instructions for what is euphemistically called opposition research—that is, digging for dirt on the opponent's background. Speaking to Jim Pinkerton, the research head of Bush's campaign, Atwater said, "'I want you to get the nerd patrol. . . . We need five or six issues, and we need them by the middle of May. . . .' I gave him a three-by-five card, and I said, 'You come back with this three-by-five card—but you can use both sides—and bring me the issues that we need in this campaign.'"[29]

The Bush campaign also picked up attack clues from Dukakis's Democratic opponents in the nominating process, such as Gore. This included the Willie Horton case and Dukakis's veto of legislation that would have mandated the recitation of the Pledge of Allegiance in schools.[30] After testing these themes in a series of focus groups, the Bush campaign consciously pursued agenda control through an attack strategy. As stated by Bush's media adviser Roger Ailes, "We felt as long as the argument was on issues that were good for us—crime, national defense, and what have you—that if we controlled the agenda and stayed on our issues, by the end we would do all right."[31]

Dukakis, however, chose a different route. He had earned the nomination by generating a sense of inevitability about his campaign. Through early fund-raising, the development of a strong organization, and cultivation of the view that he was the most electable Democrat, Dukakis was able to play the role of the long-distance runner in the race. Because his advertising generally was positive (with the exception of his timely attack on Richard Gephardt's flip-flops), he did not offend his opponents' voters. Dukakis thereby was able to gain opposition support when voters' preferred candidates bowed out. The lesson he learned from the nominating contest, then, was that if he was patient and took the high road, victory would come eventually.

According to Estrich, his campaign manager, Dukakis decided that his fall race would, among other things, center on character and integrity. She said, "An important element of our fall strategy . . . would emphasize competence . . . [and] the value of integrity. You saw this at the convention and throughout the campaign—that Mike Dukakis stood for high standards. That's the kind of campaign he would run, the kind of governor he had been, the kind of president he would be."[32] Along with the nomination experience, which had rewarded a positive campaign, this decision inevitably led to a strategy that would not respond to Bush's fall attacks.

However appropriate this approach may have been in the nominating context, with its sequential primaries and multiple candidates, it was disastrous in the two-candidate context of the general election. Dukakis's decision allowed Bush to set the tone of the campaign and to define the terms of debate. Bush's issues—flags, patriotism, tax-and-spend liberalism, and crime—became the agenda of the campaign. Little was heard about homelessness, rising poverty, and the unmet social needs of the Reagan years.

The consequences of these campaign choices are reflected in an analysis that shows the impact on voters after seeing each candidate's top ads: Bush's "Revolving Door" and Dukakis's "Family/ Education" ad. Bush was able through his "Revolving Door" commercial to widen the perception of crime as the most important problem facing the country. In contrast, exposure to Dukakis's ad decreased the importance of crime in the eyes of voters. Viewers who thought crime was the most pressing policy problem also were more likely to say they would cast ballots for Bush over Dukakis.[33]

Bush's attacks took a toll on the Massachusetts governor. Not only did the attacks allow the vice president to dictate the terms of debate in the campaign, but Dukakis's failure to respond adequately created the perception that the Democrat was not a fighter. As stated by Estrich, "The governor was hurt by the attacks on him—the mental health rumors, the attacks on patriotism, the harbor and furlough issues—and perhaps most of all by the perception that he had failed to fight back, which went to his character. . . . We did fight back on occasion. The problem is we didn't fight back effectively, and we didn't sustain it. We created a perception that we weren't fighting back, and I think that hurt us much more."[34]

Dukakis's decision was even more harmful in light of the very favorable media coverage reaped by Bush. In an intensive analysis of network news coverage in 1988, Kiku Adatto found that newscasts ran segments from the "Revolving Door" ad ten times in October and November, making it the most frequently aired commercial of the campaign. Overall, twenty-two segments about Bush's crime ads were rebroadcast during the news, compared with four for Dukakis's ads.[35]

These news reports reinforced Bush's basic message. A number of stories appeared during the general election campaign citing political professionals who believed that Bush's tactics were working and that Dukakis's strategy was a complete failure. Because these assessments appeared in the context of news programs, with their high credibility, they were more believable than if they had come from paid ads.

A Fixed Agenda

The agenda in 1992 differed significantly from 1988 in emphasizing a single topic—the economy. In 1988, the election took place in a setting characterized by a fluid agenda and no single dominating concern, but in 1992, the Clinton campaign's favorite line about the agenda was "The Economy, Stupid" in honor of a sign Clinton adviser James Carville kept posted in the Little Rock headquarters. About two-thirds of Americans identified the economy and unemployment as the crucial problems facing the country, far exceeding any other issue.

The presence of a fixed agenda altered the strategic terrain of the presidential campaign. Rather than attempting to redirect people's priorities, as had been the case in 1988 when peripheral concerns such as crime were made central to voters, candidates geared their appeals to jobs and economic development. In the case of Clinton and Perot, the message was simple: Economic performance was poor under George Bush, with gross domestic product growth in the negative range. President Bush discussed the economy, although he wavered between claiming that things were not as bad as his opponents charged and admitting that the economic picture was terrible but blaming congressional Democrats.

Bush's attempt at agenda redefinition—raising questions about Clinton's character in order to deflect attention from his own record—was not very successful. After being urged privately by Ailes to "go for the red meat [and] get on the bleeping offensive," the president challenged Clinton on numerous personal dimensions in speeches, interviews, the debates, and spot commercials.[36] In one of his most hard-hitting ads, Bush used a series of ordinary men and women to criticize Clinton's integrity: "If you're going to be president you have to be honest." "Bill Clinton hasn't been telling anything honestly to the American people." "The man just tells people what they want to hear." "About dodging the draft." "I think he's full of hot air." "I wouldn't trust him at all to be commander in chief." "I think that there's a pattern, and I just don't trust Bill Clinton." "I don't think he's honorable. I don't think he's trustworthy." "You can't have a president who says one thing and does another." "Scares me. He worries me. You know, and he'll just go one way or another."[37] It is interesting to note that the campaign edited out a criticism about Clinton's trip to Russia because backlash developed against Bush for hitting below the belt on this charge. In a play on Carville's sign, the Bush people also posted a message in their headquarters: "TRUST AND TAXES, STUPID." However, in light of Bush's decision to sign onto a congressional deficit reduction bill that raised taxes, thereby negating his well-publicized 1988 campaign pledge of "no new taxes," it was difficult for Bush to have much credibility on the trustworthiness front.

National opinion surveys demonstrated little increase in concern about Clinton's character during the fall campaign. For example, in a CBS News/*New York Times* survey taken from September 9 to September 13, 42 percent of respondents thought Clinton responded truthfully to the charge that he had avoided the draft, and 25 percent did not. Seventy-nine percent felt the allegation would have no effect on their vote.[38] In an October 12 to October 13 CBS News/*New York Times* poll, 79 percent of respondents claimed that their votes were unaffected by Bush's attacks on Clinton's antiwar activities at Oxford University.[39] Clinton's focus groups revealed little damage: "Many people indicated that they thought he [Clinton] had been evasive or had even lied, but they said that wouldn't affect their vote."[40]

Bush's efforts to redefine the agenda were unsuccessful because of unfavorable media coverage and the strategic response by Clinton and Gore. Although the media devoted considerable time and space to Bush's allegations, the spin on the story generally was negative toward Bush and his chief adviser, Jim Baker. Headlines repeatedly emphasized Bush's "assaults" on Clinton and "smears" on Clinton's character. Spokespeople for the Arkansas governor meanwhile labeled the tactics *McCarthyite*. News of State Department searches of the passport records of Clinton, as well as of his mother, brought this stinging rebuke from Gore: "The American people can say we don't accept this kind of abuse of power. We've had the Joe McCarthy technique and the smear campaign; now we have the police state tactics of rummaging through personal files to try to come up with damaging information."[41] Combined with sympathetic news coverage, this response undermined the legitimacy of Bush's attack strategy.

In addition, Bush's advertising attacks suffered because they were unfocused. After the election, Bush's advisers said their efforts were hampered because "we never knew if we were focusing on Arkansas or Clinton's character or big spending. I don't think it ever clicked. I don't think the character assault was framed very well."[42] Bush's focus groups furthermore revealed a boomerang effect from voters on the trust issue: "They didn't trust Clinton's word or Bush's performance." For a while, Bush's advisers had the candidate substitute *truth* for trust. But new wording did not change the final outcome.[43]

A Fluid Agenda

The biggest change in the agenda between 1992 and 1996 was the move from a fixed agenda dominated by the economy back to a fluid one that was broader and more diffuse. Whereas 60 percent of voters in 1992 cited the economy as the most important problem facing the country, the types of issues named in 1996 were quite varied: government spending, high taxes, crime rates, the drug problem, and the possible budget reduction of Medicare and Medicaid.

Overall, voters were far more positive about the economy. In 1996, according to network exit polls on election night, 59 percent of Americans rated the economy as excellent or good. In 1992, 19 percent had given the economy excellent or good ratings. This upturn in consumer confidence raised people's spirits and made a majority of voters feel the country was headed in the right direction.

The fluidity of the agenda in 1996 made that year look more like 1988 than 1992. Rather than having to frame every part of their message around the 800-pound gorilla of the economy, Clinton, Dole, and Perot enjoyed greater strategic flexibility. The result was that the campaign centered on competing conceptions about the country's direction. Clinton successfully framed the election's choice as a referendum on the Republican revolution of downsizing government. Did voters want to "CUT MEDICARE," "SLASH EDUCATION," and "GUT THE ENVIRONMENT"? Through ads, speeches, and news events, Clinton pounded home the message that Republicans were uncaring, insensitive, and not to be trusted with America's future.

Dole, by contrast, attempted to redefine the agenda along several different dimensions. His first frame, developed at the Republican convention and continued through mid-September, was on his economic plan of a 15-percent across-the-board tax cut. Unfortunately for him, only one-quarter of Americans believed he would actually deliver a tax cut for them, according to a national public opinion poll. When his economic program failed to arouse much voter interest, Dole shifted to crime and drugs in September. He aired the MTV ad, accused the president of failed liberal policies, and made some short-term gains in the polls. But the movement in his direction did not persist. It was not until the closing weeks of the campaign, when a series of Democratic fund-raising misdeeds came to light and Dole began to push the character attack, that polls tightened, and by Election Day Dole did better than expected. Rather than losing by the expected fifteen points, Dole lost by eight. Polls in congressional races around the country also showed a movement in a Republican direction in the last two weeks, which helped the GOP retain control of Congress. The character issue had resonated with people in a way the tax-cut issue and attacks on Clinton's crime and drug policies had not. The allegations of the Democratic National Committee's fund-raising illegalities were designed to portray Clinton as a politician not to be trusted. This turned out to be Dole's most successful effort at agenda redefinition during the fall campaign.

A Varied Agenda

Education, health care, taxes, and Social Security dominated the 2000 policy agenda, along with complaints about George W. Bush's inexperience and Gore's lack of trustworthiness. Each candidate attacked the policy prescriptions and personal weaknesses of his opponent. A CBS News/*New York Times* survey at the end of September found that 71 percent of respondents believed Gore had prepared himself well enough to be president, compared with only 49 percent who felt that way about Bush. Gore also was given an edge with voters in the areas of affordable health care (56 percent thought he would handle that issue better, compared with 35 percent who believed that of Bush) and caring about people (66 percent said Gore was caring, whereas 53 percent said Bush was). However, more voters believed that Bush would make U.S. defenses stronger (53 percent, compared with Gore's 18 percent) and that Bush would reduce taxes (43 percent, compared with Gore's 27 percent).[44]

By the end of October, though, some of these impressions had changed. After weeks of criticizing Gore's trustworthiness, Bush gained an advantage. A CBS News/*New York Times* survey found that 48 percent believed Bush said what he really believed rather than what he thought people wanted to hear, compared with 37 percent who said that of Gore. More people also gave higher marks to Bush (48 percent) for personal honesty and integrity than to Gore (42 percent).[45]

These opinions were reinforced by late-night comedians and *Saturday Night Live* skits that lampooned both major presidential candidates. In looking at the "joke war," Gore was the object of more jokes in August (78 to 43 for Bush), Bush was more ridiculed in September (94 to 34 for Gore), the two were virtually tied in October (126 lampooning Bush and 120 making fun of Gore), and the campaign closed with thirty-four jokes about Bush and eleven about Gore in the first week in November. Overall, from January 1 to November 6, Bush was the subject of 548 jokes, whereas Gore was the butt of 386. For example, making fun of Bush's mangling of the word "subliminable," David Letterman said, "Earlier today, George W. Bush said that he has one goal for these debates. He wants to show the American people that he's presidentiamable." In regard to Gore, Jay Leno laughed about Gore's lies and exaggerations, saying, "You've gone from George Washington, who could not tell a lie, to Bill Clinton, who could not tell the truth, to Al Gore, who can't tell the difference."[46]

In this situation, the candidates used ads to sway voter opinion. In his commercials and public statements, Bush complained that Gore had a tendency to exaggerate and that if you couldn't trust him, how could you trust his policy proposals? For his part, Gore aired an ad in the closing days of the campaign asking whether Bush was "ready to lead" the country. Voter concerns were heightened when, a few days before the general election, a Maine attorney uncovered information concerning a 1976 arrest record for Bush for driving under the influence of alcohol. The resulting media clamor forced Bush off message and helped fuel a last-minute surge by Gore that led to the closest election result in recent history. Following several weeks of ballot recounts and legal wrangling over contested voting in Florida, Bush eventually was declared the winner by five Electoral College votes.

A Bifurcated Agenda: Terrorism versus the Economy

The agenda in 2004 featured a battle between an agenda bifurcated between terrorism and security concerns on the one hand and domestic economic issues on the other. American elections typically center much more on domestic than foreign policy considerations, but the September 11, 2001, attacks and the subsequent wars in Afghanistan and Iraq placed foreign policy directly onto the political agenda. In terms of campaign-related topics, Bush attempted to portray Kerry as a flip-flopping liberal out of touch with the American mainstream.

For example, in early advertising in spring 2004 Bush complained that Kerry would penalize drivers with a 50-cent-per-gallon gasoline tax, would "raise taxes by at least $900 billion," would "weaken the Patriot Act used to arrest terrorists," opposed "body armor for troops in combat," and "opposed weapons vital to winning the war on terror—Bradley Fighting Vehicles, Patriot missiles, B-2 stealth bombers, F-18 fighter jets."[47] A Bush spokesperson justified these attacks by saying "Kerry sailed through the Democratic primary process with little or no scrutiny. In order to make an informed judgment about whether Kerry is a suitable choice for president, voters need to have this information." However, the Kerry campaign saw a more nefarious motive. Strategist Michael Donilon complained that Bush staffers "have decided that the only way to win this election is to destroy John Kerry."[48]

For his part, Kerry attempted to characterize Bush as "a corporate toady who wants to foul the air and water, outlaw abortion, and export U.S. jobs overseas." Among other claims, ads by the Massachusetts Democrat argued that Bush "wants to roll back the Clean Air and Clean Water acts," name "anti-choice justices" to the U.S. Supreme Court, and supports "sending jobs overseas."[49]

In general, however, Kerry's early ads were much more positive than Bush's. One study found that 52 percent of claims in Bush's spots were attack-oriented, compared to 19 percent for Kerry.[50] This was in keeping with the general thrust of the Bush organization to paint Kerry in negative terms while he still was relatively unknown to the electorate as a whole.

When asked at the beginning of the campaign which one issue they most wanted to hear the presidential candidates discuss, voters named the war in Iraq (23 percent), economy and jobs (20 percent), health care and Medicare (13 percent), and education (5 percent).[51] However, by the fall, these priorities had shifted somewhat. Public interest in the economy and jobs was ranked the number one priority (20 percent), followed by the war in Iraq (18 percent), health care and Medicare (15 percent), and defense (4 percent).[52]

Throughout the fall, Bush attempted to maintain the focus on terrorism. One of his more provocative ads was called "Wolves." In it, a wolf runs through a forest, while a female announcer warns: "In an increasingly dangerous world, even after the first terrorist attack on America, John Kerry and the liberals in Congress voted to slash America's intelligence budget by $6 billion. Cuts so deep they would have weakened America's defenses. [Image of a pack of wolves resting on a hill] And weakness attracts those who are waiting to do America harm."[53]

Within a day, individuals outside the campaign had put up a new Web site titled WolfpacksforTruth.org, which advertised the "real story" on Bush's "Wolves" commercial. Taking on the voice of the wolves, the site explained that they'd been tricked by George W. Bush. "They told us we were shooting a Greenpeace commercial! When the camera crew showed up, we wondered why they were all driving Hummers. . . . Little did we know we were being tricked into this vicious campaign attack ad! We are not Terrorists. . . . We are a peaceful pack of wolves. All we want in life is: Live in tree-filled forests. Drink clean water from our rivers and streams. Breathe fresh and clean air."

And not to be outdone by animal imagery, Kerry started broadcasting an ad featuring an eagle and an ostrich: "The eagle soars high above the earth. The ostrich buries its head in the sand. The eagle can see everything for miles around. The ostrich? Can't see at all. . . . Given the choice, in these challenging times, shouldn't we be the eagle again?"[54]

On Election Day, though, it was clear how much Bush's effort at focusing the agenda on terrorism and moral values had paid off for him. National exit polls revealed a clear tie between seeing particular issues as most important and voting for the president. Bush won 85 percent of the votes of those who cited terrorism as their most important issue, compared to 15 percent for Kerry. Seventy-eight percent of those naming moral values as the most important consideration in the election cast ballots for Bush, compared to 19 percent who did so for Kerry. In contrast, Kerry's top issues were the economy and jobs (he received 81 percent of the vote of individuals saying this was their most important issue), education (76 percent of their vote), and Iraq (75 percent).

These results suggest how potent a combination cultural values and security concerns have become for the general public. While American elections generally have centered on domestic economic concerns, Bush successfully redefined the national agenda away from the economy, education, and health care to cultural and security issues. His unstated but clearly visible mantra during the campaign became, "It's Terrorism, Stupid." In so doing, he took advantage of voter anxiety in the post–September 11 world and repositioned his party as the one that would best defend the United States against both foreign and domestic threats.

It's Still the Economy, Stupid!

The 2008 agenda saw the country's financial meltdown and weak economy return to the forefront. In the spring, when asked what the most important problem facing the country was, Americans named the economy, followed by the Iraq War, health care, and high gas prices; by October, when the country slid into negative growth, all eyes centered on the domestic economy.

Obama's early ads focused on his record of emphasizing ethics reform and working in a bipartisan fashion. One spot, "America's Leadership," focused on the senator's bipartisan work with GOP senator Richard Lugar of Indiana. His commercials complained that McCain had accepted contributions from Big Oil and then turned around and proposed major tax cuts for these same companies. His ad "Pocket" ended with the memorable tagline: "After one president in the pocket of Big Oil, we can't afford another."

By October, though, Obama had shifted to such traditional Democratic issues as the economy, health care, and education. With the stock market having fallen by more than 40 percent and unemployment rising, the Democrat broadcast ads showing how voters in large industrial states such as Ohio and Pennsylvania were suffering from hard times. People's health care benefits were dwindling or lost altogether, and jobs were being shipped overseas. Complaining about McCain's shifting stance on fiscal matters, Obama's ads argued that the Arizona senator was "erratic" and had "careened from stance to stance." The result, according to the Democrat, was that he had "poured gasoline on the economic mess."

For his part, McCain sought to distract people from the dismal economic news by tying Obama to such controversial figures as alleged terrorist William Ayers, convicted Chicago financier Tony Rezko, and political machine fixture William Daley. One spot ended with the tagline: "With friends like that, Obama is not ready to lead." Another McCain commercial, "Dangerous," alleged that Obama was a risky individual who did not support U.S. troops. An ominous announcer claimed that Obama was "too risky for America."

By the end of the campaign, McCain had employed Joe Wurzelbacher, whom he called "Joe the Plumber," to make the point that taxes would rise on middle-class workers if Obama was elected president. One ad used footage from an encounter between Obama and Wurzelbacher to criticize Obama's response that he would "spread the wealth" and benefit everyone. This ad ended by saying "Barack Obama: Higher Taxes. More Spending. Not Ready."

Conclusion

Since voters are not able to focus on every important issue, campaigners seek to prioritize elections by focusing attention on a few items. If they can set the agenda in a way favorable to their own electoral interests, this is a tremendous help in the campaign as a whole. Some issues, such as national security, often are viewed as favoring Republicans, whereas topics such as health care generally help Democrats. As seen in a number of different elections, setting the agenda through advertisements is one of the major strategic goals in any campaign.

As argued in previous chapters, candidates cannot make an issue important if it is not already salient with voters. It is impossible to create relevance that does not previously exist. If the campaign features a fixed agenda with one dominant item, candidates have to address that topic. However, they have greater strategic flexibility when the agenda is fluid or varied. In that situation, their speeches and ads can increase or decrease the perceived saliency of a topic by giving it more attention. Raised issues can confer major electoral advantages if a candidate is seen as having greater competence or credibility on that particular topic.

Chapter 7

Priming and Defusing

Politics is one of many activities for American voters. The traditional notion that individuals review every option before making choices has been supplanted by models that incorporate information grazing, or sporadic searches for material.[1] *Priming* is a perspective that builds on this way of thinking about political information. Developed in regard to the evening news, this approach proposes that people use readily available material to evaluate candidates and that in the media age one of the most accessible sources is television. By its patterns of coverage, television can influence voters' choices between candidates by elevating particular standards of evaluation. For example, television shows that devote extensive coverage to defense matters can increase the importance of defense policy in citizens' assessments. Likewise, news accounts that dwell on environmental concerns can raise the importance of those matters in voting choices.[2]

Priming has attracted growing attention in relation to television news, but little attention has been paid to its conceptual counterpart, *defusing*. This term refers to efforts on the part of candidates to decrease the importance of particular standards of evaluation. Candidates often have problematic features, such as being seen as weak on defense or lacking a clear vision for the future. It obviously is in their interest to defuse their shortcomings. They can do this either by lessening the overall importance of a topic to the public or by shortening the distance between the candidates to the point where the subject no longer affects the vote.

The concepts of priming and defusing are particularly applicable to the study of campaign advertising. In the same way that the news can alter voter judgments, television commercials can prime (or defuse) the electorate by shifting the standards of evaluation. This chapter examines priming and defusing through campaign ads and demonstrates that commercials can alter the importance of various factors in voters' decision-making. There are a number of examples (such as George H. W. Bush in 1988 and Bill Clinton in the 1990s) in which political ads helped campaigners prime and defuse citizens' concerns.[3]

Informational Shortcuts

To understand priming, it is crucial to understand the notion of information costs. Acquiring information costs people time and effort. It is not easy for ordinary citizens to compile a full record of candidates' backgrounds, policy views, and personal attributes, particularly during election campaigns. Citizens lack the inclination to search for all relevant material, given this expense. Instead, people look for informational shortcuts, or what Daniel Kahneman, Paul Slovic, and Amos Tversky call *heuristics*.[4] Rather than conducting a complete search that incorporates every nugget of material about the candidates, voters use readily available cues. In the media era, television provides some of the most accessible material. By its patterns of coverage and emphasis on particular information, the electronic medium plays a significant role in influencing the standards of evaluation used in voters' selection of candidates.

For most elections, voters call on many standards to evaluate candidates—views about the candidates' prospects for election, assessments of their positions on issues, and feelings about their personal attributes. Candidates attempt to prime the electorate by promoting standards that benefit themselves. If their strength lies in foreign policy as opposed to domestic policy, as was true for George Bush Sr. in 1992, they seek to elevate foreign policy considerations in voters' decision-making. If their strength is being seen as the most knowledgeable or trustworthy candidate, such as with George W. Bush and Al Gore in 2000, they will try to persuade voters to make those traits the basis of evaluation.

Candidates conversely attempt to defuse matters that are problematic. They try to lessen the salience of problem areas. George Bush, for example, was seen as wimpish and uncaring at the start of the 1988 presidential campaign. He obviously was not able to remake his personality, but Bush did alter the terms of the campaign in a way that defused those perceptions, emphasized his toughness, and focused voters' attention on other matters not as problematic for him.[5]

Considerable evidence has surfaced about the ability of television to prime viewers, although little attention has been devoted to defusing. Shanto Iyengar, Donald Kinder, and Jon Krosnick have undertaken path-breaking work on priming; they have shown that television can shape standards of evaluation in regard to presidents and political candidates.[6] Iyengar and Kinder document the power of priming through the evening news: "By calling attention to some matters while ignoring others, television news influences the standards by which governments, presidents, policies, and candidates for public office are judged."[7]

Krosnick and Kinder demonstrate the importance of priming with regard to a real-world issue—the Iran-contra affair—which was demonstrably salient to voters in late 1986. Using data from surveys taken before and after the revelation of the scandal, this study showed that intervention in Central America "loomed larger" in popular evaluations of President Ronald Reagan after saturation coverage by the media than before the event was publicized. Priming was also more likely to occur among political novices than among experts.[8]

In addition, Nicholas Valentino shows how crime news affects support for political candidates. Using a novel experimental study, he found that "evaluations of Clinton's performance on crime was primed powerfully by exposure to crime news, and this effect was largest when the suspects in the story were nonwhite." Issues such as crime and welfare are "race-coded," meaning that media coverage activates stereotypes about minorities. In these situations, viewers often react in prejudiced ways to stories about crime.[9]

None of these projects, though, addressed the role of television commercials in altering voters' standards. Candidates have obvious incentives to attempt to change the importance of matters in ways that benefit themselves.[10] In fact, based on recent campaigns, political commercials appear to be particularly influential as a means of altering voters' assessments of candidates. Ads are designed to be persuasive, and campaigners frequently seek to shift voters' standards of evaluation. The power to mold the judgments of voters through commercials is a major strategic resource for the contesting of elections.

Standards of Evaluation

The study of priming during election campaigns is complicated by uncertainties concerning the kind of standards used to judge candidates.[11] Past work has devoted little attention to the mechanism by which a voter's heightened interest in a subject leads to the incorporation of that factor into the voter's assessments of candidates.

For example, Krosnick and Kinder assumed in their study of the Iran-contra affair that the increased coverage of the scandal led to the decline in support for Reagan. However, Richard Brody and Catherine Shapiro argue that the criticism of Reagan by elites of both parties, not simply news of the arms-for-hostages deal, was the crucial factor in the decline.[12]

Both studies, though, ignore a third possibility: the strategic behavior of the participants. In the campaign arena, voters' assessments depend on media coverage, the views of political elites, and the strategic actions of the candidates. In fact, the candidates' activities may be the crucial mechanism because they generate coverage by news organizations and reaction by political elites. Electoral strategies generally involve efforts to alter voters' concerns about domestic and foreign policy, views about the personal traits of candidates (such as leadership, trustworthiness, and the appearance of caring), and impressions of the electability of particular candidates. The large number of determinants distinguishes electoral from nonelectoral priming. Government scandals, such as the Iran-contra affair, typically provoke a change in policy standards. But in the electoral arena, other types of standards are also important to voters' assessments.[13]

Experimental studies have solved the problem of how to determine which standards are most salient to voters by making assumptions. Iyengar and Kinder conducted a series of experiments in which viewers were shown newscasts emphasizing defense.[14] But outside of the experimental setting, there is no way of knowing whether citizens would incorporate defense as a factor in their vote choices. Other studies, such as that of Krosnick and Kinder, ensure salience by using an issue—in this case the Iran-contra scandal—that had obvious relevance for citizens.[15] Iran-contra received saturation coverage from the mass media over a period of several months.

Another way to address the saliency matter is to ask citizens which factors were most crucial in their voting choices. In 1984 and 1988, CBS News/*New York Times* surveys inquired about which general factors were most important to voters. In 1984, the survey asked in its pre- and post-election waves, "When you vote/voted for president on Tuesday, what will be/was more important in deciding how you vote/voted—the economy of this country, or the U.S. military and foreign policy, or mainly the way you feel/felt about Reagan and Mondale?" In 1988, the item was, "Some people choose among presidential candidates by picking the one closest to them on important issues. Some other people choose the one who has the personal characteristics—like integrity or leadership—they most want in a president. Which is most important when you choose—issues or personal characteristics?" The results show that the top factor cited by voters in 1984 was the economy (49 percent), followed by the candidates (37 percent), and foreign policy (14 percent). In 1988, 76 percent of respondents named issues as the most important factor, and 24 percent cited personal characteristics as most important.

The crucial question is: As people saw and paid more attention to ads, did their standards of evaluation change? A voting model that reflects how the importance of particular standards changed with different levels of ad exposure can be used to investigate the interpretations of priming, defusing, and no effect. A priming effect is present when the impact of the factor on the vote rises with level of ad exposure. In contrast, a defusing effect is evidenced by a reduction in the importance of the factor, and no effect is demonstrated by a flat line for importance of the factor based on ad exposure or a zigzag line revealing random fluctuations.

I undertook an analysis of the effect of each of the factors on the 1984 and 1988 votes, respectively. Four levels of ad exposure, from low to high, were incorporated, as were controls for intervening factors (party identification, education, age, gender, race, ideology, political interest, and [for 1988] media exposure). Vote choice was a measure of candidate preference for Reagan or Walter Mondale in 1984 and for Bush or Michael Dukakis in 1988.

In 1988, there was little evidence of priming or defusing for people who felt that issues or personal characteristics were important. The lines zigzagged, indicating that among those with low or high ad exposure, there was no systematic difference in the weighting of issues or personal characteristics as factors in vote choice.

However, in 1984, there was significant evidence of priming. Foreign policy moved from unimportant to important as a determinant of the vote as level of exposure to television ads increased. Those who watched ads were much more likely than were those who did not to cite foreign policy matters as influencing their vote for Reagan. There was also a significant priming effect for economic matters. The more ads people saw, the more likely they were to cite economic matters as an influence on their vote.

Although a number of media stories proclaimed the power of Reagan's personal traits, there was no evidence of ad priming in regard to personal candidate qualities in 1984. Politicians were unable to shift standards in this area despite journalists' reporting on Reagan's "Great Communicator" status. According to voters, ads had more influence on substantive than on personal dimensions of evaluation.

Nixon and the Politics of Inevitability

Ads can influence general standards of evaluation, but it remains to be seen whether political commercials can prime or defuse specific factors in vote choice. Elections from 1972 through 2008 represent an interesting opportunity to examine ad priming and defusing in greater detail. Individual elections need to be investigated to determine exactly how ad exposure influenced the factors generally considered to have been important standards of evaluation. The 1972 presidential general election is an interesting setting for an examination of priming. Richard Nixon's general strategy in this race was to characterize himself as a trusted, capable, and responsible leader, in sharp contrast to what he portrayed as an irresponsible and not very trustworthy George McGovern. Nixon also sought to portray the McGovern candidacy as hopeless in a clear effort to elevate electability as a standard of evaluation.[16]

The question in this case is whether the president's ads shifted the standards of evaluation to magnify the significance of personal traits and electability. Respondents were asked to rate the importance of various personal qualities. Trustworthiness was the most commonly cited trait (61 percent), whereas foreign affairs (36 percent) and the economy (33 percent) were ranked as the most important problems. Respondents were also asked to assess Nixon's electability to determine how important a factor that may have been in their choice.

There were weak priming effects in regard to the policy problems of foreign affairs and the economy. Neither played a strong role in voters' decision-making, and there appears to have been little significant variation based on exposure to campaign ads. However, there were stronger priming effects for personal traits and electability. The more ads viewers saw, the more likely they were to elevate trustworthiness in their voting decisions. Trustworthiness went from being an unimportant consideration in the vote among those not exposed to ads to a statistically significant factor among those who watched many ads. Electability also displayed strong evidence of priming. Its role in voters' decision-making became much more important as viewers were exposed to ads. Among those who had not seen ads, electability was a statistically insignificant contributor to vote choice. But among attentive viewers, electability had a substantial impact on the vote.

There were also interesting shifts in the importance of these qualities during the course of the campaign. Between September and November, 28 percent of the sample shifted from not seeing trustworthiness as the most important trait to seeing it as such. Seven percent shifted in the opposite direction, 33 percent cited trustworthiness as most important in both waves, and 32 percent mentioned it at neither point.

Campaign advertising appears to have had some influence. Among those who consistently rated trustworthiness as important, 31 percent did not see ads and 37 percent saw many ads, a statistically significant difference of six percentage points. Political ads therefore demonstrated a priming effect over time.

These effects were consistent with the general strategy used by Nixon against McGovern. Based on his media advertising, the president appears to have shifted the standards of evaluation in a way that elevated personal traits and electability.[17] Voters who saw his ads were more likely to incorporate these factors into their decisions and to use standards favorable to the president.

Defusing Potential Problems: Bush in 1988

George Bush started his fall presidential campaign in a difficult position. Dukakis held a substantial lead in the early summer polls. Bush was reeling from bad publicity surrounding the Reagan administration's negotiations with Panamanian dictator Manuel Noriega and disclosures that Nancy Reagan had consulted an astrologer during her husband's presidency. Bush himself was seen as weak and ineffective.[18]

However, according to the theory of priming and defusing, careful advertising can help a candidate shift standards of evaluation. This is exactly what Bush set out to do in 1988. Through priming, he sought to elevate factors advantageous to himself. Meanwhile, matters that hurt him would be defused through television ads and favorable coverage from the news media. If he could not remove his own negatives, he could at least shift the standards to his advantage.

In looking at the impact of various factors on the Bush vote, there was little evidence of priming or defusing on certain issues.[19] For example, there was no shift in the importance of the death penalty or defense issues. The most significant effect was defusing the salience of the environment and the view that Bush did not care enough about people. These matters actually became less relevant to the vote as people saw more ads. As an oil-state representative, Bush had never had strong environmental credentials, but the vice president was able to defuse the issue by noting his concern about the environment in ads. In one of his most famous spots, Bush also cast doubt on Dukakis's environmental credentials by arguing that the Massachusetts governor had not cleaned up Boston Harbor.

Bush defused the personality issue by reducing its centrality to American voters. Among those who watched few ads, the matter of whether Bush cared about people was significantly linked to the vote. However, voters who saw and paid more attention to ads considered Bush's personality less relevant. These effects were consistent with the strategic goals of Bush's campaign. They demonstrate how well-organized advertising pitches can improve a candidate's fortunes. Bush achieved defusing effects, and he was therefore able to change the standards of evaluation in ways that benefited him.

Clinton and the Economy in 1992

Clinton advisers James Carville, Stanley Greenberg, and Mandy Grunwald report that in April 1992 they were worried. Their candidate had sewed up the nomination early, but they felt uneasy about the upcoming fall campaign. In a memo that month, Carville and Greenberg noted that Clinton's negatives had risen to a damaging 41 percent and that he trailed George Bush by twenty-four percentage points on the crucial dimensions of trustworthiness and honesty. Focus group participants regularly complained that "no one knows why Bill Clinton wants to be president" and called him "Slick Willie."[20]

The Clinton advisers moved into action. In a top-secret memo prepared for what Grunwald euphemistically called the Manhattan Project in honor of the 1940s program to build a nuclear bomb, Greenberg wrote, "The campaign must move on an urgent basis before the Perot candidacy further defines us (by contrast) and the Bush-Quayle campaign defines us by malice." According to the *Newsweek* account of this plan, Clinton's problem was not so much being accused of adultery by Gennifer Flowers, avoiding the draft, or having once tried to smoke marijuana, but "the belief that Bill Clinton is a typical politician." The report noted many of the inaccurate impressions people had of Clinton—that he was rich and privileged, that he and Hillary Rodham Clinton were childless, that he could not stand up to the special interests, and that "Clinton cannot be the candidate of change." The campaign, the report said, must "take radical steps" to "depoliticize" its candidate.

Early in the summer, the Clinton camp pretested its fall themes of a New Covenant, fighting for the forgotten middle class, and putting people first. At a series of focus groups in New Jersey, the reactions of voters were stunningly negative. One participant said the New Covenant was "just words . . . glib . . . insulting . . . like blaming the victims." The notion of fighting for the middle class drew these comments: "baloney . . . propaganda." After hearing these comments, Greenberg remarked, "They think he's so political, the message stuff gets completely discounted. In fact, it makes it worse."

With the help of a coordinated research program of public opinion surveys and focus groups, the Clinton campaign embarked on an effort to redefine its candidate. At a meeting late in May, Carville suggested, "We need to mention work every fifteen seconds." Grunwald agreed and said, "By the end of the convention, what do we want people to know about Clinton: that he worked his way up; that he values work; that he has moved people from welfare to work; that he has a national economic strategy to put America back to work."

The next day, they met with Bill and Hillary Clinton to lay out their plan. The proposal, as described by Greenberg, was based on the idea that "in the 1980s the few—leaders in the corporations, the Congress and the White House—neglected the many. The consequences were that work was not honored, good jobs were lost, everyone but the few felt insecure. . . . The answer for the 1990s had to be a plan to do right by the American people. A plan means a contract. It's not 'Read my lips.'" The campaign then sketched out a plan to coordinate paid ads on the economy in a small group of targeted states and hope for the future with a variety of media appearances on the network morning shows, *Larry King Live*, and the *Arsenio Hall Show*. The talk show appearances would put Clinton in more intimate settings and allow viewers to get to know him better.

This plan was remarkably successful. Because some interpretations of the 1992 elections have labeled pocketbook voting (that is, casting votes based on economic conditions) the sole reason for Clinton's victory, it is important to recognize the ways in which Clinton's media campaign encouraged economic voting. For example, Clinton was able through his advertising to focus public attention on the economy and his own ability to improve economic performance.

People who had high ad exposure were more likely than those with low exposure to make the economy a factor in their votes. They were also more likely to support the view that Clinton had the ability to improve the economy.[21] At the same time, Clinton was able through advertising to strengthen his own image on the trustworthiness and honesty dimension.

These results demonstrate that people's views about the economy do not merely reflect their daily experiences but instead can be shaped by the candidates' strategies. The 1992 election suggests that citizens' predictions for the economy can be more pessimistic than warranted on the basis of objective economic statistics. One of the reasons forecasting models based purely on economic factors failed to predict Clinton's victory was their failure to take into account the ability of candidates and the media to prime voters.[22] Clinton's advertising and the media coverage of the campaign were part of the reason that George Bush was blamed for the country's poor economic performance.

Clinton in 1996

The 1996 election featured a different dynamic than that of 1992. The country was at peace, and people generally were feeling prosperous. The recession that had aborted the reelection effort of President Bush was over, and a majority of Americans believed the country was headed in the right direction. But Clinton faced a new problem during his reelection campaign: Republicans wanted to revise the role government played in American society. The Republican Revolution proposed to downsize government and reduce the rate of growth in spending on a wide variety of social programs.

To combat this new Republican challenge, Clinton moved to the center, reclaimed his old credentials as a New Democrat, and adopted Republican language on the importance of balancing the budget and protecting American values. His first ad, aired in June 1995, touted his crime bill and showed Clinton surrounded by a bevy of police officers. In winter 1995 and spring 1996, the Democratic National Committee broadcast commercials attacking Republicans Newt Gingrich and Robert Dole for their efforts to cut popular social programs.

This two-track message of compassion for the downtrodden and a sense of fiscal responsibility was a powerful component in Clinton's reelection. The impact of each factor on the vote rose in importance as people viewed more ads. The idea that Clinton "cared about people like you" had been important in 1992 as Americans struggled with the economy and President Bush appeared oblivious to the suffering of ordinary people. It remained important in 1996 following Republican efforts to cap the social safety net. As people moved from low to high Clinton ad exposure, the sense that Clinton was caring and compassionate rose in importance to the vote.

The same was true on the crucial dimension that Clinton would bring fiscal discipline to the federal government. As people saw more ads, the president's image as fiscally responsible exerted a stronger influence on the vote. It was a strategy that helped Clinton fight off Dole and defuse the potential problem of being called a tax-and-spend liberal. As a result, he became the first Democratic president to win reelection since Franklin Roosevelt.

Bush and Gore in 2000

The year 2000 featured an open-seat election with no incumbent on the ballot. Seeking to become the first sitting vice president since George Bush in 1988 and Martin Van Buren in 1846 to win election in his own right, Gore secured the Democratic nomination over New Jersey senator Bill Bradley. George W. Bush meanwhile beat back a determined challenge from Arizona senator John McCain. Sensing that the race would be extremely close, both nominees campaigned in the middle. Bush sought to dispel the notion from the Gingrich era that Republicans were dangerous extremists not to be trusted with America's future and that he was up to the job of the presidency. For his part, Gore attempted to continue Clinton's New Democratic leanings by emphasizing targeted tax cuts and prescription drug benefits for senior citizens and by promising that he would continue Clinton's capacity for strong leadership.

Several of these messages resonated with voters. The more ads that people viewed, the stronger the connection was between believing that Gore was a strong leader and expressing a willingness to vote for him. There also was a strong link between the vote and perceived electability, which rose for both Gore and Bush as ad viewing increased. Similar to the 1992 election, academic models based on economic voting proved way off target. Scholars predicted that Gore would win comfortably, with something between 53 and 60 percent of the two-party vote. Peace and prosperity reigned in the United States, and these forecasters asserted that Gore would carry the day.[23]

However, these predictions ignored the ability of campaigns to alter the terms of debate. Just as Clinton in 1992 was able to make voters feel worse about the economy than was warranted by objective evidence, voters did not reward Gore based on the strong economy of the Clinton years. Owing to the Clinton scandal involving Monica Lewinsky, Gore distanced himself from Clinton and thereby prevented himself from being the only beneficiary of economic voting. This inability of the party controlling the presidency to benefit from the economy was one of the most surprising results of the 2000 election.

Bush and Kerry in 2004

The 2004 election saw an effort by President George W. Bush to win reelection over Democrat John Kerry. In this campaign, national conditions did not look advantageous for the sitting president. Throughout the fall, his job approval numbers ranged from the low to high 40s, well below the 50 percent threshold assumed for reelection. More than a thousand American soldiers had lost their lives in Iraq. Between 2001 and 2004, the economy lost around 2.7 million jobs. It was not until 2004 that new jobs started to be created in large numbers.

In this situation, Bush's campaign primed the electorate to see Kerry in negative terms, while Bush's own poor governing record in several respects was de-emphasized. Kerry was portrayed as a wishy-washy flip-flopper who was not to be trusted, whereas Bush was caring toward the downtrodden and interested in helping middle-income earners do better economically. Given that his administration's tax cuts went largely to the rich, the caring and compassionate dimension represented clear points of vulnerability for his reelection bid.

Bush sought to prime trust and defuse caring through a series of ads attacking Kerry's trustworthiness and penchant for changing positions. On issues such as the Iraq War, the Patriot Act, and Bush's "No Child Left Behind" education program, Bush's advertisements said Kerry had voted for the policies but later switched his position. At the same time, the president surrounded himself with images of working-class folk and made jokes about his poor speaking ability by saying, "English is not my first language." Kerry responded by seeking to undermine Bush's credibility. He broadcast commercials asserting that Bush had deceived the country by saying there were weapons of mass destruction in Iraq and had provided tax cuts for rich, corporate interests.

In looking at this fight over problem definition, polling data on trust and caring demonstrated that Bush made some gains. Voters were more likely to describe Bush (59 percent) as sticking firm to his beliefs than Kerry (37 percent). And Kerry's 51 percent advantage over Bush's 44 percent on caring was not as much of a margin as Democratic presidential candidates typically hold over their Republican counterparts.

By the end of the campaign, each candidate was using highly emotional ads to scare voters to his side. A Bush spot showed a clock ticking while a father loaded his young children into a minivan. An announcer warned, "Weakness invites those who would do us harm." A Kerry ad had images of a soldier shooting a machine gun into the air and a car bursting into a gigantic fireball. The announcer proclaimed, "Now Americans are being kidnapped, held hostage— even beheaded."[24]

Not only were there highly emotional images in the commercials, there were also highly questionable charges. Bush accused Kerry of wanting to create a huge new federal bureaucracy to oversee health care, even as Kerry said Bush would restore a military draft and privatize Social Security in a second term. In the end, Bush was able to defeat Kerry by 3.6 million votes.

McCain and Obama in 2008

The 2008 election featured a battle between senators John McCain and Barack Obama over experience versus change. As someone with more than two decades of experience in the U.S. Senate, McCain sought to prime the electorate to focus on his experience and his opponent's inexperience. Obama had served in the Senate for just a few years when he chose to run for president, and McCain ran ads arguing that the Democrat was "risky," "not ready," and "dangerous."

Similar to the 1988 campaign, when George Bush had attacked Michael Dukakis as not ready to be commander in chief, McCain used guilt-by-association tactics to suggest that Obama was not up to the job as chief executive and would lead the United States on a dangerous course. According to the common critique, Obama was too liberal, did not share mainstream values with the American public, and was poorly prepared for the office he was seeking.

In contrast, Obama sought to turn his inexperience into a strength. The Illinois senator noted that he had opposed the Iraq War at a time when many Democrats supported it and that in a situation in which more than four out of every five Americans believed the country was headed in the wrong direction, having experience in Washington wasn't the best leadership credential. He countered McCain's claims by saying his rival was an out-of-touch elitist so rich he could not answer the question of how many homes he owned. The ad "Seven" proclaimed: "Here's one house America can't afford to let John McCain move into." This helped Obama defuse McCain's attacks and turn his opponent's claims into attacks of his own.

Other Democrats' spots sought to maintain the Siamese connection between Bush and McCain. Taking advantage of Bush's low popularity, political ads showed images of the two Republicans together, riding in golf carts, and Bush kissing McCain on the top of his head. The consistent message was clear: In bad economic times and with an unpopular GOP president, McCain was the risky candidate.

Conclusion

To summarize, candidates take advantage of the fact that voters use heuristic shortcuts known as priming and defusing to alter citizen standards of evaluation at election time. Through the tie to candidate strategies, priming and defusing help citizens frame their electoral choices. Voters do not have the time or inclination to research every aspect of a politician's record. Their inability to devote a large amount of time to politics leads them to rely on information-processing shortcuts that make use of readily available material, such as media cues, when deciding which standards of evaluation are most helpful.

Past races show that campaigners research both their own and their opponents' strengths and weaknesses. Taking advantage of this material, they seek either to elevate or undermine particular standards to gain electoral advantage. This puts them in a situation in which they can set the tone of the campaign dialogue.

While not all such efforts are successful, winning candidates typically have been effective at broadcasting ads and eliciting news coverage that emphasize their strengths. Whether the trait is being the most electable candidate, the one most liked, the one worthy of trust, or someone with the most experience, these priming strategies are vital to advertising and contribute to how the election turns out. One cannot fully understand political dynamics without grasping the concepts of priming and defusing.

Chapter 8

Playing the Blame Game

B ased on recent campaigns it has become conventional wisdom that attack ads work. The widespread acceptance of this view explains in part the frequency of negative campaigns. This perspective, though, ignores some contrary evidence. In 1988, George H. W. Bush was able to dominate the agenda and prime voters with the help of political attacks. Yet it also is clear from other elections that Bush in 1992; Steve Forbes, Robert Dole, and Newt Gingrich in 1996; and John McCain in 2008 were the objects of a backlash against negative ads that enabled their opponents to attract voters.

From the candidates' standpoint, negative ads are risky as a strategic device because it is hard to benefit from an attack without being blamed for an unpleasant campaign. Attack strategies must be used with great prudence. Simply going on the offensive is not necessarily going to be effective. If attributions of blame outweigh the benefits of controlling the agenda, attacks are likely to backfire. As the case studies in this chapter reveal, for negative ads to work they must help candidates define the terms of debate without also making them come across as mean-spirited or nasty.

Blame Dukakis

In the 1988 presidential campaign, Bush played the blame game masterfully. A CBS News/*New York Times* survey that year asked voters two questions in an effort to measure attributions of responsibility for the campaign negativity: "Did most of Bush's [Dukakis's] TV commercials that you saw explain what George Bush [Michael Dukakis] stands for, or did most of the commercials attack George Bush [Michael Dukakis]?" and "Who is more responsible for the negative campaigning there has been this year, George Bush or Michael Dukakis?"

Although Bush is generally acknowledged as having been the more aggressive campaigner that year, he did not reap a disproportionate share of the blame for negativity. In October, more people saw his ads as attacking the opponent (37 percent) than as explaining his views (21 percent), but the same was true for Dukakis (34 percent thought his ads attacked the opponent and 25 percent believed they explained his views) (Table 8-1). Not until the end of the campaign did Bush receive the majority of the blame.

If one compiles the attack-to-explain response ratios for Bush and Dukakis at different points in the campaign, viewers were evenly split in their responses for Bush (1.8) and Dukakis (1.4) in October. By November, though, Bush's attack-to-explain ratio was 3.1, whereas Dukakis's was only 1.3.[1] These figures were in line with reality. A study of *CBS Evening News* stories involving ads aired during the 1988 general election reveals that 75 percent of Bush's commercials aired during the news were negative about Dukakis, whereas only 33 percent of Dukakis's ads were negative about Bush.

Blame Bush

The picture in 1992 could not have been more different. In September, almost twice as many people said George Bush's commercials attacked Bill Clinton (46 percent) than said the ads explained his own views (24 percent). In contrast, more people thought Clinton's ads explained his views (37 percent) than attacked the opponent (31 percent). People also were more likely to name Bush (39 percent) than Clinton (21 percent) as being responsible for the negative campaigning. By late October, Bush was being blamed by an even larger margin of 60 percent to 13 percent. In early November 1988, in contrast, 25 percent had blamed Bush and 16 percent Dukakis for campaign negativity.

To some extent Democrats anticipated Bush's 1992 attack ads and focused attention on the blame game.[2] In a clear contrast to Dukakis's high-road strategy, the Clinton team responded immediately to Republican onslaughts. When Bush ran attack ads in early October accusing the Arkansas governor of raising taxes, Clinton broadcast an instant rebuttal. The spot started with a bold red headline: "GEORGE BUSH ATTACK AD." The commercial went on to say, "George Bush is running attack ads. He says all these people

TABLE 8-1
Tone of Presidential Ads and Responsibility for
Negative Campaigning, 1988–2008

1988 Campaign	Oct. 21–24	Nov. 2–4	Nov. 10–15
Bush ads			
Explain his views	21%	14%	14%
Attack opponent	37	36	43
Dukakis ads			
Explain his views	25	24	24
Attack opponent	34	26	31
Responsibility for negativity			
Bush	–	25	30
Dukakis	–	16	19

1992 Campaign	Sept. 28–29	Oct. 26–31
Bush ads		
Explain his views	24%	16%
Attack opponent	46	56
Clinton ads		
Explain his views	37	46
Attack opponent	31	24
Responsibility for negativity		
Bush	39	60
Clinton	21	13

1996 Campaign	May 31–June 3	Oct. 10–13	Oct. 17–20	Oct. 28–Nov. 3
Dole ads				
Explain his views	32%	40%	24%	14%
Attack opponent	48	50	63	55
Clinton ads				
Explain his views	53	68	73	49
Attack opponent	28	19	14	21
Perot ads				
Explain his views	–	–	–	31%
Attack opponent	–	–	–	21
Responsibility for negativity				
Dole	–	–	–	52
Clinton	–	–	–	13
Perot	–	–	–	6

2000 Campaign	Sept. 27–Oct. 1	Oct. 18–21	Oct. 28–Nov. 2
Bush ads			
Explain his views	48%	55%	40%
Attack opponent	35	32	38

(Continued)

TABLE 8-1 (Continued)

2000 Campaign	Sept. 27–Oct. 1	Oct. 18–21	Oct. 28–Nov. 2
Gore ads			
Explain his views	65	61	41
Attack opponent	23	28	36
Responsibility for negativity			
Bush	—	—	28
Gore	—	—	26

2004 Campaign	Sept. 12–14	Oct. 1–3	Oct. 14–17	Oct. 28–30
Bush ads				
Explain his views	47%	41%	37%	43%
Attack opponent	45	48	56	50
Kerry ads				
Explain his views	37	35	35	32
Attack opponent	54	56	58	60

2008 Campaign	July 7–14	Aug. 15–19	Sept. 5–7	Oct. 10–13	Oct. 19–22	Oct. 25–29
McCain ads						
Explain his views	63%	38%	44%	31%	27%	20%
Attack opponent	26	52	49	61	64	64
Obama ads						
Explain his views	73	61	55	63	69	50
Attack opponent	17	26	32	27	22	30

Sources: 1988: CBS News/*New York Times* surveys; 1992: Sept. 28–29—Winston-Salem survey, Oct. 26–31—Los Angeles County survey, CBS News/*New York Times* survey; 1996: May 31–June 3, Oct. 10–13, and Oct. 28–Nov. 3—CBS News/*New York Times* surveys, Oct. 17–20—Brown University survey; 2000: Sept. 27–Oct. 1—CBS News/*New York Times* survey, Oct. 18–21 and Oct. 28–Nov. 2—Brown University surveys; 2004: CBS News/*New York Times* surveys; 2008: CBS News/*New York Times* surveys.

Note: Entries indicate percentages of individuals believing candidate explained or attacked and that the candidate was responsible for the negativity of the campaign. The "responsibility for negativity" question was not asked in 2004 or 2008. No data available.

would have their taxes raised by Bill Clinton. Scary, huh? 'Misleading,' says the *Washington Post.* And the *Wall Street Journal* says, 'Clinton has proposed to cut taxes for the sort of people featured in [Bush's] ad.'"

Bush's broadcast of an ad on the draft-evasion issue using *Time* magazine's cover story asking whether Clinton could be trusted also led Clinton's media advisers to test a commercial featuring editorial responses from throughout the country. Though the ad was never broadcast because focus groups felt it was too harsh, the spot illustrates the quick-response mentality of the Clinton team: "All across America people are hurting, and what is George Bush doing? The press calls his campaign gutter politics [*St. Petersburg Times*]. Malicious and dangerous mudslinging [*The Tennessean*]. Wrong, deceitful [*Des Moines Register*]. It's sad to see a president stoop this low [*Atlanta Constitution*]. Nasty and shrill [*New York Times*]. Deplorably sordid [*Los Angeles Times*]. Lies and attempted distraction [Hutchinson, Kan., *News*]. Bush's smear . . . new low [*USA Today*]. Cheap shot, Mr. President [*Miami Herald*]. Stop sleazy tactics and talk straight [Wilmington, Del., *News Journal*]. We can't afford four more years."[3]

The same tactic was in evidence on October 7, 1992, when Bush raised the character issue in response to a question on *Larry King Live*. Under prodding from the host, Bush attacked Clinton for leading antiwar demonstrations while he was a student at Oxford University: "I cannot for the life of me understand mobilizing demonstrations and demonstrating against your own country, no matter how strongly you feel, when you are in a foreign land. Maybe I'm old fashioned, but to go to a foreign country and demonstrate against your own country when your sons and daughters are dying halfway around the world, I am sorry but I think that is wrong." When asked in the same interview about a student trip Clinton made to Moscow in 1969, Bush said: "I don't want to tell you what I really think. To go to Moscow, one year after Russia crushed Czechoslovakia, not remember who you saw there. . . ."[4]

In 1988, Bush's attacks were reported favorably by the press and Dukakis's weak rebuttals were seen as evidence of passivity. Bush's 1992 attacks met a different fate; Clinton took the lead in responding. In the first presidential debate, he turned to Bush and accused the president of engaging in a McCarthy-style smear on his patriotism. He also reminded Bush that in the 1950s, Bush's father, Sen. Prescott Bush, had displayed courage in standing up to McCarthy.

The press response was sympathetic to Clinton, and Bush met with unfavorable headlines across the country. For example, the *Washington Post* headlined its stories, "Clinton Denounces Attacks by Bush" and "President Drops Moscow Trip Issue: Bush Denies Attacking Foe's Patriotism." The *New York Times* ran stories entitled "Clinton Says Desperation Is Fueling Bush Criticism," "Bush Camp Pursues an Offensive by Having Others Make the Attack," and "Campaign Renews Disputes of the Vietnam War Years."

The backlash against Republican attacks took their toll on President Bush. An analysis shows how attack strategies by Bush and Clinton, as well as attributions of responsibility for negative campaigning, influenced the vote. The results indicate that attacks produced a strong voter backlash. The more each candidate was perceived as attacking, the more likely voters were to blame that person for negative campaigning.[5]

These attributions are important because a negative correlation was found between blame and the vote. Voters who saw Bush as responsible for negativity were more likely to vote for Clinton. Because more people were blaming Bush than Clinton for the tone of the race, this trend clearly was a liability for Bush. Shortly after the election, Bush aide Jim Pinkerton was forced to admit in a campaign postmortem, "We've got to ask ourselves what would make a voter vote for a draft-dodging, womanizing, fill-in-the-blank sleazeball? What would drive them to it? This says a lot about us, doesn't it?"[6]

It is ironic to note that in light of its moralistic protests against Bush's attacks, the Clinton camp had prepared ads for the last week of the campaign challenging Ross Perot's suitability for the presidency. One ad featured people-on-the-street interviews with former Perot volunteers saying Perot lacked character. Another said, "Ross Perot's plan? It could make things worse. He wants a 50-cent gas tax, which hits middle-class families hardest. He wants to raise taxes on the middle class. And he wants to cut Medicare benefits." Each statement was footnoted with a page number from Perot's book, *United We Stand.*[7] The commercials were not broadcast because it became apparent right before the election that Perot represented no threat to Clinton.

Blame Forbes

The 1996 Republican primaries featured a barrage of attack ads unprecedented for a nomination campaign. Starting in September 1995, six months before the Iowa caucuses and New Hampshire primary, multimillionaire Steve Forbes broadcast wave after wave of television assaults on front-runner Bob Dole.

One ad proclaimed, "The official *Congressional Record* documents Bob Dole's vote that increased his million-dollar, tax-paid pension. But now, he denies it." [Dole in TV interview] "I never voted to increase pensions." [Announcer] "Bob Dole must have forgotten. The *Orlando Sentinel* reported the Senate pay raise that Bob Dole voted for increased senators' pensions by $26 million." [Dole on TV]

"I never voted to increase pensions." [Announcer] "Bob Dole. A Washington politician."

Another Forbes spot condemned Dole for raising taxes: "Since 1982, Bob Dole has voted for seventeen tax increases. . . . Bob Dole voted to increase income taxes. Taxes on phones, gas, even Social Security." Still another ad criticized Dole for supporting appropriations bills that funded ski slopes. In all, more than two-thirds of Forbes's ads run before Iowa were negative in tone, far above the level of negativity common in the nominating process.

Tim Forbes, senior adviser to his brother's campaign, explained the strategy this way: Because Steve Forbes had zero name recognition nationally just a few months before the election and was running against a well-known opponent who had a huge lead in the polls, the Forbes campaign needed something to "puncture the air of inevitability" surrounding Dole.[8] Because both Dole and Texas senator Phil Gramm received much more free news coverage and had much stronger ground organizations than Forbes, he had to rely on big ad buys to get his message out.

The decision to go negative, according to Tim Forbes, was predicated on the view that "people say they hate attack ads, but they actually respond to them. People see them as having greater credibility and are more likely to be swayed by them." As the attack ads rained down on television viewers, political observers began to notice similarities between Forbes's strategy and that used for years by Republican senator Jesse Helms of North Carolina. Helms's ads often featured harsh, inflammatory, and graphic appeals to gut-level issues: race, taxes, and government spending. The split-screen pictures at the end of many Forbes ads—"[picture of Dole] Washington values. [picture of Forbes] Conservative values"—paralleled the onscreen convention of Helms's commercials.

This similarity was no accident. Although Forbes tried to downplay the association, his early ads were designed by two conservative veterans of Helms's North Carolina campaigns: Tom Ellis and Carter Wrenn. These consultants were the same individuals who had devised Helms's infamous "White Hands" commercial.[9]

At one level, these television attacks were remarkably successful. In the short run, they drove down voter support for Dole. From early 1995 to early 1996, Dole's support in Iowa and New Hampshire dropped by more than thirty percentage points. The ads attached negative code words to Dole, such as "Washington politician" and "raising taxes." The commercials also temporarily increased support for Forbes. By destabilizing voter judgments about the candidates, Forbes's attack ads upset the predictability of the Republican nominating process and forced voters to take another look at their choices.

But in the midst of all his ad buys, Forbes missed two basic rules of attack politics. First, voters do not like negative ads even if they learn from them, and there always is an inevitable backlash against the person seen as responsible for those types of appeals. Second, when attacked, opponents always position themselves as the victim and focus blame on whoever started the attack.

By the end of January, Dole had redeployed his ad broadcasts against Forbes. One ad said, "Steve Forbes tells us he has the experience to cut government waste. But in his one government job, he allowed $276,000 in tax dollars to be wasted redecorating the residences of a friend who was his top aide. Forbes's top bureaucrats received government pay averaging $240,000. The press called it a 'gravy train.' Two federal audits sharply criticized this lavish waste of our tax dollars as 'improper.' Steve Forbes. Untested. Just not ready for the job."[10]

Forbes did not anticipate either voter backlash or opponent efforts to blame him for the negativity of the campaign. In this situation, Forbes could have made a strategic adjustment. He could have scaled back the attacks and mixed more positive ads with the negative spots. For example, during the 1992 general election, Clinton always tried to have one positive ad airing for every two attack commercials he was running. When questioned by opponents or journalists about why he was on the attack, Clinton always could point to a specific positive spot on the air at that moment.

In addition, Forbes could have played the blame game with opponents by inoculating himself from their complaints. Similar to Clinton, he could have warned reporters that opponents were going to go after him. After all, he was rising in the polls, and Washington politicians were feeling threatened. What else would one expect them to do but to attack him in return?

Forbes did neither of these things until it was too late. After he finished in fourth place in Iowa, he canceled his negative attacks in New Hampshire for the week prior to that primary. But the backlash had already developed and engulfed him in the blame game. An exit poll in New Hampshire the night of the state primary revealed that 65 percent of voters thought the ads in that primary had mainly attacked opponents rather than addressed the issues. A large number of voters blamed Forbes for this turn of events.

Ultimately, Forbes's attacks succeeded in weakening support for Dole, but Forbes was not the beneficiary of this change. Buchanan ended up winning New Hampshire, and Lamar Alexander came in a strong third after Dole. Forbes's candidacy was doomed in part by his slowness in anticipating voter backlash to his attacks.

Blame Dole

The fall 1996 campaign began unusually early. With Clinton having no opposition and Dole wrapping up the Republican nomination by the middle of March, both candidates aired commercials throughout March, April, May, and June. Many of these spots attacked the opposition. Clinton tied Dole to Gingrich, accusing them of gutting Medicare, Medicaid, education, and the environment. Dole, for his part, questioned the president's trustworthiness in light of the Whitewater allegations concerning Clinton's real estate and financial transactions in Arkansas.

Clinton won the spring phase of this campaign. By June, he had a lead of 54 to 35 percent among registered voters and was viewed more favorably than Dole. Whereas 48 percent viewed the president favorably and 33 percent saw him unfavorably, Dole had a favorability rating of 29 percent and an unfavorability rating of 35 percent. By early October, Dole's unfavorability rating had risen to 41 percent and his favorability rating remained at 29 percent. Clinton was viewed favorably by 47 percent and unfavorably by 36 percent. His lead in terms of vote choice was 53 percent to 36 percent.

More surprising was how well Clinton did in the blame game. When asked in a May 1996 survey whether the candidates were spending more time explaining views or attacking the opponent, more respondents blamed Dole than Clinton. Thirty-two percent of voters thought Dole was explaining his views and 48 percent believed he was attacking the opponent. In Clinton's case, 53 percent thought he was explaining his views and only 28 percent felt he was attacking the opponent.

By early October 1996, even more voters blamed Dole than Clinton. In a national survey from October 10 to 13, 50 percent of respondents believed Dole was attacking the opponent and 40 percent thought he was explaining his views. In contrast, 19 percent believed Clinton was attacking the opponent and 68 percent felt he was explaining his views.[11]

The blame directed at Dole got even worse later in October. After the final debate and a week in which Dole attacked Clinton's character on everything from the president's unsuccessful White-water real estate investment to his ethics in the White House, 63 percent felt Dole was attacking his opponent and only 14 percent believed Clinton was doing so.[12]

By the last week of the campaign, 55 percent of voters felt Dole was attacking his opponent, 21 percent believed Clinton was doing so, and 21 percent thought Perot's ads were attacking the opponent. When asked who was most responsible for the negative campaigning for that year, 52 percent cited Dole, 13 percent Clinton, and 6 percent Perot.

As they had done successfully in 1992, the Clintons used an inoculation strategy as early as April 1996 to warn people that Republicans would launch "a relentless attack" of negative advertising and misinformation. Speaking before a thousand Democratic women at an event sponsored by EMILY's List, an organization devoted to raising early money for female candidates, First Lady Hillary Clinton predicted: "Get prepared for it, and don't be surprised by it. When you've got no vision of how to make the world a better place for yourself or your children, then you go negative." After Dole went negative in the fall, Clinton White House adviser George Stephanopoulos characterized Dole's public persona this way: "All you ever see him doing on TV is carping, attacking, whining."[13]

The Clinton people shielded themselves from the backlash against negative campaigning by developing a new genre in the advertising area—the positive attack ad. Recognizing that voters do not like negative advertising, the Clinton campaign broadcast attack ads that combined negative and positive appeals. An example is an ad Clinton ran as a response to Dole's attack on Clinton's drug record. The ad criticized Dole for opposing the creation of a drug czar and Congress for cutting monies for school drug prevention programs but then went on to explain that Clinton had sought to strengthen school programs and had expanded the death penalty to drug kingpins. By using attack ads as a surgical tool, not as a sledgehammer, the Clinton campaign sought to attach negatives to the opponent while also sheltering itself from blame by voters upset about negative ads.

Blame Gingrich

The 1996 campaign was unusual in being one of the few national elections to be framed around the Speaker of the House. In 1982, Republicans had created an ad making fun of what they called

Speaker Tip O'Neill's "tired old liberalism." The ad concluded with the tagline "The Democrats are out of gas." But this targeting of a sitting Speaker was atypical. Elections are more likely to be framed around general public perceptions about the two parties, such as Republicans being uncaring and insensitive and Democrats being tax-and-spend liberals.

However, owing to Gingrich's high unpopularity in national public opinion polls, in 1996, Democrats throughout the country launched ads that directly attacked him by name. About 75,000 ads, 10 percent of all the political spots aired in 1996, were broadcast against Gingrich, according to the Speaker's own estimate. Local Republican candidates were shown standing next to him with the suggestion that they were Gingrich robots who mindlessly sought to gut Medicare, Medicaid, education, and the environment. Other Democratic spots relied on new video technology to show the local Republican being "morphed" into a picture of the Speaker. The general text of these ads was to claim that a vote for the Republican was a vote for the unpopular House Speaker.[14]

As congressional Democrats ran against Gingrich, Republicans responded with a series of ads produced by the Republican National Committee (RNC) that accused Democratic candidates of being liberal, ultra-liberal, and super-liberal. Many of these ads took the guise of issue advocacy spots designed to educate the public, not influence the election. This approach exempted the commercials from federal campaign laws and meant the party organization was not limited in how much it could spend on local races and was not forced to disclose the contributors who financed the spots.

RNC ads in 1996 continued throughout the Senate campaign, accusing the Democratic nominees, such as Jack Reed of Rhode Island, of being liberal.[15] As part of its polling, the Reed campaign tracked the percentage of voters who felt Reed was "too liberal." The number reached a high point of 29 percent midway through the campaign and dropped after that. Even after the RNC accelerated its expenditures on "Liberal Jack Reed" ads, the percentage did not rise. Reed's polls also found that more voters blamed the Republican candidate Nancy Mayer for the negativity of the campaign compared with Reed.[16]

Voters had considerable difficulty correctly identifying the sponsors of ads and distinguishing between ads run by candidates and those run by party organizations. In a campaign focus group, only 50 percent were able to correctly identify the sponsors of the ads.

Just 12 percent correctly identified the sponsor of a Republican Senatorial Campaign Committee ad. Indeed, some voters thought it was sponsored by the RNC; others believed it was sponsored by the Mayer campaign and the Republican Party.

Don't Blame Me

The hallmark of the 2000 election was repeated efforts by all the candidates to avoid blame for negativity. During the nominating process, George W. Bush often couched attacks on primary opponent John McCain with language blaming the Arizona senator for having attacked Bush previously. This was an obvious effort to lead voters to conclude that Bush's criticisms were merely a response to McCain's negativity and therefore should not be judged harshly. Friends of Bush at the Republican Leadership Council also launched inoculation ads against Forbes complaining about his penchant for negativity, in anticipation that Forbes would attack Bush in the same way he had criticized Dole in 1996.

Gore followed the same strategy as Bush with regard to Democratic challenger New Jersey senator Bill Bradley. Even while broadcasting ads critical of Bradley, Gore complained that Bradley was being negative and engaging in unfair criticisms of his proposals. This skill at playing the blame game shielded Gore from criticism that he was being the aggressor in the Democratic nominating process.

In the general election, both Bush and Gore went on the attack frequently but sought to blame each other for the harsh tone of the campaign. Indeed, each followed a good cop–bad cop routine in which each candidate tried to stay at least moderately positive, while surrogates and outside interest groups delivered more hard-hitting messages. This approach was intended to insulate the candidates from the inevitable voter backlash that arises when citizens get upset with negative campaigning.

As shown in Table 8-1, both candidates were remarkably successful at avoiding blame for negative campaigning. Early in the fall campaign, Gore fared a little better than Bush in this strategy. By a 65 percent to 23 percent margin, voters were more likely to say Gore explained his view than attacked the opponent. By comparison, Bush's ratio for explaining to attacking was 48 percent to 35 percent.

However, as the campaign wore on, Bush repositioned himself as an explainer rather than an attacker. By the end of the campaign, there was virtually no difference between the two candidates in terms of who was seen as attacking and explaining and who was held responsible for the negativity of the campaign (28 percent named Bush, 26 percent cited Gore, and the rest were undecided). It was a sign of how closely divided the presidential election had become and of the ability of both candidates to shift responsibility for negativity away from themselves.

Blame Terrorists

The 2004 presidential campaign featured the most negative advertising since 1988. Aware that the country had been closely divided in the 2000 campaign between "blue" states that had supported Gore on the Electoral College map and "red" states that had supported Bush, President Bush went on the attack early in an effort to define his Democratic opponent, John Kerry. In March and April, the president's organization broadcast $60 million in television ads designed to discredit his opponent. According to these spots, Kerry was wrong on defense, taxes, and terrorism.

Knowing that these negative ads could provoke voter backlash, Bush used several strategies designed to avoid the blame. For one, many of his attacks focused more on substantive issues than personal background. Citizens typically have unfavorable reactions to character attacks more often than to substantive attacks. They view the latter as an appropriate part of campaign dialogue, and therefore fair game for electoral criticism. In addition, Bush relied on surrogates such as Vice President Richard Cheney, cabinet officials, and RNC chairman Marc Raciot to deliver some of the attacks. This helped shield the president from having to engage in excessive criticism himself.

Finally, when confronted with the high cost of the Iraq War and large job losses during his administration, Bush invoked the specter of the September 11, 2001, attacks. This helped explain why jobs had been lost, the budget deficit had mushroomed, and the country had gone to war in Iraq. Although not everyone believed this explanation, some saw it as a national trauma that justified subsequent policy actions.

In September 2004, 54 percent of respondents thought Kerry's ads attacked Bush, whereas only 45 percent saw Bush's ads as attacking Kerry (see Table 8-1). Contrary to public perception, analysis of ad-buy data indicates that throughout most of the campaign, Bush broadcast a far higher volume of negative commercials than Kerry. For example, an analysis undertaken by Ken Goldstein of the Wisconsin Advertising Project found that in October 2004 nearly 90 percent of the Bush ads featured attacks, compared to around 10 percent of Kerry's spots.[17]

Despite this situation, the public blame directed toward Kerry continued. By mid-October, voters had shifted to nearly equal blame for Bush (56 percent) and Kerry (58 percent). However, by the end of October, 60 percent of voters saw Kerry as spending most of his time attacking his opponent, compared to only 50 percent who felt that way about Bush. This meant that in the crucial blame game, Bush had clearly out-foxed Kerry. In spite of objective evidence to the contrary, more voters saw Kerry as being the prime instigator and proponent of campaign negativity. The ability to influence how voters perceived the televised air wars was a major strategic victory for Republicans.

Blame Bush and McCain

The 2008 presidential campaign featured a referendum on the two-term presidency of George W. Bush. With the war in Iraq stretching into its sixth year, the economy in recession, and oil and gas prices fluctuating, Democrats ran against McCain on the platform of "Bush's Third Term." One of the first Democratic National Committee ads broadcast against McCain showed him hugging Bush and Bush kissing him on the forehead while the announcer said that McCain planned to continue many of Bush's foreign and domestic policies.

The rationale behind this ad was that Bush was at record-low popularity levels. In most national polls, his approval rating hovered around 30 percent for most of the election. Equally ominous for Republicans was the fact that nearly 90 percent of Americans believed the country was headed in the wrong direction. It was the "perfect storm" of public opinion that gave heartburn to GOP candidates up and down the ticket.

In a situation in which the public opinion climate was not sympathetic to his party, McCain ran a campaign that sought to turn the election into a referendum on his opponent by charging that Obama lacked the policy vision and personal character to serve as president. For example, the spot "Celebrity" compared Obama to Paris Hilton and Britney Spears and claimed he was a vacuous celebrity who knew nothing and was not ready to lead.

TABLE 8-2
Tone of Presidential Campaign Compared to
Previous Elections, 1988–2008

	More Positive	More Negative	Same
1988	7%	61%	28%
1992	2	39	35
1996	28	16	54
2000	—	—	—
2004	8	51	38
2008	15	35	48

Sources: CBS News/*New York Times* surveys.
— No data available.

Later advertisements sought to tie Obama to controversial figures and argued that he was a tax-and-spend liberal out of touch with the political mainstream. At campaign stops, McCain noted that Obama had a more liberal Senate voting record than Bernard Sanders of Vermont, a man who earlier in his career had called himself a socialist.

In July, when this line of attack barrage started, neither candidate was seen as responsible for negative campaigning. A national survey found that only 26 percent of voters saw McCain as going on the attack, compared to 17 percent who thought Obama was spending most of his time attacking his opponent. However, as shown in Table 8-1, by mid-August, voter perceptions had shifted against McCain. A new national survey at that time found that 52 percent believed he was attacking Obama, while only 26 percent felt Obama was attacking him. These dismal numbers for McCain got worse as the general election unfolded. By October, 64 percent of voters believed he was on the attack and only 22 percent felt that way about Obama. The Illinois senator had won the crucial blame game centering on who was responsible for negative campaigning. In the voter's eyes, McCain was being much more negative.

However, national surveys also showed that the 2008 campaign was not seen to be as negative in tone as the 2004 campaign. Table 8-2 lists voter responses to the question of whether a particular election was more positive, more negative, or about the same as the previous presidential race. In 2008, 35 percent believed that general election was more negative. But in 2004, 51 percent felt that year was more negative. Both years, though, were dwarfed by the 1988 campaign. That was the time when the largest number of voters (61 percent) believed the general election was more negative than in preceding years.

Conclusion

Candidates must use negative ads very carefully. Although there is evidence that these kinds of attacks can be effective at framing the election and tarring the opposition, research also demonstrates that citizens do not like this style of discourse: mean-spiritedness or attacks that are seen as unfair upset voters and make them cynical about politicians.

For this reason, candidates hope to use critical ads to pin negatives on the opponent without incurring the inevitable backlash. As the cases in this chapter suggest, campaigners have developed a number of blame-game strategies designed to insulate themselves from voter dissatisfaction with campaign discourse. This includes using surrogates to deliver the attacks, adopting rhetoric that blames the opponent for having started the fight, using finely honed surgical strikes on the opposition, questioning the legitimacy or fairness of the attacks, and blaming outside forces. When blame is skillfully avoided, candidates can use attack ads to gain electoral advantage.

Chapter 9

Ads in Congressional Elections

<hr />

Campaign ads have long been a major expenditure in presidential races, but they also have become a prominent part of House and Senate races throughout the country. According to recent studies, congressional candidates devote 40 percent of their overall campaign budgets to advertisements, which is below the 60 percent spent by presidential campaigners but still a significant portion of the campaign effort.[1]

In many respects, advertisements for Congress are similar to those run during presidential campaigns. Such spots are produced to shape public views and news media coverage, and they represent the major strategic tool for presenting a campaign to voters. In terms of public presentation, congressional spots feature a blend of positive and negative appeals. Citizens' responses to these spots vary depending on ad content, media coverage, and voter predispositions.

But congressional campaigns differ from presidential contests in some key respects. With many House and Senate incumbents facing no challengers or very weak opponents, congressional campaigns are more one-sided than is typically the case at the presidential level. In addition, congressional races are less visible to the general public and attract little media coverage, which affects the context in which television ads are seen.

Features of Congressional Campaigns

The most important quality of congressional contests is their general lack of competitiveness. Through the power of incumbency, the ability of Senate and House members to raise money and attract press attention, and the opportunities incumbents have to serve constituents, around 95 percent of House members and 90 percent of senators seeking reelection win.

Over the past few decades, incumbents have taken advantage of so many officeholder benefits that it is virtually impossible to beat them short of a personal scandal or a major partisan shift in voting habits. As illustrated by the 1994 elections, even when Republicans gained control of the House and Senate in a historic upset, most new GOP victories took place in open-seat contests in which no incumbent was on the ballot.

Incumbents are much better known than challengers owing to the formers' press coverage and ability to generate favorable publicity for themselves. This gives congressional incumbents an enormous advantage in terms of political advertising. Television ads are most effective when the public brings little previous knowledge to the election. If voters do not know much about one of the candidates, campaign spots can be used to fill in that profile. If a challenger has a lot of money, that individual can use ads to create a public image. However, if the challenger is not widely known, advertisements and news coverage generated by the incumbent can construct an unfavorable portrait of the opposition.

A classic illustration of this situation took place in Massachusetts when Democratic senator Edward Kennedy was challenged by Republican Mitt Romney in 1994. Well-funded and armed with attacks ads against Senator Kennedy, Romney initially appeared to be a strong opponent. However, after information was unearthed through opposition research about one of Romney's companies denying health care coverage to employees, Kennedy advertisements raised the negatives of the challenger and effectively ended the threat to Kennedy's reelection.

Because incumbents have so many advantages, it is difficult for congressional challengers to raise money, run ads, and mount serious threats to public officeholders. Through the ability of incumbents to use the perks of the office, deliver goods and services to their states, and keep their names in the press, most congressional races are not terribly competitive.

Historical Congressional Ads

The 1950 campaign of Sen. William Benton, D-Conn., is credited as the first in which television ads were used to promote a congressional candidate. The year before, Benton had been appointed by

Gov. Chester Bowles to a vacant Senate seat. Benton had worked on radio ads in the 1930s and then for Encyclopedia Britannica Films in the 1940s, so he was perfectly positioned to understand the power of the new medium of television. During his 1950 campaign, he produced five ads that helped him gain victory in that contest.[2]

Since that time, many congressional candidates have used television to advance their political careers. Candidates from the West have used the visual imagery of horses, cattle, and the frontier to appeal to voters who feel distant from Washington, D.C. Those from New England often play to their Yankee roots and the rustic sense of the region. And more than one Texan has relied on the Stetson hat to convey a down-home image of a regular person who can relate to ordinary voters.

As at the presidential level, some challengers have successfully used political attacks against incumbents. In 1984, for example, Kentucky GOP challenger Mitch McConnell, then a county chief executive, beat Democrat Dee Huddleston by running a series of ads called "Hound Dogs," which featured several hounds attempting to sniff out the trail of the incumbent, who had missed several key votes while speaking at resort events. The spots created a compelling narrative that portrayed Huddleston as being out of touch with ordinary voters.

During the middle of the Reagan era, Kent Hance, a congressman from Texas running against fellow Democrat Lloyd Doggett, was accused of being a servant of the rich because of his key role in passing the 1981 tax cut. Doggett's ad "Butler" used the imagery of a butler serving tax cuts on a silver platter to an affluent man to claim that Hance favored the wealthy.

In 1980, the Republican National Committee demonized Democratic House Speaker Tip O'Neill by showing a man who looked like O'Neill as passenger in a car that ran out of gas. This ad, a generic spot broadcast in a number of House districts across the country, played to voter beliefs that Democrats had been in power too long and were out of touch.

After Newt Gingrich and the Republicans captured control of Congress in 1994 and proceeded to pass legislation designed to downsize government, Democrats responded with a variety of ads portraying the new Speaker as a dangerous extremist not to be trusted with Medicare, Medicaid, education, and the environment. To defend itself in 1996, the GOP tried to associate Democrats with labor union "bosses" in an attempt to make the point that returning Democrats to power would hand over the political process to a special interest group.

That year, a research team looking at the thirty-four Senate races across the country found that 106,438 spots were aired by Senate candidates. Of these, 54,456 were broadcast by Republicans; 51,982 by Democrats. In addition, interest groups and party organizations ran 36,814 spots (23,567 for the GOP and 13,247 on behalf of Democrats). In the twenty races involving incumbents, challengers spent $3 million, compared with the $5.2 million spent by incumbents. Not surprisingly, nineteen of the twenty incumbents seeking reelection won. Overall, this project documented that exposure to ads raised the probability that viewers would vote for the candidate sponsoring the spot.[3]

The Fight for a Democratic House

Six years after the Gingrich Revolution, Republicans remained in control of Congress. Ever since 1994, the GOP had controlled congressional committees, appointed staff members, and dominated the legislative agenda. With the help of outside interest groups, Republicans pursued their agenda of promoting tax cuts, controlling the rate of growth in entitlement programs, and strengthening the military. In the 2000 election, Democrats made a concerted effort to regain control of the House.

Because of the advantages of incumbency, most Republican and Democratic House members held safe seats and were not at risk of losing. Ads in these districts tended to be low key and positive if there were any ads at all. In the remaining thirty to forty competitive districts, however, the television air war resembled a presidential campaign: lots of spending; attack ads; extensive media coverage; and advertising by candidates, interest groups, and parties.

Consider, for example, the 27th District in California. Rep. James Rogan, a Republican conservative who had won in 1998 with only 50.1 percent of the vote and served as one of the House impeachment managers in the Senate trial of President Bill Clinton, was the target of an effort by Democratic challenger Adam Schiff. Before the race was over, Rogan had raised $6 million, whereas Schiff had garnered $4 million, making this the first $10 million House race in U.S. history. Outside interest groups devoted another $2.5 million to this contest.

With senior citizens comprising 22 percent of the district, Schiff advocated the importance of a prescription drug benefit, the need for health maintenance organization reform, and money to save

Social Security. The Rogan campaign responded by arguing, "Adam Schiff is talking about it, but Congressman Rogan is doing it. The Congress just voted again for a lockbox to protect 100 percent of Social Security funds from being spent on other programs. Congress also modernized Medicare this year."[4] In the end, though, Schiff became one of the few challengers to defeat a member of the House, winning 52 percent to 44 percent.

The national parties also took advantage of Internet technology to poke fun at the opposition. For example, the National Republican Congressional Committee sponsored a site at www .retaintheminority.com, which criticized House Democrats. It included a "Weenie of the Week" feature that publicized Democratic miscues and a survey allowing viewers to predict the Democratic incumbent most likely to lose in November.[5]

By the time the national House elections ended, Democrats had picked up three seats but not majority control. In one of the closest congressional elections in recent memory, Republicans retained control of the House 221 to 212 (with 2 Independents). For the fourth consecutive election starting with 1994, Republicans held the reins of power.

The Fight for the Senate

While the two parties jockeyed for control of the House, there were a large number of competitive Senate races. When the dust settled, six incumbents had lost: five Republicans and one Democrat. The larger than usual number of senators who lost was noteworthy, but most incumbents who sought reelection won.

In the contests in which incumbents lost, some races had idiosyncratic features. In one of the most unusual Senate races in history, Missouri Republican John Ashcroft lost to Gov. Mel Carnahan, who died unexpectedly in a plane crash a few weeks before the election. Though dead, Carnahan won the election—his term served by his widow and appointed successor, Jean Carnahan. Eighty-year-old William Roth, a Republican incumbent senator from Delaware, lost after fainting twice during the campaign, once in front of a television camera. The remaining losses took place in districts in which there was a strong challenger and the incumbents had voting records either more moderate or more conservative than those of their states as a whole.

The Senate race that emerged as the closest of the year was in Washington State, where Sen. Slade Gorton was locked in a close match with Democratic challenger Maria Cantwell. A multimillionaire, Cantwell bankrolled most of her own campaign. Social Security and the environment were major subjects in the ad wars. For example, she broadcast an ad that claimed Gorton had broken his 1988 pledge never to cut Social Security. Gorton responded by calling her commercial "a lie."[6]

In another spot, Cantwell attacked a company that received a state permit for a gold mine despite a possible threat to the environment. Her commercial opened with an image of a mountain with birds singing. A black cloud then engulfed the screen and a young girl was seen taking a drink from a faucet. In a debate, Gorton blasted the ad, saying it was "totally false" in its implication that the mine would poison the local water supply. He accused Cantwell of using "typical, big government plans" to push her election.[7] When the election was over and the absentee ballots had been counted, however, Cantwell won by several thousand votes.

Clinton versus Giuliani and Lazio

The most prominent Senate race in 2000 occurred in the state of New York. Hillary Clinton sought to make history by becoming the only first lady to win elective office in her own right. Emboldened by surveys showing her as a strong candidate for the open Senate seat in New York, Clinton passed the word that she would run against likely GOP candidate Rudolph Giuliani, the mayor of New York City.

Initially, the race looked improbable. Clinton had never lived in New York prior to her Senate bid, thereby inviting the age-old criticism that she was a carpetbagger. Both she and her husband had been attacked for a variety of personal scandals: Whitewater, Travelgate, the Lewinsky affair, and the exchange of overnight visits in the Lincoln bedroom for campaign contributions. Public opinion on Clinton was polarized. Some loved her; others hated her. Few people appeared to be in the middle.[8]

Yet the first public survey in February 1999 showed Clinton with a 53 percent to 42 percent lead over Giuliani. Her numbers were boosted by a wave of public sympathy resulting from her husband's admission of infidelity and the subsequent congressional impeachment effort. Women, minorities, and young people provided a solid base of support for her campaign.

However, during 1999, Clinton's numbers faded while Giuliani's support increased. In March 1999, a Marist College poll showed her lead had dropped three points (48 percent to 45 percent). By April, a *New York Post* survey put the mayor ahead of the first lady 46 percent to 42 percent, the first to show him leading. In fall 1999, Giuliani's lead ranged from four to seven points, depending on the survey. Each candidate held similar favorability ratings. In an October 1999 CBS News/*New York Times* survey, 39 percent indicated they were favorable toward Giuliani, whereas 34 percent were unfavorable. For Clinton, 37 percent were favorable, whereas 38 percent were unfavorable.

Even more interesting were voter impressions of which candidate would do a better job handling important issues. Clinton was seen as better able to reform health care (63 percent to 22 percent) and improve education (60 percent to 27 percent); Giuliani was seen as more adept at reducing crime (75 percent to 15 percent), having experience (67 percent to 44 percent), and getting things done (69 percent to 59 percent).[9] Despite the early stage of the election, voters had formed relatively clear impressions of the two campaigners.

A series of gaffes by Giuliani improved the first lady's numbers. A jury acquittal of police officers charged in the shooting death of Amadou Diallo and another police shooting of an unarmed man, Patrick Dorismond, combined with inflammatory statements by the mayor, gave Clinton a lead of 49 percent to 41 percent, according to an April 2000 CBS News/*New York Times* survey. In that survey, not only did Giuliani's numbers drop, but voters blamed him for the negativity of the campaign, a crucial indicator of who was winning the blame game. Fifty-two percent of respondents believed Giuliani was spending most of his time attacking Clinton, whereas only 29 percent felt that way about her.[10]

In early summer 2000, however, the race took a surprising turn. In a completely unexpected move, Giuliani withdrew from the race after being diagnosed with prostate cancer. His spot on the GOP ticket was taken by Rep. Rick Lazio of Long Island. The switch of candidates redefined the dynamics of the campaign. Unlike Giuliani, who had statewide appeal but high negatives, Lazio was not well known statewide and had few negatives in the eyes of voters. Early polls revealed that within a few weeks of his candidacy, Lazio had come within eight points (52 percent to 44 percent) of Clinton. Only 10 percent viewed him unfavorably, compared with 31 percent for Clinton.

Still, Clinton had a major advantage in terms of voters' feeling about the blame game. Many more voters felt she was explaining her views rather than attacking Lazio, a clear contrast with how voters saw him. Seventy-four percent believed she was spending more time explaining her opinions, whereas only 9 percent believed she was on the attack. In contrast, 37 percent felt Lazio was explaining his views and 30 percent believed he was attacking his opponent.[11]

The fall air wars started with a barrage of advertisements, fueled by $80 million in fund-raising ($27 million by Clinton, $33 million by Lazio, and $20 million by Giuliani). Clinton attacked Lazio for missing key votes in Congress. How could he be an effective senator, she asked, when he was not even fulfilling his basic House responsibilities? He returned the fire by attacking her failed 1993 health care reform effort. Her proposals represented "bad medicine for New York," his ads argued. She noted in return that his budget votes had cost New Yorkers billions in health care financing. Her ad tagline ran, "Rick Lazio: The more you know, the more you wonder."[12]

Each candidate broadcast ads virtually around the clock. On October 4, for example, Clinton ran ads in the New York City area from 8:00 a.m. until 11:30 p.m. Her ads ran on ABC every half hour except 11:30 to noon, 3:30 to 4:00, 5:30 to 6:00, and 9:30 to 11:30. Lazio matched Clinton in nearly every time slot. Whereas many candidates in less well-endowed races hoard their ad buys for airing around news and public affairs shows, Clinton and Lazio targeted news shows, entertainment shows, and game shows. Both candidates purchased time during such shows as *Oprah Winfrey, Judge Judy, Wheel of Fortune,* and *Hollywood Squares.* Each spent $35,000 to air a single spot during ABC's hit show *Who Wants to Be a Millionaire?* Overall, Lazio spent $6 million in New York City in September, and Clinton spent $5 million.[13]

As the race neared its end, Clinton ran spots featuring former mayor Ed Koch holding up a picture of Lazio shaking hands with Palestinian leader Yasir Arafat. One of Lazio's final ads showed a dark picture of Clinton's face while an announcer warned, "Hillary Clinton: You can always trust her to do what's right—for Hillary Clinton."[14]

The closing CBS News/*New York Times* poll showed Clinton with a 52 percent to 44 percent lead over Lazio. Fifty percent of voters had a favorable view of her, whereas only 37 percent held a favorable impression of him. Many more felt she had the maturity and experience to be a senator and care about ordinary people. On the crucial issue of honesty and integrity, the two were virtually tied: fifty-three percent felt Lazio was honest; 51 percent believed that of Clinton.[15] She had effectively defused a possible negative for herself from Whitewater and Travelgate.

On Election Day, Clinton won 55 percent to 44 percent. Network exit polls revealed that the male vote was split evenly at 49 percent each for Clinton and Lazio, but Clinton triumphed among women, with 60 percent favoring her and only 39 percent preferring Lazio. Among those who said the issues were most important for their vote, 62 percent voted for Clinton, whereas only 36 percent favored Lazio. However, among those saying personal qualities were most important, Lazio beat Clinton 54 percent to 43 percent. On the crucial blame game, 54 percent of voters felt Clinton had attacked her opponent unfairly; 65 percent believed that of Lazio.[16]

2004 Senate Campaigns

The race for control of the U.S. Senate in 2004 came down to eight states. Although thirty-four seats were up for grabs, only one-quarter of these were competitive: South Dakota, Oklahoma, Colorado, Alaska, North Carolina, South Carolina, Florida, and Louisiana. In every one of these states, with the exception of Florida, President George W. Bush would go on to win reelection by a sizeable margin. His popularity in these states forced Democrats to run a campaign based on local, not national, issues.

For example, in South Dakota, where Senate minority leader Tom Daschle faced a strong challenge from Republican John Thune, Daschle broadcast television ads touting his success at bringing the state federal money to build bridges and highways and finance various water projects in the state. He also positioned himself as a champion of the working class. One ad featured voters who said Thune "gets pushed around by Wall Street and the big boys in Washington," while "Daschle cuts taxes for the middle class." [17]

Thune responded by airing ads that accused the Senate leader of being out of touch with local voters. One ad criticized the incumbent as someone who "says one thing in South Dakota and votes the other way in Washington." Thune's yard signs said, "It's time," suggesting Daschle had been in office for too long.[18] Although South Dakota has a relatively small population of 750,000, Daschle spent more than $18 million, compared to $13 million by Thune. The average television viewer within the state saw thirty commercials a week from each side; Daschle ran ads more than a year before the November election.[19]

The close contest attracted outside groups and political parties to the ad wars (although Daschle refused the help of outside groups).

Organizations such as the U.S. Chamber of Commerce and Club for Growth devoted millions to ads attacking the Senate minority leader on tax and legal reform issues. The National Republican Senatorial Committee ran an ad showing pictures of liberal Democrats John Kerry and Edward Kennedy that proclaimed Daschle was "leading the Democratic attack on President Bush."[20] In the end, Thune defeated Daschle and helped the Republicans pick up four seats that year.

Another state that had a very close Senate race was Colorado. Republican Pete Coors, scion of the family's beer business, ran against Democratic attorney general Ken Salazar. Each man raised millions ($7 million for Salazar and $6 million for Coors). The Democrat emphasized his centrist roots as a law-and-order attorney general, whereas Coors opposed the death penalty and defended beer drinking by young people. Environmental groups spent almost a million dollars attacking Coors's record and put together a Web site: www.PolluterPete.com.[21] With the help of these attacks, Salazar was able to defeat Coors.

The Wisconsin Senate race between Republican Tim Michels and Democrat Russell Feingold featured an ad showing an image of a burning World Trade Center tower. Against the backdrop of this image, Michels's commercial said, "Russ Feingold voted against the Patriot Act and the Department of Homeland Security." The spot concluded by showing pictures of Michels holding his young daughter and expressing his support for the U.S. military and the Patriot Act.[22] Despite this graphic attack, Feingold was reelected by a comfortable margin.

2006 House and Senate Campaigns

The political context had changed dramatically by the 2006 elections.[23] According to a CBS News/*New York Times* survey undertaken right before the election, top issues included the Iraq War (26 percent), economy (11 percent), terrorism and immigration (7 percent), health care (5 percent), foreign policy (4 percent), defense and military matters (3 percent), jobs and unemployment (3 percent), and education (2 percent).[24]

The indictments, convictions, and resignations of several Republicans gave Democrats the opportunity to campaign against Washington and call for a change in the national course. In California, an ad for Democrat Francine Busby compared Republican Brian Bilbray to convicted Rep. Randy Cunningham and warned, "We don't need another congressman in jail."

Meanwhile, actor Michael J. Fox appeared in a commercial supporting federal funding for stem cell research and calling for the election of Missouri Democratic senatorial candidate Claire McCaskill.[25] Fox also called for the election of a new Democratic senator in Virginia by saying, "A vote for Jim Webb is a vote for hope and a better quality of life for Americans."[26] Republican George Allen responded by pointing out that Webb had written books that stereotyped women as sex objects: "His novels? Some are graphic, even deviant," the advertisement warned.[27]

Many of the ads across the country were unrelentingly negative. Indeed, of the spots broadcast by the national party committees, 91 percent of National Republican Congressional Committee ads were judged negative, while 81 percent of those sponsored by the Democratic Congressional Campaign Committee fell into that category. Expert commentators, such as Kathleen Hall Jamieson, said that 80 percent of the ads in 2006 were negative, compared to 60 percent of commercials in 2004.[28]

With a wave of attack ads sweeping the major House and Senate races, Democrat Ned Lamont of Connecticut produced a spoof ad that mocked attacks on him. "Meet Ned Lamont," the ad stated, "He can't make a decent cup of coffee." As the candidate shuffled papers, flashy red text appeared on the screen warning "Messy Desk."[29] This commercial, though, did not save the man's campaign. He lost to independent Joe Lieberman in the Senate campaign.

Rather than scaring voters into believing a terrorist attack was imminent, ads played to citizens worried about a war in Iraq that was not going well. In national surveys, only 29 percent of Americans approved of the way in which Bush was managing the war, and 70 percent did not believe the president had a plan to end the war.[30] After more than $250 billion and nearly three thousand dead U.S. soldiers, Republicans were on the defensive and Democrats framed the election as a referendum on President Bush. Overall spending on advertisements topped $2 billion, up from the $1.6 billion spent in 2004.[31]

Democratic candidates across the country ran advertising campaigns that played to voter discontent with Bush. One ad against Republican House member Dave Reichert of Washington criticized the legislator by saying he "just sides with Bush on Iraq. Iraq is just a disaster. Iraq is a complete disaster. It's heartbreaking." Another spot targeting Republican congressman Rob Simmons of Connecticut said, "Despite a war gone wrong and no plan for victory, politicians like Rob Simmons keep voting to stay the course again and again, following George Bush's failed leadership no matter what the cost."[32]

Republicans meanwhile centered their response on questioning the values and backgrounds of their Democratic opponents. In Tennessee, the Republican National Committee financed an independent ad against senatorial candidate Harold Ford Jr. that featured a scantily clad white woman claiming to have met the African American Democrat at a Super Bowl party sponsored by *Playboy* magazine. The young woman leered into the camera and pleaded, "Harold, call me."[33] After critics condemned the advertisement for playing on racial fears about a black man dating a white woman, the commercial was pulled. The damage was done, though. Ford lost his electoral bid to Republican Bob Corker 51 percent to 48 percent. Corker also aired more ads (12,007) than Ford (7,239) between August 1 and October 15, which helped cement his victory.[34]

Not to be outdone, Pennsylvania senator Rick Santorum linked his opponent Bob Casey Jr. to terrorist Osama bin Laden and North Korean dictator Kim Jong II. In an ad entitled "The Stakes," Casey was accused of being soft on terrorism and risking nuclear war.[35] But in an environment in which nearly two-thirds of voters thought the country was headed in the wrong direction, Santorum ultimately lost his bid for reelection.

During the 2006 midterm elections, candidate ads sought to elevate or undermine particular standards of evaluation, often related to candidate character. Republican challenger Paul Nelson attacked Democratic House member Ron Kind by saying his opponent supported federal grants for studies of human sexuality. "Ron Kind Pays for Sex!" shouted one ad, while visual text splashed "XXX" across his face. According to the commercial, Kind wanted "to pay teenage girls to watch pornographic movies with probes connected to their genitalia." Republican Rep. John Hostettler aired radio spots saying that if Nancy Pelosi of California became the new Democratic Speaker, she would "put in motion her radical plan to advance the homosexual agenda."[36]

Another spot paid for by the National Republican Congressional Committee accused Kind of calling a sex hotline and attempting to charge it to taxpayers. More detailed scrutiny of this ad claim, though, found that the call was a wrong number made by an associate of the Democratic candidate and that it lasted only a few seconds.[37]

At the end of this hard-fought midterm election, the Democratic strategy of nationalizing the election and raising the negatives of

Republican opponents on Bush and Iraq reaped tremendous dividends. Democrats regained majority control of the House and Senate. They picked up thirty-three seats in the House and six seats in the Senate, thereby ensuring that there would be a Democratic Congress for the first time since 1994.

2008 Senate Campaigns

The 2008 race saw Democrats pick up a large number of seats in the Senate. Befitting a public opinion climate hostile to the GOP, Democrats emphasized the bad economy, a long war in Iraq, and an unpopular Republican president. Senate Republicans had to defend three states in which a GOP incumbent was retiring (New Mexico, Colorado, and Virginia) and five states in which incumbent senators were vulnerable (Minnesota, North Carolina, New Hampshire, Alaska, and Oregon). In three other states (Kentucky, Georgia, and Mississippi), upsets were considered possible in the closing days of the campaign.

One of the nastiest races took place in North Carolina where Democrat Kay Hagan was challenging incumbent Elizabeth Dole. More than $34 million in ad money was spent, a state record. Seeking to take advantage of Dole's age of seventy-two, Democrats broadcast an advertisement complaining that the Republican was ninety-three. "Ninety-three?" asked an amazed bystander. "Yup," the ad pointed out, "she ranks ninety-third in effectiveness." The person is perplexed and asks, "After forty years in Washington?" Her friend replies that "after forty years in Washington, Dole is ninety-third in effectiveness, right near the bottom." The spot closed with the tagline of "What happened to the Liddy Dole I knew? She's just not a go-getter like you and me."[38] Dole immediately denounced this spot as unfair ageism on the part of her opponent.

After this spot blanketed the state, Dole broadcast her own controversial commercial. Learning that Hagan had held a fund-raiser in Boston organized by Woody Kaplan, a member of the Godless Americans political action committee, Dole's ad proclaimed, "Godless Americans and Kay Hagan. She hid from cameras. Took godless money. What did Hagan promise in return?" The ad closed by showing a picture of Hagan with a female voiceover saying, "There is no God." Hagan was so upset that she sued for defamation and ran her own response ad entitled "Belief," which noted her Christian faith and accused Dole of "bearing false witness against fellow

Christians." The ad complained that her opponent "faked my voice in her TV ad to make you think I don't believe in God. Well, I believe in God. I taught Sunday school. My faith guides my life."[39] In one of the year's upsets, Hagan unseated Dole and took the seat once held by Jesse Helms.

Other states saw equally large amounts of money spent on campaign ads. In Minnesota, for example, the race between Republican Norm Coleman and Democrat Al Franken saw more than $30 million in ad expenditures. The Oregon battle between Republican Gordon Smith and Democrat Jeff Merkley saw more than $34 million spent in advertisements. The Colorado contest between Democrat Mark Udall and Republican Bob Schaffer generated more than $35 million in ad spending.[40]

In most of these races, Democrats emphasized that it was "time for a change." Bush's unpopularity helped them link the chief executive to any local Republican seeking national office. Big Oil was a target, as was the weak economy and out-of-touch incumbents. These themes resonated with voters and helped Democrats build a large majority in the U.S. Senate.

Conclusion

House and Senate campaigns feature different dynamics than presidential races. They generally do not attract as much media attention as national contests, and voters are not as engaged in the final results. In addition, incumbents have far greater advantages over challengers in congressional campaigns than in presidential campaigns.

For these reasons, ads in House and Senate contests face fewer counterweights than at the presidential level. In presidential campaigns, voters may be influenced by news coverage, debates, or objective economic or international events. These other forces restrain the power of advertisements and empower a variety of alternative forces. In congressional contests, some of these constraining factors are absent, making advertisements potentially even more important. If candidates have the money to advertise in a congressional contest, it can be a very powerful force for electoral success.

Chapter 10

Advertising and Democratic Elections

In this book, I have investigated television advertising from a number of perspectives: What is the strategic use of political commercials? How do the media cover ads? What impact do campaign spots have on viewers? In brief, I found that commercials influence how voters learn about the candidates (chapter 5), what they identify as priorities (chapter 6), their standards of assessment (chapter 7), and attributions of blame (chapter 8). Ads have their strongest impact with little-known candidates and electoral settings of low visibility and in situations in which journalistic coverage reinforces an ad's message. Strategic elements within each election are also crucial. Both the timing and content of ads and decisions on when and where to attack shape viewer responses to advertisements.

This chapter examines the implications of these results for democratic elections, which are crucial to democratic systems. They are a means by which citizens choose who occupies positions of formal responsibility. There is little doubt that ads have altered the way citizens make electoral decisions. Yet the research reported here has shown that not all electoral arenas face the same problems. Because the impact of an advertisement depends considerably on the campaign context, the same type of commercial can pose very different challenges in various settings.

Democratic Expectations

Few aspects of democracy have been discussed over the course of U.S. history as much as the quality of information provided during the election process. Candidates are expected to address the subjects at stake in a given election and to indicate where they stand in regard to those matters. In fact, this information allows voters to hold leaders accountable. Failure to provide suitable material undermines the representative basis of American democracy.[1]

As an intermediary institution, the media are expected to devote enough attention to candidates' character attributes and to the issues to help voters bridge the gaps left by candidates' communications. Not many people directly experience election campaigns. Voters are dependent on the media to help them interpret political realities. When reporters provide the type of information that educates citizens regarding the choices facing them, the election process is significantly enhanced.

However, there is disagreement over exactly how detailed the information from candidates and the media should be. The classical model of democracy calls for specific, issue-oriented material.[2] Candidates are expected to have detailed positions on the major issues facing the country and to communicate these views clearly to voters. Issue-based voting models as well as textbook descriptions of U.S. elections emphasize the policy aspects of campaigns.

Other scholars, though, have argued that popular control can be achieved through other approaches. For example, the *party-responsibility model* uses partisanship as the means of accountability. Parties foster representation because they encapsulate general lines of thinking about major policy positions. According to this model, voters can make substantive judgments about candidates based purely on party labels.[3] In a similar way, retrospective evaluations have become widely accepted as a means of popular control. Advocates of this system argue that a candidate's approach to issues alone is not an appropriate test because voters can be sophisticated and rational without engaging in issue-based voting. As long as leaders can be held accountable for the broad direction of government performance, democratic tenets are satisfied.[4]

Still others have argued that knowledge about the character of potential leaders is vital to democratic elections.[5] Elections are seen as a means of evaluating the judgment of the leaders who will do the deliberating in a representative democracy. According to this perspective, assessments about leadership qualities and character are quite relevant to voters' decision-making.

The emergence of thirty-second ads and short sound bites as the primary means of political communication represents a potential challenge to each of these models.[6] Because classical democratic theory places a premium on detailed policy information, the chief danger under this model is deception and distortion by the candidates regarding their positions on issues. Ads that mislead viewers or distort an opponent's record are particularly dangerous. Numerous campaigners have used ads to create impressions of themselves that turned out to be inaccurate (including Lyndon Johnson as the peace candidate in 1964 and George Bush as the "no new taxes" man of 1988). The same logic applies to models centered on leaders' judgment. The primary danger of ads in this view is their potential to alter or reinforce citizen opinions about personal traits. In 1984, for example, Gary Hart was remarkably successful at getting people to see Walter Mondale, who had formidable Washington experience and interest group support, in a negative light as just another old-style politician currying favor with special interests.

But these are not the only consequences from advertisements. The party-responsibility model assumes that long-term party identification will protect ad viewers against excesses by candidates. Yet even this model recognizes that party attachments have shifted in recent years and that new arenas based on intraparty nominating contests have arisen. These settings are precisely where ads achieve their greatest impact. The combination of unknown candidates, volatile preferences, and shared party labels gives ads enormous influence. The emergence of independent candidates, such as Ross Perot and Ralph Nader, has put the party-responsibility model in even greater danger in regard to general elections, because party ties are less decisive in a three-way race. In these settings, advertising takes on great strategic significance. The ability to win with a plurality of the vote encourages candidates to use commercials to appeal to narrow pockets of voters.

The *pocketbook-voting model* also raises important questions. This approach appears on the surface to be the least vulnerable to ads because vote choice is presumed to be based on citizens' views about the economy, which are in turn rooted in people's personal experiences, so ads would not seem to be too influential on electoral decisions. A closer inspection, however, reveals that even this model requires voters to assign blame for unsatisfactory performance and assess candidates' capabilities to deal with economic matters.[7] In 1992, for example, Bill Clinton—primarily through advertising—was able to boost public perceptions about his ability to improve the economy and show people that he was a caring individual. The same arguments hold for 2008. Barack Obama benefited from voter perceptions of bad economic performance under the Republican Party.

Attributions of responsibility are particularly open to media influence. Through techniques based on priming and defusing, ads can elevate or lower particular standards of evaluation (see chapter 7). In fact, during eras of scarce resources, elections often rest on how well candidates play the blame game.[8] Therefore, although traditional voting models diagnose the problem of advertisements quite differently, each one identifies particular dangers regarding the quality of information presented to voters and the ability of citizens to engage in informed decision-making.

The Risk of Manipulation

The concerns expressed about U.S. elections did not originate with television. Writers have long complained about the dangers of outside influences on voters. Nineteenth-century reformers, for example, fought outright bribery in an era when cash payoffs to citizens in exchange for votes were quite common. The extension of voting rights in that century precipitated wild debates regarding the impact of external agents: Opponents of expanded suffrage claimed that newly enfranchised women would be unduly influenced by their husbands and that Catholic immigrants would become pawns of the pope!

Several features of democratic systems have been thought to reduce the danger of external manipulation. Foremost is vigorous electoral competition. In a two-party system in which there is equity of funding and each candidate has a reasonable opportunity to get his or her message out to the general public, voters should have enough information to protect themselves from ad distortion and manipulation. The assumption is that even though voters may not pay close attention to politics, they can garner enough material through party labels, issue information, views about the economy, and impressions of candidate qualities to reach informed decisions.

Widespread acceptance of the democratic culture by political elites is seen as providing a sufficient guarantee of fair and open competition. Self-regulation, it is said, weakens the threat from candidates and helps ensure that election appeals are made fairly. At the same time, a variety of intermediary institutions supposedly protect citizens from overly ambitious campaigners. People can express opinions and hold leaders accountable through organizations representing their political perspectives. Parties and interest groups have been seen as the most important links in modern theories of democracy. Because these organizations facilitate the joint activity of citizens having common points of view, they are a means of bridging the gap between citizens and leaders.

The problem with this view of democracy is that its proponents have been strangely quiet about key aspects of leadership behavior. In the rush to reconcile less than optimistic views of citizens' behavior with hopes for democracy, observers have lost sight of the crucial responsibilities of candidates in the election process. Some perspectives, for example, ignore the facts that elite competition can go beyond the bounds of fair play when there is no referee to penalize players for making deceptive appeals and that partisan competition can tax public respect for the political system. With powerful advertising tools at candidates' disposal, citizens are exposed to potent and sometimes misleading campaign appeals.[9]

In addition, problems sometimes arise in terms of equity of electoral discourse. One candidate may be better funded or have access to greater resources than others, which can create an unfair advantage. This is particularly a problem in some presidential nomination contests (such as George W. Bush versus John McCain in 2000, in which Bush had twice as much money as his challenger and Barack Obama and McCain in 2008, in which Obama again raised more money than McCain) and in House races in which incumbents routinely raise and spend many times that which is available to challengers.

The decline of self-regulation by candidates' organizations would not be as problematic if a universally acknowledged body existed to protect citizens against subtle manipulation of their standards of evaluation. Unfortunately, there is no external referee with the authority to police electoral competition. Political parties and interest groups have lost some of their organizational grip on elections. Meanwhile, government agencies (such as the Federal Election Commission and the Federal Communications Commission) cannot regulate campaign appeals, because political speech is constitutionally protected.

The weakness of external regulators at a time when candidates control influential communication technologies has given candidates great incentive to attempt manipulation of voters through the airwaves. The classic problem of electoral deception involves *substantive manipulation*, whereby leaders deceive citizens about policy matters. According to Benjamin Page and Robert Shapiro, "To the extent that the public is given false or incorrect or biased information, or is deprived of important relevant information, people may make mistaken evaluations of policy alternatives and may express support for policies harmful to their own or society's interests, or in conflict with values they cherish."[10]

If elections were primarily about public policy, substantive manipulation would remain the most dangerous threat to the political system. However, contests involve perceptions about electability and personal images as well. Many races in recent years have turned on questions of momentum, likability, and mistakes. How the game is played often has become more important than the task of setting the future course of government action.

The fact that elections generally involve short-term campaign phenomena creates another type of deception, which I call *strategic manipulation*. In this situation, efforts are made to shift impressions of the campaign in a direction favorable to particular candidates. For example, candidates often seek to influence short-term evaluations. Specifically, spot commercials can be used to alter views about an opponent's likability, they can lead to exaggerated claims regarding a contender's electoral prospects, or they can be used to change campaign dynamics and distract voters from pressing matters of the day. There are a number of common techniques for viewer manipulation through advertising. Prevalent tactics include using visual trickery, condemning an opponent for a position you also hold, telling half the story, taking votes out of context, playing with definitions, and using lapses in grammar that create misleading impressions.[11]

Television commercials are particularly problematic because they combine audio and visual technologies. Sounds, colors, and visual presentations can be used in deceptive ways, as discussed in the opening chapter. For example, Pat Buchanan's ad consultants in 1992 occasionally sped up or slowed down George Bush's physical movements to create unfavorable impressions of the president. Independent ad producer Floyd Brown also admitted that he had doctored a 1992 ad showing President Clinton's hand raised high with Massachusetts senator Edward Kennedy's. The joint picture was faked by combining separate pictures of the men alone.[12]

In the 1996 U.S. Senate race in Virginia, Republican senator John Warner was forced to fire consultant Greg Stevens after Stevens admitted to doctoring a photo used in a spot linking Democratic opponent, Mark Warner, with President Clinton by replacing the head of Sen. Charles Robb with Warner's.[13] This type of editing, which tried to link Mark Warner with other candidates said to be liberal, poses obvious problems for viewers. People may remember the visual image but not be in a position to recognize electronic chicanery.

In 2004, George W. Bush's campaign was forced to redo a commercial when ad producers were found to have doctored an ad called "Whatever It Takes." Featuring Bush talking at the Republican National Convention, the spot also showed images of Bush speaking in front of soldiers. However, a liberal Web site, Daily Kos.com, found that faces of the same soldiers appeared in several places of the crowd scene. It turned out that the ad maker had digitally expanded the crowd by cutting and pasting the same individuals into the picture. This made it look like Bush was addressing a large group of soldiers, not the small audience that actually had been present. Democrats had a field day linking this electronic deception to what they said were larger questions of truthfulness in the Bush presidency. According to Kerry's spokesperson Joe Lockhart, "If they won't tell the truth in an ad, they won't tell the truth about anything else."[14]

The 2008 presidential race featured a large number of advertisements that contained misleading or inaccurate information. McCain accused Obama of supporting comprehensive sex education for kindergarten children when the legislation actually sought to help young kids identify possible sexual predators. Obama broadcast misleading spots accusing his GOP rival of wanting to cut Social Security and having torpedoed immigration reform.

Strategic manipulation has not attracted as much study as substantive or symbolic manipulation, but in a media era it is a serious threat. A campaign structure that is open, volatile, and heavily dependent on media coverage gives candidates clear incentives to seek strategic advantage through doctored images or video manipulation. The rise of new technologies and the employment of professional campaign managers in the United States have broadened the range of tactics considered acceptable and given campaigners extraordinary tools for influencing voters.

Different Arenas, Different Threats

The susceptibility of voters to advertising appeals has long generated despair from political observers. Joe McGinniss's book, *The Selling of the President,* and Robert Spero's *The Duping of the American Voter* express common fears about the dangers of advertisements.[15] But these authors failed to recognize that not all electoral arenas are subject to the same threat. The visibility of the setting makes a big difference.

The major threat in highly visible arenas, such as presidential general election campaigns, is substantive manipulation. The 1988 general election gave a textbook illustration of this danger, as the relatively unknown Michael Dukakis saw his entire campaign shattered by George Bush's successful efforts to move the campaign from past performance to flags, furloughs, and patriotism. Bush used advertising on tax and spending matters as well as crime to fill in the public profile of the relatively unknown Dukakis. The vice president was able to dominate the campaign because few voters knew much about the Massachusetts governor, 1988 was a year with a fluid policy agenda, and Dukakis did not successfully defend himself. Bush portrayed Dukakis as an unrepentant liberal who was soft on crime and out of touch with the American people. To some voters, this portrait was accurate; for others it was an example of image redefinition.

Similar problems arose in the 2008 presidential election. In the closing days of the campaign, both candidates made a number of debatable charges. McCain accused Obama of being a socialist because he wanted to "spread the wealth." Obama meanwhile said that if McCain were elected, he would cut Social Security and thereby undermine the social safety net for the elderly.

Less visible electoral arenas, such as presidential nomination campaigns, are particularly vulnerable to strategic manipulation. Because they are less visible contests that are heavily influenced by campaign dynamics, they contain fewer countervailing forces than are present in presidential general elections. Democrats compete against Democrats and Republicans against Republicans in a sequential nominating process.[16] In this situation, party identification is not central to vote choice. The setting limits the power of long-term forces and makes it possible for short-term factors, such as advertising and media coverage, to dominate.

Senate races share some features with nominating races. These contests are susceptible to ad appeals because relatively unknown candidates compete in races that resemble roller-coaster rides. Wild swings in electoral fortunes often occur during a campaign. The absence of prior beliefs about the candidates makes advertising especially influential.[17] It is easier to create a new political profile (for one's self or one's opponent) than to alter a well-defined image. Candidates who are the least known are the most able to use advertisements to influence the public. But they also are the most susceptible to having opponents create unfair images of them with television ads.

Slicing and Dicing the Electorate

Campaign advertisements also pose problems for democratic elections on the systemic level. Even if ads influence voting behavior only in certain circumstances, they have consequences for the way in which a campaign is viewed. Advertisements are one of the primary means of communication, and much of how people feel about the electoral system is a product of how campaign battles are contested.

In contemporary elections, political consultants commonly divide voters into three advertising segments based on public opinion polls and focus groups: the committed (those who are for you), the hopeless (those who are against you and about whom little can be done), and the undecided (those who could vote either way). The last group, of course, is the central target of campaign tactics.

New digital communications make it possible to target even more precisely based on demographics, geography, lifestyle, or ideological beliefs. It is possible to run ads on Internet sites that micro-target small groups of voters. The narrow-casting model of cable television has given rise to micro-niches of voter appeals.

Ads are developed to stir the hopes and fears of the 20 percent to 30 percent of the electorate who are undecided, not the 70 percent to 80 percent who are committed or hopeless. Narrow pockets of support are identified and targeted appeals are made. Many Americans complain that campaign discussions do not reflect their concerns. Their complaints are legitimate. With advertising appeals designed for the small group of voters who are undecided, it is little wonder many voters feel left out.

In this system of segmentation and targeted appeals, candidates have clear incentives to identify pockets of potential support and find issues that will move these voters. Whether it is the backlash against affirmative action among white rural dwellers in North Carolina (one of the winning issues for Sen. Jesse Helms in 1990) or George Bush's attacks on Clinton for his 1969 antiwar demonstrations (which did not save the election for Bush), the current electoral system encourages candidates to find divisive issues that pit social group against social group.

It is not surprising that in this situation Americans feel bad at the end of election campaigns. Candidates engage in an electronic form of civil war not unlike what happens in polarized societies. The battleground issues often touch on race, lifestyle, and gender, which are among the most contentious topics in the United States. Ads and sound bites are the weapons of choice in these confrontations. The long-term dangers of the electronic air wars are ill feelings and loss of a sense of community.

What Can Be Done

The controversies that have arisen concerning television campaign ads have produced cries for serious reform. These calls undoubtedly reflect deep frustration over the uses of advertisements in the United States.[18] But it is far too simple to blame ads for electoral deficiencies: The problem of political commercials is as much a function of campaign structure and voters' reactions as of candidates' behavior. Structural and attitudinal changes have loosened the forces that once restrained elite strategies. The rise of a mass-based campaign system at a time when candidates have powerful means of influencing viewers rewards media-centered campaigns.

At the same time, voters are vulnerable to candidates' messages because the forces that used to provide social integration have lost their influence. Intermediary organizations no longer control people's impressions of political reality. With the end of the Cold War, consensus has broken down on key domestic and foreign policy questions. Voters are bombarded with spot ads precisely because of their proven short-term effectiveness.

Because ads are a form of expression, they are subject to constitutional protection and thereby quite difficult to restrict.[19] Most attempts at direct regulation have been resisted as unconstitutional encroachments on free speech.[20] Self-monitoring efforts, such as those proposed by the National Association of Political Consultants, have been of limited value. Vigorous electoral competition is the ultimate form of protection for voters, but too many times, inequity in resources tilts campaign discourse in favor of incumbents or well-funded individuals.

However, an informal mechanism in the advertising arena offers voters some help: the media. Journalists who focus on deceptive or misleading commercials help the public hold candidates accountable for ads that cross the threshold of acceptability. Currently, reporters devote plenty of attention to candidates' ads but not necessarily in a way that informs citizens on important issues. For example, the media are more likely to use ads to discuss the horse race than the policy views of the candidates. But with a different approach to ad coverage, television could become a more enlightening force in U.S.

elections. Journalists in the United States have an unusually high credibility with the public. American reporters are seen as being more fair and trustworthy than are reporters in other countries. Whereas 69 percent of Americans surveyed in a comparative study had great confidence in the media, only 41 percent of Germans and 38 percent of the British gave high ratings to journalists.[21]

Both Kathleen Hall Jamieson and David Broder have suggested that journalists should exercise their historical function of safeguarding the integrity of the election process.[22] The media could use their high public credibility to improve the functioning of the political system. Candidates periodically make exaggerated claims in their efforts to win votes. Journalists need to look into their claims and report to voters on their accuracy.[23]

These efforts are valuable, but journalists must go beyond fact checking to true oversight. The media have some responsibility to expose blatant manipulation, distortion, and deception, not just inaccurate use of facts. Reporters should bring to task candidates who exceed the boundaries of fair play. Unfair tactics or misleading editing need to be publicized. Commercials that engage in obvious appeals to racism, for example, should be condemned. While it is difficult for reporters to compete with the volume of advertisements run in major campaigns, it remains important to have an independent checks-and-balance system on the claims of candidates for office.

Television has a special obligation because it is the medium through which most Americans receive their political news. Ad watches are especially important in spots involving race, lifestyle issues, gender, or other topics with emotional overtones.[24] Reporters are the only major group with the credibility vis-à-vis the American public to arbitrate electoral advertising. In fact, a Gallup poll revealed that citizens would like the media to undertake an aggressive watchdog role.[25]

There is some danger for the media in openly assuming this role. Many Americans already are concerned about what they believe is excessive influence and bias on the part of the news media.[26] If journalists aggressively challenge candidates' statements, they may be viewed as part of the problem rather than the solution. There are increasing signs of a backlash against the media, and reporters could become subject to more stringent criticism regarding their overall influence and objectivity.

In 1991, for example, Louisiana gubernatorial candidate David Duke tried to foster antipathy toward the media through a last-minute ad directly criticizing coverage of his campaign: "Have you ever heard such weeping and gnashing of teeth? The news media have given up any pretense of fair play. The liberals have gone ballistic. The special interests have gone mad. The politicians who play up to them are lining up on cue. Principles lie abandoned and hypocrisy rules the day. I raise issues that must be discussed, and get back venom instead. Try a little experiment. Next time you hear them accuse me of intolerance and hatred, notice who is doing the shouting."

George Bush attempted to build support for his 1992 reelection with the slogan, "Annoy the Media: Reelect Bush." In 1996, Robert Dole attacked the "liberal press," saying, "They don't put any anti-Clinton stories in the *New York Times*. Only anti-Dole stories in the *New York Times*."[27] Along with his 2008 vice-presidential nominee Sarah Palin of Alaska, McCain complained about a liberal press that was soft on Obama. (A study undertaken by the Project for Excellence in Journalism supported McCain's claim, finding that 60 percent of the McCain news stories following the GOP convention were negative compared to 29 percent for Obama news coverage.[28])

A national survey conducted during the last week of the 2000 campaign found that 49 percent of respondents believed the media had done a good or excellent job of covering the fall presidential election, 31 percent felt the job was only fair, 11 percent thought it was poor, and 9 percent were unsure. This poll also asked whether news coverage had been biased against any individual candidate. Twenty-eight percent said yes, whereas 58 percent did not feel there had been any bias. When asked which candidate had received the most biased coverage against him, 49 percent cited George W. Bush, 25 percent named Al Gore, 17 percent claimed Nader, 9 percent mentioned Buchanan, and 1 percent were unsure.[29]

In 2004, a national survey by the Pew Research Center found that 37 percent of voters thought the press had been unfair to President Bush; 27 percent believed the media had been unfair to John Kerry. In terms of the overall campaign coverage, 54 percent rated it excellent or good, 28 percent said it was only fair, 16 percent believed the coverage was poor, and 2 percent were unsure. When asked how much influence news organizations have on which candidate becomes president, 62 percent of voters said they believed the media had too much influence.[30]

Conclusion

Despite the possible drawbacks, oversight by the media is vital enough to the political system to warrant the risk of backlash. The quality of information presented during elections is important enough to outweigh the practical difficulties facing the media. Nothing is more central to democratic elections than electoral discourse. Without informative material, voters have little means of holding leaders accountable or engaging in popular consent. By encouraging candidates to address the substantive concerns of the electorate, media watchdogs help voters make meaningful choices.

Appendix

Memorable Ads, 1984–2008

Walter Mondale, "Future," 1984

Crosby, Stills, Nash, and Young sing portions of their song "Teach Your Children," while images of missiles shooting from underground silos are juxtaposed with close-ups of children's faces. The ad concludes with a picture of a forest shaking from an explosion and a young girl's face appearing on screen. Then a globe fills the screen and the words "Mondale/Ferraro" rotate into view.[1]

Ronald Reagan, "Bear in the Woods," 1984

[A bear lumbers through the woods.] "There's a bear in the woods. For some people the bear is easy to see; others don't see it at all. Some people say the bear is tame; others say it's vicious and dangerous. Since no one can be sure who is right, isn't it smart to be as strong as the bear—if there is a bear!"[2]

George H. W. Bush, "Revolving Door," 1988

[Dissonant sounds are heard: a drum . . . music . . . metal stairs.] "As governor, Michael Dukakis vetoed mandatory sentences for drug dealers." [A guard with a rifle climbs the circular stairs of a prison watchtower. The words "The Dukakis Furlough Program" are superimposed on the bottom of the prison visual.] "He vetoed the death penalty." [A guard with a gun walks along a barbed wire fence.] "His revolving door prison policy gave weekend furloughs to first-degree murderers not eligible for parole." [A revolving door formed of bars rotates as men in prison clothing walk in and back out the door in a long line. The words "268 Escaped" are superimposed on the screen.] "While out, many committed other crimes like kidnapping and rape."

[The camera comes in for a closer shot of the prisoners in slow motion revolving through the door.] "And many are still at large." [The words "And Many Are Still At Large" are superimposed on the screen.] "Now Michael Dukakis says he wants to do for America what he's done for Massachusetts." [The picture changes to a guard on a roof with a watchtower in the background.] "America can't afford that risk!" [A small color picture of Bush appears, and the words "Paid for by Bush/Quayle '88" appear in small print.][3]

Michael Dukakis, "Family/Education," 1988

[A young man is shown flipping dough in a pizza parlor at night.] "Jimmy got accepted to college, but his family couldn't afford tuition." [Dukakis appears on the screen.] A voice-over says: "Mike Dukakis wants to help. . . . If a kid like Jimmy has the grades for college, America should find a way to send him."[4]

Bill Clinton, "The Plan," 1992

[Clinton speaks into the camera.] "The people of New Hampshire know better than anyone. America is in trouble; our people are really hurting. In the eighties, the rich got richer, the middle class declined, poverty exploded. Politicians in Washington raised their pay and pointed fingers. But no one took responsibility. It's time we had a president who cares, who takes responsibility, who has a plan for change. I'm Bill Clinton, and I believe you deserve more than thirty-second ads or vague promises. That's why I've offered a comprehensive plan to get our economy moving again, to take care of our own people, and regain our economic leadership. It starts with a tax cut for the middle class and asks the rich to pay their fair share again. It includes national health insurance, a major investment in education, training for our workers, tough trade laws, and no more tax breaks for corporations to move our jobs overseas. Take a look at our plan and let me know what you think. I hope you'll join us in this crusade for change. Together we can put government back on the side of the forgotten middle class and restore the American Dream."[5]

Bill Clinton, "How're You Doing?" 1992

[Picture shows George Bush.] A voice-over says, "Remember President Bush saying, 'And if you elect me president, you will be better off four years from now than you are today'?" The announcer responds, "Average family income down $1,600 in two years"

(Commerce Department Bureau of Census 9/1/92). A voice-over says, "President Bush says, 'You will be better off four years from now than you are today.' " The announcer responds, "Family health care costs up $1,800 in four years" (Health Insurance Association of America, 1988; KPMG Peat Marwick 1992). A voice-over says, "President Bush says, 'You will be better off in four years.' " The announcer responds, "The second biggest tax increase in history" (Congressional Budget Office Study 1/30/92; *New York Times* 8/7/92). A voice-over says, "President Bush says, 'If you elect me president, you will be better off four years from now than you are today.' " The announcer asks, "Well, it's four years later. How're you doing?"[6]

George H. W. Bush on Clinton Economics, 1992

An announcer says, "Bill Clinton says he'll only tax the rich to pay for his campaign promises. But here's what Clinton economics could mean to you. [Picture shows a male steamfitter.] $1,088 more in taxes. [Picture shows a female scientist.] $2,072 more in taxes. 100 leading economists say his plan means higher taxes and bigger deficits. [Picture shows a professional couple.] $1,191 more in taxes. [Picture shows a black housing lender.] $2,072 more in taxes. You can't trust Clinton economics. It's wrong for you. It's wrong for America."[7]

Ross Perot on Job Creation, 1992

[Background picture shows a ticking clock; text scrolls up the screen.] "It is a time when the threat of unemployment is greater than the threat of war. It is a time that the national debt demands as much attention as the national security. It is a time when the barriers to a better life are rising and the barriers between nations are falling. The issue is the economy. And it is a time that demands a candidate who is not a business-as-usual politician, but a business leader with the know-how to balance the budget, rebuild the job base and restore the meaning of 'Made in the U.S.A.' In this election, we can choose a candidate who has made the free enterprise system work, who has created thousands of jobs by building successful businesses. The candidate is Ross Perot. The election is November 3. The choice is yours."[8]

Ross Perot on National Debt and Children, 1992

[Background picture shows children's faces; text scrolls up the screen.] "Our children dream of the world that we promised them as parents, a world of unlimited opportunity. What would they say to us if they knew that by the year 2000, we will have left them with a national debt of $8 trillion? What would they say to us if they knew that we are making them the first generation of Americans with a standard of living below the generation before them? We cannot do this to our children. In this election, we have the opportunity to choose a candidate who is not a career politician, but a proven business leader with the ability to take on the tasks at hand, to balance the budget, to expand the tax base, to give our children back their American dream. The candidate is Ross Perot. The issue is our children. The choice is yours."[9]

Bill Clinton, "Wrong in the Past, Wrong for Our Future," 1996

[Scenes are shown of a calendar flipping backward.] "Let's go back in time." [The sixties.] "Bob Dole's in Congress. Votes against creating Medicare. Against creating student loans." [The seventies.] "Against the Department of Education. Against a higher minimum wage." [The eighties.] "Still there. Against creating a drug czar. Against the Brady Bill." [The nineties.] "Against the Brady Bill. Against family and medical leave. Against vaccines for children. Against Medicare, again. Dole-Gingrich tried to cut $270 billion. Bob Dole. Wrong in the past. Wrong for our future."[10]

Bob Dole, "MTV Drug Use," 1996

[Scenes are shown of school children inspecting a plastic bag filled with marijuana and then passing around a marijuana cigarette.] "We send them off to school. And we worry. Teenage drug use has doubled since 1992. And Bill Clinton? He cut the White House Drug Office 83 percent. His own surgeon general considered legalizing drugs. And in front of our children, on MTV, the president himself." [Scene switches to black-and-white clip of MTV audience member asking a question.] "If you had it to do over again, would you inhale?" [President Clinton.] "Sure, if I could. I tried before." [Announcer.] "Bill Clinton doesn't get it. But we do." [Screen graphic: "Clinton's liberal drug policy has failed."][11]

Ross Perot, "Where's Ross?" 1996

"He's put together a bona fide campaign." [Woman.] "Where's Ross?" [Narrator.] "He won the debates in '92." [Woman.] "Where's Ross?" [Narrator.] "Set the campaign agenda and won 19 percent of the vote." [Woman.] "Where's Ross?" [Narrator.] "He's been allocated $30 million of federal funds." [Woman.] "Where's

Ross?" [Narrator.] "Seventy-six percent of Americans want him in the debate. But a Washington commission with no legal standing, headed by career politicians and meeting behind closed doors, said no." [Woman.] "Where's Ross?" [Narrator.] "He's on the ballot in all fifty states. Vote for a change. Vote for Perot."[12]

Republican National Committee, "Talk Is Cheap," 1996

[Footage shows Bill Clinton offering different projections for when he would balance the federal budget.] [Announcer.] "For four years you've heard a lot of talk from Bill Clinton about balancing the budget." [President Clinton.] "I would present a five-year plan to balance the budget." "... we could do it in seven years." "... I think we can reach it in nine years." "... balance the budget in ten years." "... I think we could reach it in eight years." "... so we're between seven and nine now." [Announcer.] "No wonder Bill Clinton opposes a constitutional amendment to balance the budget." [President Clinton.] "7 ... 9 ... 10 ... 8 ... 5" [Announcer.] "Talk is cheap. Double talk is expensive. Tell Mr. Clinton to support the balanced budget amendment."[13]

AFL-CIO, "Cutting Medicare," 1996

[Black-and-white pictures show the sad and weathered faces of several elderly people.] "Congressman George Nethercutt voted to cut our Medicare benefits. George Nethercutt knows it. And so do we. Fact: On November 17, 1995, Nethercutt voted with Newt Gingrich to cut $270 billion from Medicare funding, while voting for tax breaks for the wealthy. Now he's trying to deny it. Tell George Nethercutt we know the truth about his vote to cut our Medicare benefits. Another vote is coming. This time we'll be watching."[14] [This was a cookie-cutter ad in which the AFL-CIO filled in the blank with local candidates.]

Al Gore, "Ready to Lead," 2000

[Picture shows George W. Bush, followed by images of an oil rig, a young mother, a polluting factory, and a middle-aged couple going over bills.] "As governor, George W. Bush gave Big Oil a tax break while opposing health care for 220,000 kids. Texas now ranks fiftieth in family health care." [Picture shows a child with the following graphic: "Texas now ranks 50th in family health care."] "He's left the minimum wage at $3.35 an hour, let polluters police themselves. Today, Texas ranks last in air quality. Now Bush promises the same $1 trillion for

Social Security to two different groups. He squanders the surplus on a tax cut for those making over $300,000. [Picture shows a Mercedes-Benz and an expensive home.] Is he ready to lead America?"[15]

George W. Bush "Hyperbole," 2000

"Remember when Al Gore said his mother-in-law's prescription cost more than his dog's?" [Picture shows newspaper headline, "Aides Concede Gore Made Up Story."] "His own aides said the story was made up. Now Al Gore is bending the truth again. The press calls Gore's Social Security attacks 'nonsense.'" [Visual text shows the word "Nonsense."] "Governor Bush sets aside $2.4 trillion to strengthen Social Security and pay all benefits." [Image shows Bush in hard hat, with graphic "Governor Bush: $2.4 trillion to strengthen Social Security & pay all benefits."] [Picture shows Gore.] Mr. Gore: "There has never been a time in this campaign when I have said something that I know to be untrue. There has never been a time when I have said something untrue." [Picture shows Gore debating Bill Bradley.] "Really?"[16]

John Kerry, "Jobs," 2004

[Image of American flag waving against a black background.] "There are many reasons to be hopeful about America's future. And one of them is that Election Day is coming, so we can choose a new direction." [Image from Bush ad citing nearly two million reasons to be hopeful.] "Because under George Bush, we've lost 2.7 million manufacturing jobs." [Visual text reads: "George Bush. Lost 2.7 million manufacturing jobs."] "He's supported tax breaks for companies that export jobs. Wages are down. The cost of living is up. Middle-class families are getting squeezed. Only Herbert Hoover had a worse record on jobs. It's time for a new direction." [Visual text reads: "Only Herbert Hoover had a worse record on jobs."] [Image of John Kerry at a campaign rally.][17]

Democratic National Committee, "Eagle," 2004

[Video of flying eagle.] "The eagle soars high above the earth." [Image of ostrich with head in the sand.] "The ostrich buries its head in the sand. The eagle can see everything for miles around. The ostrich? Can't see at all. The eagle knows when it's time to change course. The ostrich stands in one place. Given the choice, in these challenging times, shouldn't we be the eagle again?" [Tagline: "America Can Do Better."]

George W. Bush, "Wolves," 2004

[Image of trees and dense forest.] "In an increasingly dangerous world, even after the first terrorist attack on America, John Kerry and the liberals in Congress voted to slash America's intelligence operations by $6 billion." [Image of wolf running through forest.] "Cuts so deep they would have weakened America's defenses." [Image of a pack of wolves on top of a hill.] "And weakness attracts those who are waiting to do America harm."[18]

George W. Bush, "Windsurfing," 2004

[Viennese waltz music in background throughout ad.] [Image of John Kerry.] "In which direction would John Kerry lead?" [Successive images of John Kerry windsurfing in opposite directions.] "Kerry voted for the Iraq War, opposed it, supported it, and now opposes it again. He bragged about voting for the $87 billion to support our troops before he voted against it. He voted for education reform and now opposes it. He claims he's against increasing Medicare premiums, but voted five times to do so." [Image of John Kerry.] "John Kerry. Whichever way the wind blows."[19]

Swift Boat Veterans, "Any Questions?" 2004

[Image of a young John Kerry as a soldier. Video of John Edwards saying, "If you have any questions about what John Kerry is made of, just spend three minutes with the men who served with him." Spoken statements from several Swift Boat veterans against backdrop images of soldiers.] "I served with John Kerry." "I served with John Kerry." "John Kerry has not been honest about what happened in Vietnam. He is lying about his record." "I know John Kerry is lying about his first Purple Heart because I treated him for that injury." "John Kerry lied to get his Bronze Star. I know, I was there. I saw what happened." "His account of what happened and what actually happened are the difference between night and day." "John Kerry has not been honest." "And he lacks the capacity to lead." "When the chips were down, you could not count on John Kerry." "John Kerry is no war hero." "He betrayed all his shipmates. He lied before the Senate." "John Kerry betrayed the men and women he served with in Vietnam." "He dishonored his country. He most certainly did." "I served with John Kerry. John Kerry cannot be trusted." [Image of a young John Kerry as a soldier.][20]

John McCain, "Original Mavericks," 2008

[Images of McCain and Palin throughout.] [Narrator.] "The original mavericks. He fights pork-barrel spending. She stopped the 'Bridge to Nowhere.' He took on the drug industry. She took on Big Oil. He battled Republicans and reformed Washington. She battled Republicans and reformed Alaska. They'll make history. They'll change Washington. McCain. Palin. Real Change."[21]

John McCain, "Joe the Plumber," 2008

Barack Obama: "I think when you spread the wealth around it's good for everybody." First woman: "I'm Joe the Plumber." Second woman: "I'm Joe the Plumber." Third woman: "I'm Joe the Plumber." [Narrator.] "Spread the wealth?" First man: "I'm supposed to work harder." Second man: "Just to pay more taxes." Third man: "Obama wants my sweat to pay for his trillion dollars in new spending?" Fourth woman: "I'm Joe the Plumber." [Narrator.] "Barack Obama. Higher taxes. More spending. Not ready."[22]

Barack Obama, "Original," 2008

[Narrator.] "He's the original maverick." [Graphic: "Really?"] John McCain: "The president and I agree on most issues. There was a recent study that showed I voted with the president over 90 percent of the time." [Narrator.] "John McCain supports Bush's tax cuts for millionaires [Image of golf course], but nothing for 100 million households. [Image of middle-class neighborhood.] He's for billions in new oil company give-aways, while gas prices soar. [Image of oil rig and gas pump.] And for tax breaks for companies that ship jobs overseas. [Image of overseas workers sewing.] The original maverick? Or just more of the same?" [Picture of Bush and McCain.][23]

Barack Obama, "Honor," 2008

[Video of John McCain saying, "I will not take the low road to the highest office in this land." Graphic: "John McCain, then."] [Narrator.] "What's happened to John McCain? [Quoting news sources.] He's 'running the sleaziest ads ever.' 'Truly vile.' 'Dishonest smears' that he repeats even after it's been 'exposed as a lie.' The 'truth be damned.' A 'disgraceful, dishonorable campaign.' After voting with Bush 90 percent of the time, proposing the same disastrous economic policies. It seems deception is all he has left."[24]

Notes

Chapter 1: Overview of Ads

1. Ira Chinoy, "In Presidential Race, TV Ads Were Biggest '96 Cost by Far," *Washington Post*, March 31, 1997, A19.
2. Michael Franz, Paul Freedman, Kenneth Goldstein, and Travis Ridout, *Campaign Advertising and American Democracy* (Philadelphia: Temple University Press, 2007).
3. Kathleen Jamieson, *Packaging the Presidency*, 2nd ed. (New York: Oxford University Press, 1992), 6–7.
4. "Ads for a Web Generation," *New York Times*, August 24, 1998, D7.
5. Jamieson, *Packaging the Presidency*, 50.
6. Quoted in Jamieson, *Packaging the Presidency*, 195. For a description of Johnson's strategy, see Edwin Diamond and Stephen Bates, *The Spot* (Cambridge: MIT Press, 1984), 127–140.
7. "How Bush Won," *Newsweek*, November 21, 1988, 117. Also see Paul Taylor and David Broder, "Early Volley of Bush Ads Exceeded Expectations," *Washington Post*, October 28, 1988.
8. Richard Berke, "Democrats See, and Smell, Rats in G.O.P. Ad," *New York Times*, September 12, 2000, A1.
9. Howard Kurtz, "Presidential Attack Ads Move from Land to Water— and Back," *Washington Post*, September 23, 2004, A9.
10. Jim Rutenberg, "Kerry Ads Draw on Saudis for New Attack on Bushes," *New York Times*, October 5, 2004, A16.
11. Elizabeth Kolbert, "Secrecy over TV Ads, or, the Peculiar Logic of Political Combat," *New York Times*, September 17, 1992, A21.
12. Emmett Buell and Lee Sigelman, *Attack Politics: Negativity in Presidential Campaigns since 1960* (Lawrence: University Press of Kansas, 2008).
13. Paul Farhi, "Ad Says Kerry 'Secretly' Met with Enemy; but He Told Congress of It," *Washington Post*, September 22, 2004, A8.
14. Ken Dilanian, "Defenders Say Wright Has Love, Righteous Anger for USA," *USA Today*, March 19, 2008.
15. Darrell M. West and John Orman, *Celebrity Politics* (Upper Saddle River, N.J.: Prentice Hall, 2003).

16. "Anti-Bush Ad Contest Includes Hitler Images," *Washington Post,* January 6, 2004, A4.
17. Howard Kurtz, "Ads Aiming Straight for the Heart," *Washington Post,* October 27, 2004, A1.
18. Darrell M. West, *Patrick Kennedy: The Rise to Power* (Upper Saddle River, N.J.: Prentice Hall, 2000).
19. Harry Berkowitz, "Campaigns Aim at Economy," *Newsday,* September 28, 1996, A13.
20. Marjorie Connelly, "A 'Conservative' Is (Fill in the Blank)," *New York Times,* November 3, 1996, E5.
21. Howard Kurtz, "Bush's Health Care Ads Not Entirely Accurate," *Washington Post,* October 13, 2004, A8.
22. David Kirkpatrick, "Republicans Admit Mailing Campaign Literature Saying Liberals Will Ban the Bible," *New York Times,* September 24, 2004, A20.
23. Paul Begala, "A Good Dirty Fight," *New York Times,* November 4, 2004, A25.
24. Glen Justice, "In Final Days, Attacks Are in the Mail and below the Radar," *New York Times,* October 31, 2004, A30.
25. Sandra Maler, "'French' Becomes Campaign Slur," *Seattle Times,* October 27, 2004, A5.
26. "Today on the Presidential Campaign Trail," *Washington Post,* October 30, 2008.
27. Wisconsin Advertising Project, "Presidential TV Advertising Battle Narrows to Just Ten Battleground States," October 12, 2004, press release.
28. Graeme Zielinski, "Michels Makes Case with Images from 9-11," *Milwaukee Journal Sentinel,* October 19, 2004, A1.
29. Martin Schram, *The Great American Video Game* (New York: William Morrow, 1987), 25–26. For a reassessment of the differential impact of radio and television viewers on the 1960 debates, see David Vancil and Sue Pendell, "The Myth of Viewer-Listener Disagreement in the First Kennedy-Nixon Debate," *Central States Speech Journal* 38 (Spring 1987): 16–27.
30. Kathleen Hall Jamieson, *Everything You Think You Know about Politics . . . and Why You're Wrong* (New York: Basic Books, 2000).
31. Daniel Stevens, "Separate and Unequal Effects: Information, Political Sophistication and Negative Advertising in American Elections," *Political Research Quarterly* 58, no. 3 (September 2005): 413–425; and Ted Brader, "Striking a Responsive Chord: How Political Ads Motivate and Persuade Voters by Appealing to Emotions," *American Journal of Political Science* 49, no. 2 (April 2005): 388–405.
32. The Media Studies Center poll is reported in *Providence Journal,* "Hype Swells as First Presidential Debate Approaches," September 29, 1996, A7. The CBS News/*New York Times* numbers come from Richard Berke, "Should Dole Risk Tough Image? Poll Says He Already Has One," *New York Times,* October 16, 1996, A1.
33. Kathleen Hall Jamieson, "Context and the Creation of Meaning in the Advertising of the 1988 Presidential Campaign," *American Behavioral*

Scientist 32 (1989): 415–424. Also see Marion Just et al., *Cross Talk: Citizens, Candidates, and the Media in a Presidential Campaign* (Chicago: University of Chicago Press, 1996).

34. James Ceaser, *Presidential Selection* (Princeton: Princeton University Press, 1979).
35. Karen DeWitt, "Tsongas Pitches Economic Austerity Mixed with Patriotism," *New York Times,* January 1, 1992, A10.
36. Ken Goldstein and Paul Freedman, "New Evidence for New Arguments: Money and Advertising in the 1996 Senate Elections," *Journal of Politics* 62 (2000): 1087–1108.
37. Daron Shaw, "The Methods behind the Madness: Presidential Electoral College Strategies, 1988–1996," *Journal of Politics* 61 (1999): 893–913. Also see his "The Effect of TV Ads and Candidate Appearances on Statewide Presidential Votes, 1988–96," *American Political Science Review* 93 (1999): 345–361.
38. Thomas Patterson and Robert McClure, *The Unseeing Eye* (New York: Putnam's, 1976). Also see Martin Wattenberg, *The Rise of Candidate-Centered Politics* (Cambridge: Harvard University Press, 1991); and Richard M. Perloff, *Political Communication: Press, Politics, and Policy in America* (Mahway, N.J.: Erlbaum, 1998).
39. The Harold Mendelsohn and Irving Crespi quote comes from their book, *Polls, Television, and the New Politics* (Scranton, Penn.: Chandler, 1970), 248.
40. Craig Leonard Brians and Martin Wattenberg, "Campaign Issue Knowledge and Salience: Comparing Reception from TV Commercials, TV News, and Newspapers," *American Journal of Political Science* 40 (February 1996): 172–193; and Xinshu Zhao and Steven Chaffee, "Campaign Advertisements versus Television News as Sources of Political Issue Information," *Public Opinion Quarterly* 59 (Spring 1995): 41–65.
41. Lynn Vavreck, Constantine Spiliotes, and Linda Fowler, "The Effects of Retail Politics in the New Hampshire Primary," *American Journal of Political Science* 46 (2002): 595–610.
42. Alliance for Better Campaigns, "Spot Comparison," *The Political Standard* 3 (June 2000): 1. See also Jonathan Krasno and Daniel Seltz, "Buying Time: Television Advertising in the 1998 Congressional Elections," Brennan Center for Justice, undated.
43. Elizabeth Kolbert, "Test-Marketing a President: How Focus Groups Pervade Campaign Politics," *New York Times Magazine,* August 30, 1992, 18–21, 60, 68, 72.
44. Quoted in John Foley, Dennis Britton, and Eugene Everett Jr., eds., *Nominating a President: The Process and the Press* (New York: Praeger, 1980), 79.
45. William McGuire, "Persuasion, Resistance, and Attitude Change," in *Handbook of Communication,* ed. Ithiel de Sola Pool (Chicago: Rand McNally, 1973), 216–252; and "The Nature of Attitudes and Attitude Change," in *Handbook of Social Psychology,* 2nd ed., vol. 3, ed. Gardner Lindzey and Elliot Aronson (Reading, Mass.: Addison-Wesley, 1969), 136–314.

46. Quote taken from David Runkel, ed., *Campaign for President: The Managers Look at '88* (Dover, Mass.: Auburn House, 1989), 142.

47. Howard Kurtz, "Some Kerry Spots Never Make the Air," *Washington Post,* October 20, 2004, A6.

48. Michael Robinson, "Public Affairs Television and the Growth of Political Malaise," *American Political Science Review* 70 (1976): 409–432.

49. David Peterson and Paul Djupe, "When Primary Campaigns Go Negative," *Political Research Quarterly* 58, no. 1 (March 2005): 45–54.

50. Larry Rohter, "Ad on Sex Education Distorts Obama Policy," *New York Times,* September 11, 2008, A22.

51. Howard Kurtz, "Ads Push the Factual Envelope," *Washington Post,* October 20, 2004, A1.

52. Seymour Martin Lipset and William Schneider, *The Confidence Gap* (New York: Free Press, 1983), 17; Paul Abramson, John Aldrich, and David Rohde, *Change and Continuity in the 1996 Elections* (Washington, D.C.: CQ Press, 1997); James Campbell, *The Presidential Pulse of Congressional Elections,* 2nd ed. (Lexington: University Press of Kentucky, 1997); and Bruce Keith, *The Myth of the Independent Voter* (Berkeley: University of California Press, 1992).

53. Thomas Holbrook and Scott McClurg, "The Mobilization of Core Supporters: Campaigns, Turnout, and Electoral Composition in United States Presidential Elections," *American Journal of Political Science* 49, no. 4 (October 2005): 689–703.

54. Alexis de Tocqueville, *Democracy in America,* trans. George Lawrence (Garden City, N.J.: Doubleday, 1969), 198.

Chapter 2: Buying Air Time

1. Darrell M. West, *Making Campaigns Count* (Westport, Conn.: Greenwood Press, 1984), 29, 45.

2. Marilyn Roberts, "Advertising Strategy, Recall, and Effectiveness in the 1992 Presidential Campaign" (paper presented at the annual meeting of the American Political Science Association, Washington, D.C., September 1993), 5. Also see Jonathan Krasno and Daniel Seltz, "Buying Time: Television Advertising in the 1998 Congressional Elections," Brennan Center for Justice, undated.

3. Darrell M. West, Montague Kern, Dean Alger, and Janice Goggin, "Ad Buys in Presidential Campaigns," *Political Communication* 12 (July–September 1995): 275–290.

4. Amy Keller, "Campaign Media Pros Fight Back against Overcharging by TV Stations," *Roll Call,* May 30, 1996, 9, 12. Also see James Bennet, "New Tool in Political Combat: Computers to Track TV Ads," *New York Times,* June 6, 1996, A1; and Graeme Browning, "Medium Cool," *National Journal,* October 19, 1996, 2223–2225.

5. James Bennet, "Aftermath of '96 Race: 1,397 Hours of TV Ads," *New York Times,* November 13, 1996, A16. The breakdown in ads run by Clinton and Dole, respectively, come from Kenneth Goldstein, "Political Advertising and Political Persuasion in the 1996 Presidential

Campaign" (paper presented at the annual meeting of the American Political Science Association, Washington, D.C., August 28–31, 1997).

6. Brennan Center, "Candidates Come to Strategic Fork in California," October 30, 2000.

7. "New Tax-Exempt Groups Donating Millions," *Providence Journal,* November 4, 2000, A11; and Wisconsin Advertising Project, "Over Half a Million TV Spots Have Been Aired in the 2004 Presidential Race," August 27, 2004, press release.

8. Jim Rutenberg, "Obama's Ad Effort Swamps McCain and Nears Record," *New York Times,* October 18, 2008.

9. Adam Nagourney and Janet Elder, "Bush Opens Lead Despite Unease Voiced in Survey," *New York Times,* September 18, 2004, A1.

10. Reported by Brooks Jackson on *Inside Politics,* CNN, September 26, 1996.

11. Marci McDonald, "Whassup with Those Boring Election Ads?" *U.S. News and World Report,* November 13, 2000, 52.

12. Ron Fournier, "Advertising Blitz Signals a Close, Negative Campaign," *Providence Journal,* August 26, 2000, A1.

13. "Candidates Court Hispanics with TV Ads," *USA Today,* October 19, 2000, www.usatoday.com.

14. Brennan Center, "Candidates Come to Strategic Fork in California," October 30, 2000.

15. Howard Kurtz, "In Advertising Give and Take, Clinton Camp Took and Responded," *Washington Post,* November 6, 1992, A10.

16. Adam Clymer, "The Republican Prescription," *New York Times,* August 29, 2000, A17; and Adam Clymer, "Democrats Release Their Volley on Prescription Drugs," *New York Times,* August 30, 2000, A17.

17. Peter Marks, "Attacking Bush's Record on Children's Health Care," *New York Times,* September 6, 2000, A20.

18. Michael Kranish, "Bush Strategy Centers on Five States," *Boston Globe,* September 27, 2000, A1.

19. John Broder, "Taking On Gore on Trust and Education," *New York Times,* September 15, 2000, A22.

20. Peter Marks, "Commercial Attacking Bush Is Most Hostile of Campaign," *New York Times,* November 3, 2000, A22; and Peter Marks, "Focusing on Gore Hyperbole," *New York Times,* November 1, 2000, A27.

21. "A General Enlists," *New York Times,* October 30, 2000, A17.

22. *Inside Politics,* CNN, March 20, 1996.

23. Susan Garland with Richard Dunham and Sandra Dallas, "Bill's First-Strike TV Blitz," *Business Week,* July 8, 1996, 126–128. Also see *Newsweek,* Special Election Issue, November 18, 1996.

24. "Clinton's Comments on Ads and Money," *New York Times,* October 21, 1997, A20.

25. "The Great Ad Wars of 2004," *New York Times,* November 1, 2004, A22.

26. Ibid.

27. Ibid.

28. Ibid.
29. Carl Hulse, "G.O.P. Now Sees Obama as Liability for Ticket," *New York Times,* April 26, 2008, A13.
30. *Boston Globe,* "Perot Steps Up Spending in Final Days," November 1, 1996, A24.
31. Tom Raum, "Bush, Gore in Election Eve Blitz," AP Online, November 6, 2000.

Chapter 3: Ad Messages

1. This quote is taken from Jonathan Moore, ed., *Campaign for President: The Managers Look at '84* (Dover, Mass.: Auburn House, 1986), 206. An example regarding the use of focus groups to influence Mondale's advertising themes against Hart is found on 78–79.
2. This quote comes from Joe McGinniss, *The Selling of the President* (New York: Simon and Schuster, 1969), 34.
3. Robert Spero, *The Duping of the American Voter* (New York: Lippincott and Crowell, 1980).
4. The 1988 results were taken from the October 21–24 CBS News/*New York Times* poll. The 1992 figures come from a poll of southern states undertaken by the *Atlanta Journal-Constitution,* October 24–27. The 1996 numbers were reported in Richard Berke, "Should Dole Risk Tough Image? Poll Says He Already Has One," *New York Times,* October 16, 1996, A1.
5. Marion Just, Ann Crigler, Dean Alger, Timothy Cook, Montague Kern, and Darrell M. West, *Cross Talk: Citizens, Candidates, and the Media in a Presidential Campaign* (Chicago: University of Chicago Press, 1996).
6. Richard Joslyn, "The Content of Political Spot Ads," *Journalism Quarterly* 57 (1980): 97.
7. See C. Richard Hofstetter and Cliff Zukin, "TV Network News and Advertising in the Nixon and McGovern Campaigns," *Journalism Quarterly* 56 (1979): 106–115, 152; Thomas Patterson and Robert McClure, *The Unseeing Eye* (New York: Putnam's, 1976); and Michael Robinson and Margaret Sheehan, *Over the Wire and on TV* (New York: Russell Sage, 1983), 144–147.
8. Samuel Popkin argues that voters can take cues about more general matters from small bites of information. See Popkin, *The Reasoning Voter* (Chicago: University of Chicago Press, 1991).
9. One of the most obvious ways in which the strategic behavior of campaigns is manifest in the advertising arena is through ad buys. Unfortunately, it is impossible to reconstruct accurate time-buy information for all ads before the 1990s.
10. Kathleen Jamieson, *Packaging the Presidency,* 2nd ed. (New York: Oxford University Press, 1992). Presentations of more than five minutes were not included.
11. For example, 1960 is underrepresented by Jamieson. She mentioned only two Republican spot ads that ran during that general election,

compared with twelve for Kennedy in the fall. In general, though, it still is preferable to rely on ad historians in 1960 than a list of ads discussed in newspapers and on television.

12. Jamieson, *Packaging the Presidency,* 83.
13. Darrell M. West and Burdett Loomis, *The Sound of Money* (New York: Norton, 1998).
14. Angus Campbell, Philip Converse, Warren Miller, and Donald Stokes, *The American Voter* (New York: Wiley, 1960).
15. Jamieson, *Packaging the Presidency,* 115.
16. Norman Nie, Sidney Verba, and John Petrocik, *The Changing American Voter,* enl. ed. (Cambridge: Harvard University Press, 1979).
17. Jamieson, *Packaging the Presidency,* 242.
18. The prominent ad listing underrepresents commercials on women's issues because, according to Jamieson, a long historical section dealing with the subject in her book *Packaging the Presidency* was cut from the final manuscript. Among the ads not described in her book that did appeal to social issues were Ellen McCormick's ads on abortion in 1976, Mondale's on Jerry Falwell in 1984, the Roslyn Carter ad in 1980, and several 1972 Florida primary ads on busing.
19. Jamieson, *Packaging the Presidency,* 411.
20. The 1992 congressional advertising involving abortion is discussed by Keith Glover in "Campaigning Crusaders Air Graphic Anti-Abortion Ads," *Congressional Quarterly Weekly Report,* September 26, 1992, 2970–2972.
21. Quote taken from Kevin Sack, "Georgia Republican Takes Abortion Stand," *New York Times,* June 16, 1996, 18. The election results are cited in Kevin Sack, "Abortion Opponents Prevail in 3 Republican Primaries," *New York Times,* August 8, 1996, B8.
22. The quotes come from Jamieson, *Packaging the Presidency,* 342, 384. Edwin Diamond and Stephen Bates describe Carter's strategy in their book, *The Spot* (Cambridge: MIT Press, 1984), 221–257.
23. Jamieson, *Packaging the Presidency,* 338, 386.
24. David Gopoian, "Issue Preferences and Candidate Choice in Presidential Primaries," *American Journal of Political Science* 26 (1982): 523–546; and Larry Bartels, "Issue Voting under Uncertainty," *American Journal of Political Science* 30 (1986): 709–728.
25. Jamieson, *Packaging the Presidency,* 338, 386, 395.
26. Tina Kelley, "Candidate on the Stump Is Surely on the Web," *New York Times,* October 19, 1999, A1.
27. "Bush Ad on Yahoo!" *New York Times,* April 13, 2000, A21; and Frank Bruni, "Bush on Taxes," *New York Times,* April 18, 2000, A18.
28. John Tierney, "Can't Buy Me Populism," *New York Times,* July 11, 2004, 16.
29. Brian Faler, "Campaigns Spending Little on Web Ads," *Washington Post,* October 4, 2004, A6.
30. Jim Rutenberg, "The Man behind the Whispers about Obama," *New York Times,* October 13, 2008.
31. Ibid.

32. Quoted in Robert Lineberry with George Edwards, *Government in America,* 4th ed. (Glenview, Ill.: Scott, Foresman, 1989), 153.
33. Howard Kurtz, "Attack Ads Carpet TV," *Washington Post,* October 20, 1998, A1. For a more extended discussion, see Kathleen Hall Jamieson, Paul Waldman, and Susan Sherr, "Eliminate the Negative? Defining and Refining Categories of Analysis for Political Advertisements" (paper presented at the conference on Political Advertising in Election Campaigns, American University, Washington, D.C., April 17, 1998).
34. William Riker, "Why Negative Campaigning Is Rational: The Rhetoric of the Ratification Campaign of 1787–1788" (paper delivered at the annual meeting of the American Political Science Association, Atlanta, August 1989).
35. Jamieson finds lower levels of "opposition" ads from 1952 to 1988. But she restricts her analysis to presidential general elections and adopts a different definition from mine. According to her formulation, the ad is oppositional "if more than 50 percent of the ad focuses on the record of the opponent without providing comparative information about what the sponsoring candidate would have done or germane information about the sponsoring candidate's record." My formulation classifies an ad as negative if at least half of it is unflattering or threatening or if pejorative statements are made, regardless of whether comparative information is provided. See Kathleen Hall Jamieson, *Dirty Politics: Deception, Distraction, and Democracy* (New York: Oxford University Press, 1992), 270 (chart 4–3).
36. Jamieson, *Packaging the Presidency,* 197.
37. Ibid., 232.
38. Diamond and Bates, *The Spot,* 179.
39. Jamieson, *Packaging the Presidency,* 245.
40. Jamieson, *Packaging the Presidency,* 407. Also see L. Patrick Devlin, "Contrasts in Presidential Campaign Commercials of 1980," *Political Communications Review* 7 (1982): 11–12.
41. L. Patrick Devlin, "Contrasts in Presidential Campaign Commercials of 1984," *Political Communications Review* 12 (1987): 26.
42. L. Patrick Devlin, "Contrasts in Presidential Campaign Commercials of 1988," *American Behavioral Scientist* 32 (1989): 390.
43. Cited in Harry Berkowitz, "Accentuating the Negative," *Newsday,* June 10, 1996, A10.
44. Devlin, "Contrasts in Presidential Campaign Commercials of 1988," 389.
45. See Karen Johnson-Cartee and Gary Copeland, "Southern Voters' Reaction to Negative Political Ads in 1986 Election," *Journalism Quarterly* 66 (1989): 888–893, 986.
46. Stephen Ansolabehere and Shanto Iyengar, *Going Negative* (New York: Free Press, 1995).
47. Richard Berke, "Polls: Social Issues Don't Define G.O.P. Vote," *New York Times,* March 31, 1996, 24.
48. Martin Wattenberg and Craig Brians, "Negative Campaign Advertising: Demobilizer or Mobilizer?" *American Political Science Review* 93 (December 1999): 891–899; Steven Finkel and John Geer, "A Spot

Check: Casting Doubt on the Demobilizing Effect of Attack Advertising," *American Journal of Political Science* 42 (April 1998): 573–595; Kim Kahn and Patrick Kenney, "Do Negative Campaigns Mobilize or Suppress Turnout?" *American Political Science Review* 93 (December 1999): 877–889; Paul Freedman and Ken Goldstein, "Measuring Media Exposure and the Effects of Negative Campaign Ads," *American Journal of Political Science* 43 (October 1999): 1189–1208; and Richard Lau, Lee Sigelman, Caroline Heldman, and Paul Babbitt, "The Effects of Negative Political Advertisements: A Meta-Analytic Assessment," *American Political Science Review* 93, no. 4 (December 1999): 851–875. Also see the response by Stephen Ansolabehere, Shanto Iyengar, and Adam Simon, "Replicating Experiments Using Aggregate and Survey Data: The Case of Negative Advertising and Turnout," *American Political Science Review* 93 (December 1999): 901–909.

49. Richard Lau and Gerald Pomper, "Effectiveness of Negative Campaigning in U.S. Senate Elections," *American Journal of Political Science* 46 (January 2002), 44–66.

Chapter 4: Media Coverage of Ads

1. See Theodore White, *The Making of the President 1960* (New York: Atheneum, 1961), for an early example of White's style of analysis. For example, White shows how Nixon's paranoia about the press pervaded his entire staff. One aide said in June 1960: "Stuff the bastards. They're all against Dick anyway. Make them work—we aren't going to hand out prepared remarks; let them get their pencils out and listen and take notes," 366.

2. Byron Shafer, *Quiet Revolution: The Struggle for the Democratic Party and the Shaping of Post-Reform Politics* (New York: Russell Sage, 1983); and Martin Wattenberg, *The Rise of Candidate-Centered Politics*(Cambridge: Harvard University Press, 1991).

3. Henry Brady and Richard Johnston, "What's the Primary Message: Horse Race or Issue Journalism?" in *Media and Momentum*, ed. Gary Orren and Nelson Polsby (Chatham, N.J.: Chatham House, 1987), 162; and Doris Graber, *Mass Media and American Politics* (Washington, D.C.: CQ Press, 1996), 190.

4. Michael Robinson and Margaret Sheehan, *Over the Wire and on TV* (New York: Russell Sage, 1983), 149.

5. Bernard Berelson, Paul Lazarsfeld, and William McPhee, *Voting* (Chicago: University of Chicago Press, 1954), 106. Also quoted in Thomas Patterson, *The Mass Media Election* (New York: Praeger, 1980), 105.

6. Patterson, *The Mass Media Election*, 105.

7. Hugh Winebrenner, *The Iowa Precinct Caucuses* (Ames: Iowa State University Press, 1987).

8. Press coverage was divided between the nominating period, which was defined as January 1 to the time of the California primary (or a candidate secured enough delegates for the nomination) in each election

year, and the general election, which ran from September 1 to Election Day. The study of television news proceeded along similar lines. Using the *Vanderbilt Television News Index and Abstracts,* which summarizes news stories for each network, reviewers tabulated the number and content of stories about political commercials that appeared Monday through Friday for the nominating process and general election each presidential year. The CBS analysis starts in 1972 because that was the first full presidential election year for which the abstracting service at Vanderbilt University compiled transcripts for the network evening news. CBS is used as the network of record in order to maintain comparability with past studies.

9. For similar results on the general election from 1972 to 1988 based on all three networks, see Lynda Lee Kaid, Rob Gobetz, Jane Garner, Chris Leland, and David Scott, "Television News and Presidential Campaigns: The Legitimization of Televised Political Advertising," *Social Science Quarterly* 74 (June 1993): 274–285.

10. The early 1960s, though, were an exception to the pattern just described. There was little coverage of ads during the close campaign of 1960 and during those of earlier years. Remember that advertising was in its infancy at that time.

11. Robinson and Sheehan, *Over the Wire and on TV.*

12. Quote cited in David Runkel, ed., *Campaign for President: The Managers Look at '88* (Dover, Mass.: Auburn House, 1989), 136.

13. Kathleen Jamieson, *Packaging the Presidency,* 2nd ed. (New York: Oxford University Press, 1992), 198.

14. Quoted in Jamieson, *Packaging the Presidency,* 200–201.

15. Leslie Wayne, "Infamous Political Commercial Is Turned on Gore," *New York Times,* October 27, 2000, A26.

16. See Kiku Adatto, "Sound Bite Democracy: Network Evening News Presidential Campaign Coverage, 1968 and 1988" (Research Paper R-2, Joan Shorenstein Barone Center for Press, Politics, and Public Policy, June 1990); and Kiku Adatto, "The Incredible Shrinking Sound Bite," *New Republic,* May 29, 1990, 20–23.

17. Jim Rutenberg, "Anti-Kerry Ad Is Condemned by McCain," *New York Times,* August 6, 2004, A15; and Glen Justice and Kate Zernike, "'527' Groups Still at Work Raising Millions for Ads," *New York Times,* October 16, 2004, A10.

18. Jim Rutenberg, "Kerry Denounces New Ad on Bush's Service in Guard," *New York Times,* August 18, 2004, A17.

19. Kate Zernike and Jim Rutenberg, "Friendly Fire: The Birth of an Anti-Kerry Ad," *New York Times,* August 20, 2004, A1.

20. Adam Nagourney and Janet Elder, "Bush Opens Lead despite Unease Voiced in Survey," *New York Times,* September 18, 2004, A1.

21. Michael Cooper and Jim Rutenberg, "McCain Barbs Stirring Outcry as Distortions," *New York Times,* September 13, 2008.

22. Kevin Sack, "Obama Attacks McCain on Health Care and Medicare, in Some Ways Inaccurately," *New York Times,* October 18, 2008.

23. June Kronholz, "Ready, Aim, Backfire: Nasty Political Ads Fall Flat," *Wall Street Journal,* October 16, 2008.

24. Ad in *New York Times,* October 1, 1996, A15.
25. Lawrie Mifflin, "Clinton and Dole Accept Plan for Campaign Time on Fox TV," *New York Times,* September 11, 1996, B8; and Lawrie Mifflin, "CBS to Give Clinton and Dole Free Air Time on Radio and TV," *New York Times,* September 28, 1996, 11. For an evaluation of these efforts, see Howard Kurtz, "Campaign for Free Air Time Falls Short of Organizers' Goals," *Washington Post,* October 31, 1996, A17.
26. Martha Moore, "A Minute of the Voters' Time," *USA Today,* September 18, 1996, 4A.
27. Lawrie Mifflin, "Time for Local Candidates," *New York Times,* September 25, 1996, C16; and "Belo to Offer Free Airtime to Candidates," *Providence Journal,* October 5, 1996, B10.
28. Kathleen Jamieson described the development of ad watches in a telephone conversation with me on January 30, 1992. Also see Michael Milburn and Justin Brown, "Busted by the Ad Police" (Research Paper R-15, Joan Shorenstein Barone Center for Press, Politics, and Public Policy, July 1995).
29. Quoted in Howard Kurtz, "In Advertising Give and Take," *Washington Post,* November 6, 1992, A10. For reviews, see John Tedesco, Lori Melton McKinnon, and Lynda Lee Kaid, "Advertising Watchdogs," *Harvard International Journal of Press/Politics* 1 (Fall 1996): 76–93; and Joseph Capella and Kathleen Hall Jamieson, "Broadcast Adwatch Effects," *Communication Research* 3 (1994): 342–365.
30. The question was, "How helpful to viewers would you say these stories about campaign ads have been? (1) very helpful, (2) somewhat helpful, or (3) not very helpful."
31. Telephone interviews with Howard Kurtz, April 8, 1992, and with Mara Liasson, April 27, 1992.
32. Stephen Ansolabehere and Shanto Iyengar, *Going Negative* (New York: Free Press, 1995); and Stephen Ansolabehere and Shanto Iyengar, "Can the Press Monitor Campaign Advertising? An Experimental Study," *Harvard International Journal of Press/Politics* 1 (Winter 1996): 72–86.
33. *Inside Politics,* CNN, January 19, 1996; and Kathleen Jamieson, "Truth and Advertising," *New York Times,* January 27, 1996, 21.
34. Interview with Martha Moore, July 19, 1996.
35. Samuel Schreiber of the Committee for the Study of the American Electorate helped collect these data.
36. Focus group conducted at Brown University in fall 1996.
37. Ibid.
38. Ibid.

Chapter 5: Learning about the Candidates

1. Thomas Patterson and Robert McClure, *The Unseeing Eye* (New York: Putnam's, 1976).
2. Ronald Mulder, "The Effects of Televised Political Ads in the 1975 Chicago Mayoral Election," *Journalism Quarterly* 56 (1979): 25–36; Charles Atkin, Lawrence Bowen, Oguz Nayman, and Kenneth Sheinkopf,

"Quality versus Quantity in Televised Political Ads," *Public Opinion Quarterly* 37 (1973): 209–224.

3. Kathleen Jamieson, *Packaging the Presidency*, 2nd ed. (New York: Oxford University Press, 1992); Edwin Diamond and Stephen Bates, *The Spot* (Cambridge: MIT Press, 1984); L. Patrick Devlin, "Contrasts in Presidential Campaign Commercials of 1988," *American Behavioral Scientist* 32 (1989): 389–414.

4. Larry Bartels, *Presidential Primaries and the Dynamics of Public Choice* (Princeton: Princeton University Press, 1988); Edie Goldenberg and Michael Traugott, *Campaigning for Congress* (Washington, D.C.: Congressional Quarterly Press, 1984), 85–91.

5. See Stanley Kelley Jr. and Thad Mirer, "The Simple Act of Voting," *American Political Science Review* 68 (1974): 572–591.

6. Quoted in Patterson and McClure, *The Unseeing Eye*, 130.

7. On hearing this story at a post-election campaign seminar, John Anderson quipped that Dole's fourteen seconds consisted of a news report about his car breaking down in New Hampshire. Both stories are taken from Jonathan Moore, ed., *Campaign for President: 1980 in Retrospect* (Cambridge, Mass.: Ballinger, 1981), 129–130.

8. For question wording, see Darrell M. West, *Air Wars: Television Advertising in Election Campaigns, 1952–1996*, 2nd ed. (Washington, D.C.: CQ Press, 1997), chap. 6, note 8.

9. Ibid., note 9.

10. Quoted in "How He Won," *Newsweek*, November/December 1992 (special issue), 64.

11. For question wording, see West, *Air Wars*, 2nd ed., chap. 6, note 11.

12. Ibid., note 12.

13. Ibid., note 13.

14. Ibid., note 14.

15. Michael Kelly, "Clinton, after Raising Hopes, Tries to Lower Expectations," *New York Times*, November 9, 1992, A1.

16. For question wording, see West, *Air Wars*, 2nd ed., chap. 6, note 16.

17. Interview with Elizabeth Kolbert, July 20, 1992.

18. "How He Won," 40.

19. Marion Just, Ann Crigler, Dean Alger, Timothy Cook, Montague Kern, and Darrell M. West, *Cross Talk* (Chicago: University of Chicago Press, 1996).

20. For question wording, see West, *Air Wars*, 2nd ed., chap. 6, note 21.

21. Ibid., note 21.

22. Just et al., *Cross Talk*.

23. Jack Germond and Jules Witcover, *Whose Broad Stripes and Bright Stars?* (New York: Warner, 1989), 283–286.

24. Ibid., 290.

25. An example of the two-stage model can be found in Benjamin Page and Calvin Jones, "Reciprocal Effects of Policy Preferences, Party Loyalties and the Vote," *American Political Science Review* 73 (1979): 1071–1089.

26. The direct effect of electability on the vote in this two-stage analysis was .47 (p .001). Other coefficients that were significant included race (.13; p .001), party identification (-.05; p .01), and gender (-.11; p .01).

27. The best predictors of views regarding electability were exposure to Dukakis ads (.18; p .01) and party (.06; p .01). The significant relationship for advertisements remains even after preferred candidate choice is included in the model as a control factor.

28. The direct effect of electability on the vote in this two-stage analysis was .47 (p .001). The effect on electability from exposure to Dukakis ads was .20 (p .001) and from exposure to Gore ads was .06 (not significant). The following variables were included as control variables: party identification, education, age, gender, race, ideology, political interest, and media exposure.

29. Bob Woodward documents the massive bureaucratic infighting that preceded the insertion of the "read my lips" line in Bush's 1988 convention speech in "Origin of the Tax Pledge," *Washington Post*, October 4, 1992, A1.

30. The direct effect of electability on the vote in this two-stage analysis was .40 (p .001). People who saw Bush ads were less likely to say they would vote for him (-.02; p .05). Exposure to Buchanan ads had no significant impact on the vote. The effect on electability from exposure to Bush ads was -.02 (p .10) and from exposure to Buchanan ads was .01 (not significant). The following variables were included in the analysis as control variables: party identification, education, age, gender, race, ideology, political interest, and media exposure.

31. This information on Bush's ads comes from an interview of Montague Kern with Robin Roberts on April 10, 1992.

32. Brown University survey conducted January–February 1996.

Chapter 6: Setting the Agenda

1. The classics in this area are E. E. Schattschneider, *The Semisovereign People* (Hinsdale, Ill.: Dryden Press, 1960); Roger Cobb and Charles Elder, *Participation in American Politics: The Dynamics of Agenda-Building*, 2nd ed. (Baltimore: Johns Hopkins University Press, 1983); John Kingdon, *Agendas, Alternatives, and Public Policies* (Boston: Little, Brown, 1984).

2. Good examples include Maxwell McCombs and Donald Shaw, "The Agenda-Setting Function of Mass Media," *Public Opinion Quarterly* 36 (1972): 176–187; Ray Funkhouser, "The Issues of the Sixties: An Exploratory Study in the Dynamics of Public Opinion," *Public Opinion Quarterly* 37 (1973): 62–75; Jack McLeod, Lee Becker, and James Byrnes, "Another Look at the Agenda-Setting Function of the Press," *Communication Research* 1 (1974): 131–166; Lutz Erbring, Edie Goldenberg, and Arthur Miller, "Front-Page News and Real-World Cues: A New Look at Agenda-Setting by the Media," *American Journal of Political Science* 24 (1980): 16–49; David Weaver, *Media Agenda-Setting in a Presidential Election* (New York: Praeger, 1981).

3. Shanto Iyengar and Donald Kinder, *News that Matters* (Chicago: University of Chicago Press, 1987), 112; Samuel Kernell, *Going Public*, 2nd ed. (Washington, D.C.: CQ Press, 1993). Also see Benjamin Page, Robert Shapiro, and Glenn Dempsey, "What Moves Public Opinion?" *American Political Science Review* 81 (1987): 23–44.

4. Stanley Feldman, "Economic Self-Interest and Political Behavior," *American Journal of Political Science* 26 (1982): 446–466. Also see Euel Elliott, *Issues and Elections* (Boulder, Colo.: Westview Press, 1989).
5. Paul Light, *The President's Agenda* (Baltimore: Johns Hopkins University Press, 1982).
6. Cobb and Elder, *Participation in American Politics*, 91–92. Also see Arthur Miller, Edie Goldenberg, and Lutz Erbring, "Type-Set Politics: Impact of Newspapers on Public Confidence," *American Political Science Review* 73 (1979): 67–84; Michael MacKuen, "Exposure to Information, Belief Integration, and Individual Responsiveness to Agenda Change," *American Political Science Review* 78 (1984): 372–391; Michael MacKuen, "Political Drama, Economic Conditions, and the Dynamics of Presidential Popularity," *American Journal of Political Science* 27 (1983): 165–192.
7. Good examples include McCombs and Shaw, "The Agenda-Setting Function of Mass Media"; McLeod, Becker, and Byrnes, "Another Look at the Agenda-Setting Function of the Press."
8. Gladys Lang and Kurt Lang, *The Battle for Public Opinion* (New York: Columbia University Press, 1983).
9. Kingdon, *Agendas, Alternatives, and Public Policies*, 61–64.
10. Ibid., 63.
11. Quoted in Light, *The President's Agenda*, 96. For congressional studies, see Barbara Sinclair, "The Role of Committees in Agenda Setting in the U.S. Congress," *Legislative Studies Quarterly* 11 (1986): 35–45; Roberta Herzberg and Rick Wilson, "Results on Sophisticated Voting in an Experimental Setting," *Journal of Politics* 50 (1988): 471–486; Darrell M. West, *Congress and Economic Policymaking* (Pittsburgh, Pa.: University of Pittsburgh Press, 1987).
12. Charles Atkin and Gary Heald, "Effects of Political Advertising," *Public Opinion Quarterly* 40 (1976): 216–228.
13. Thomas Bowers, "Issue and Personality Information in Newspaper Political Advertising," *Journalism Quarterly* 49 (1972): 446–452; Bowers, "Newspaper Political Advertising and the Agenda-Setting Function," *Journalism Quarterly* 50 (1973): 552–556.
14. For a review of the character issue, see Peter Goldman, Tom Mathews, and Tony Fuller, *The Quest for the Presidency 1988* (New York: Simon and Schuster, 1989); Jack Germond and Jules Witcover, *Whose Broad Stripes and Bright Stars?* (New York: Warner, 1989).
15. Nelson Polsby also discusses this quality of press coverage in "The News Media as an Alternative to Party in the Presidential Selection Process," in *Political Parties in the Eighties*, ed. Robert Goldwin (Washington, D.C.: American Enterprise Institute, 1980), 50–66.
16. For question wording, see Darrell M. West, *Air Wars: Television Advertising in Election Campaigns, 1952–1996*, 2nd ed. (Washington, D.C.: CQ Press, 1997), chap. 7, note 16.
17. For the text of this speech, see "Bush's Presidential Nomination Acceptance Address," *Congressional Quarterly Weekly Report* 46 (1988), 2353–2356.

18. See Eric Uslaner and Margaret Conway, "The Responsible Electorate: Watergate, the Economy, and Vote Choice in 1974," *American Political Science Review* 79 (1985): 788–803.

19. The CBS News/*New York Times* post–general-election surveys in 1984 and 1988 did not include measures for free media exposure.

20. The 1984 analysis of individual ads does not include a measure of media exposure; the October 1988 CBS News/*New York Times* survey regarding Bush's "Revolving Door" and Dukakis's "Family/ Education" commercials incorporates media exposure as a control factor.

21. There often has been confusion between the Bush-produced "Revolving Door" ad, which did not mention Horton directly by name, and the Horton ad aired by an independent political action committee, which used his name and picture. It is not clear whether viewers actually distinguished the two, because both ads dealt with crime and Dukakis's lack of toughness.

22. Marjorie Hershey, "The Campaign and the Media," in *The Election of 1988*, ed. Gerald M. Pomper (Chatham, N.J.: Chatham House, 1989), 95–96.

23. Criticisms about Dukakis's failure to respond to Bush, however, were influenced by personal circumstances. People in the Northeast, those aged forty-five years or older, and women were most likely after viewing Dukakis advertising to conclude Dukakis had erred in not responding to Bush's attacks.

24. "How He Won," *Newsweek*, November/December 1992 (special issue), 78.

25. I also confirmed this result through a logistic regression analysis that included an interaction term for gender and exposure to Bush's "Revolving Door" ad. The coefficient for the interaction term was 1.39 with a standard error of .62 (p .05), indicating a strong relationship in the expected direction.

26. Quote taken from David Runkel, ed., *Campaign for President: The Managers Look at '88* (Dover, Mass.: Auburn House, 1989), 113–114.

27. For a related argument, see Darrell M. West, "Television and Presidential Popularity in America," *British Journal of Political Science* 21 (1991): 199–214.

28. Stephen Ansolabehere and Shanto Iyengar, "The Electoral Effects of Issues and Attacks in Campaign Advertising" (paper delivered at the annual meeting of the American Political Science Association, Washington, D.C., August 1991).

29. Quote taken from Runkel, *Campaign for President*, 110. In anticipation of similar treatment, Clinton in 1992 hired someone to do opposition research on himself. See Sonni Efron and David Lauter, "Spy vs. Spy: Campaign Dirt Game," *Los Angeles Times*, March 28, 1992, 1.

30. Following the election, Atwater claimed that it was Gore, during the Democratic nominating process, who first criticized Dukakis on the Horton furlough issue. See Runkel, *Campaign for President*, 115.

31. Ibid., 221.

32. Ibid., 9.

33. In this two-stage analysis of the 1988 CBS News/*New York Times* survey data, the direct effect on the vote of citing crime as the most important problem was .70 (*p* .05). People who saw Bush's "Revolving Door" ad were more likely to cite crime (.10; *p* .01), whereas those who saw Dukakis's family education ad were less likely to name crime (-.06; *p* .05). The following variables were included in the analysis as control variables: party identification, education, age, gender, race, ideology, political interest, and media exposure. Because neither ad had a direct effect on the vote, those links were removed from the path model. Other agenda items displaying significant correlations with the vote included social welfare problems and jobs.
34. Quote taken from Runkel, *Campaign for President*, 9.
35. See Kiku Adatto, "Sound Bite Democracy: Network Evening News Presidential Campaign Coverage, 1968 and 1988" (Research Paper R-2, Joan Shorenstein Barone Center for Press, Politics, and Public Policy, June 1990), 9, 26–27. On October 25, 1988, CBS reporter Lesley Stahl corrected the revolving-door claim that "268 escaped" by pointing out that four first-degree murderers escaped while on parole. Other reporting on the furlough ad can be found on ABC on September 22, CBS on October 28, *Meet the Press* and *Face the Nation* the last weekend in October, and *Good Morning America* in early October.
36. "How He Won," 84.
37. Richard Berke, "The Ad Campaign: Mixing Harshness with Warmth," *New York Times,* October 22, 1992, A20; Leslie Phillips, "Bush Ads Revive 'Man on the Street,'" *USA Today,* October 23, 1992, A2.
38. Robin Toner, "Clinton Retains Significant Lead in Latest Survey," *New York Times,* September 16, 1992, A1.
39. Robin Toner, "Clinton Fending Off Assaults, Retains Sizable Lead, Poll Finds," *New York Times,* October 15, 1992, A1.
40. "How He Won," 81.
41. Toner, "Clinton Fending Off Assaults." After the election, it was revealed that searches had been made of Perot's passport file, too.
42. Quoted in Howard Kurtz, "In Advertising Give and Take, Clinton Camp Took and Responded," *Washington Post,* November 6, 1992, A10.
43. "How He Won," 84.
44. Richard Berke and Janet Elder, "Candidates Given High Marks in Poll on Fitness to Lead," *New York Times,* October 3, 2000, A1.
45. Richard Berke and Janet Elder, "In Final Days, Voters Still Wrestle with Doubts on Bush and Gore," *New York Times,* October 23, 2000, A1.
46. Center for Media and Public Affairs, "Bush Is Still Biggest Joke on Late Night TV," October 18, 2000, press release and "Candidate Jokes by Month in 2000," November 18, 2000, press release found at www.cmpa.com.
47. Howard Kurtz, "Candidates' Ads Switch the Focus to Kerry," *Washington Post,* May 9, 2004, A4.
48. Ibid.
49. Ibid.
50. Ibid.

51. CBS News/*New York Times* Poll, June 23–27, 2004.
52. Ibid., October 14–17, 2004.
53. Liz Sidoti, "New Bush Ad Uses Wolves to Suggest Terrorists Would Seize on Kerry Presidency," Associated Press, October 22, 2004.
54. Ibid.

Chapter 7: Priming and Defusing

1. See Herbert Simon, *Models of Thought* (New Haven: Yale University Press, 1979); S. E. Asch, "Forming Impressions of Personality," *Journal of Abnormal and Social Psychology* 41 (1946): 258–290; and B. Fischhoff, P. Slovic, and S. Lichtenstein, "Knowing What You Want," in *Cognitive Processes in Choice and Decision Behavior,* ed. T. Wallsten (Hillsdale, N.J.: Erlbaum, 1980).
2. A number of studies have investigated this relationship. See George Bishop, Robert Oldendick, and Alfred Tuchfarber, "Political Information Processing: Question Order and Context Effects," *Political Behavior* 4 (1982): 177–200; C. Turner and E. Krauss, "Fallible Indicators of the Subjective State of the Nation," *American Psychologist* 33 (1978): 456–470; and Amos Tversky and Daniel Kahneman, "The Framing of Decisions and the Psychology of Choice," *Science* 211 (1981): 453–458.
3. Peter Goldman, Tom Mathews, and Tony Fuller, *The Quest for the Presidency, 1988* (New York: Simon and Schuster, 1989); Jack Germond and Jules Witcover, *Whose Broad Stripes and Bright Stars?* (New York: Warner, 1989).
4. Daniel Kahneman, Paul Slovic, and Amos Tversky, *Judgment under Uncertainty: Heuristics and Biases* (New York: Cambridge University Press, 1982).
5. Goldman, Mathews, and Fuller, *The Quest for the Presidency, 1988;* and Germond and Witcover, *Whose Broad Stripes and Bright Stars?*
6. Shanto Iyengar and Donald Kinder, *News That Matters* (Chicago: University of Chicago Press, 1987), 63–64. Also see Jon Krosnick and Donald Kinder, "Altering the Foundations of Popular Support for the President through Priming: Reagan and the Iran-Contra Affair," *American Political Science Review* 84 (1990): 497–512.
7. Iyengar and Kinder, *News That Matters,* 63.
8. Krosnick and Kinder, "Altering the Foundations of Popular Support."
9. Nicholas Valentino, "Crime News and the Priming of Racial Attitudes during Evaluations of the President," *Public Opinion Quarterly* 63 (Autumn 1999): 293–320.
10. Lawrence Jacobs and Robert Shapiro, "Issues, Candidate Image, and Priming: The Use of Private Polls in Kennedy's 1960 Presidential Campaign" (Unpublished paper, Columbia University, 1992).
11. Michael Robinson and Margaret Sheehan, *Over the Wire and on TV* (New York: Russell Sage, 1983); and F. Christopher Arterton, "Campaign Organizations Confront the Media-Political Environment," in *Race for the Presidency,* ed. James David Barber (Englewood Cliffs, N.J.: Prentice Hall, 1978), 3–24.

12. Richard Brody and Catherine Shapiro, "Policy Failure and Public Support," *Political Behavior* 11 (1989): 353–369. A more general discussion of this argument can be found in Richard Brody, *Assessing the President: The Media, Elite Opinion, and Public Support* (Stanford, Calif.: Stanford University Press, 1991).
13. Jeff Fishel, *Presidents and Promises* (Washington, D.C.: Congressional Quarterly Press, 1985); and Gerald Pomper with Susan Lederman, *Elections in America*, 2nd ed. (New York: Longman, 1980).
14. Iyengar and Kinder, *News That Matters,* 66–68.
15. Krosnick and Kinder, "Altering the Foundations of Popular Support."
16. Descriptions of the 1972 presidential campaign can be found in Thomas Patterson and Robert McClure, *The Unseeing Eye* (New York: Putnam's, 1976); and Warren Miller and J. Merrill Shanks, "Policy Directions and Presidential Leadership: Alternative Interpretations of the 1980 Presidential Election," *British Journal of Political Science* 12 (1982): 299–356.
17. Theodore White, *The Making of the President, 1972* (New York: Atheneum, 1973).
18. Goldman, Mathews, and Fuller, *The Quest for the Presidency, 1988*; and Germond and Witcover, *Whose Broad Stripes and Bright Stars?*
19. For question wording, see West, *Air Wars,* 2nd ed., chap. 8, note 18.
20. This and the following description of the Clinton strategy can be found in "How He Won," *Newsweek,* November/December 1992 (special issue), 40–56. Also see Michael Kelly, "The Making of a First Family: A Blueprint," *New York Times,* November 14, 1992, 1.
21. For question wording, see West, *Air Wars,* 2nd ed., chap. 8, note 26.
22. For example, Yale economist Ray Fair's model, based on national economic growth, boldly predicted a big Bush reelection. What he failed to recognize, though, was the cumulative nature of economic fears and the ability of candidates to influence attributions of responsibility. A discussion of 1992 forecasting models is found in Richard Morin, "For Political Forecasters, Key Variable Is the Winner," *Washington Post,* September 5, 1992, A1. Only two of the five forecasters cited in this newspaper article correctly predicted a Clinton victory.
23. D. W. Miller, "Election Results Leave Political Scientists Defensive over Forecasting Models," *Chronicle of Higher Education,* November 17, 2000, A24.
24. Jim Rutenberg, "Scary Ads Take Campaign to a Grim New Level," *New York Times,* October 17, 2004, A1.

Chapter 8: Playing the Blame Game

1. Panel data from before and after the election show 58 percent of respondents felt in both the pre- and post-election surveys that Bush was responsible for negative campaigning. Among low ad viewers, 46 percent consistently cited Bush as the culprit, whereas among high viewers, 67 percent named him.
2. Discussions of voter backlash against Bush can be found in Howard Kurtz, "Bush's Negative Ads Appear to Be Backfiring," *Washington*

Post, October 10, 1992, A12; Renee Loth, "Ads Afford View of Camps' Strong, Weak Spots," *Boston Globe,* October 22, 1992, 19; Howard Kurtz, "Negative Ads Appear to Lose Potency," *Washington Post,* October 26, 1992, A1; Howard Kurtz, "Perot Escalates Costly TV Ad Blitz Targeting Media, Parties, Pundits," *Washington Post,* October 27, 1992, A1; and Leslie Phillips, "Hopefuls May Spend Record $300 Million," *USA Today,* October 23–25, 1992, A1.

3. Text shown in Howard Kurtz, "In Advertising Give and Take, Clinton Camp Took and Responded," *Washington Post,* November 6, 1992, A10.

4. The first quote comes from Michael Kelly with David Johnston, "Campaign Renews Disputes of the Vietnam War Years," *New York Times,* October 9, 1992, 1. The second quote is taken from Michael Isikoff, "Clinton Denounces Attacks by Bush," *Washington Post,* October 9, 1992, A1.

5. In this two-stage analysis of the September 1992 Winston-Salem, North Carolina, data, the direct effect on the vote of attributions of responsibility for negative campaigning was -.24 (*p* .001). People who saw Bush as attacking were more likely to attribute responsibility to him (.31; *p* .001), whereas those who saw Clinton as attacking were more likely to attribute responsibility to him (.32; *p* .001). The following variables were included in the analysis as control variables: party identification, education, age, gender, race, ideology, political interest, and media exposure.

6. Quote cited in David Hilzenrath, "GOP Aide Slams Administration," *Washington Post,* November 6, 1992, A18.

7. See Kurtz, "Advertising Give and Take," A10; and Ross Perot, *United We Stand* (New York: Hyperion, 1992).

8. Personal interview, May 25, 1996.

9. Michael Crowley, "Forbes' Henchmen," *Pittsburgh Post-Gazette,* January 14, 1996, B4.

10. Author's transcription.

11. The June numbers were reported in Richard Berke, "Voter Ratings for President Change Little," *New York Times,* June 5, 1996, A1, B7. The early October numbers come from Richard Berke, "Should Dole Risk Tough Image? Poll Says He Already Has One," *New York Times,* October 16, 1996, A1. For September numbers, see Richard Berke, "Some Images Stick. Some Don't. Why?" *New York Times Week in Review,* September 15, 1996, 1.

12. Richard Berke, "Aggressive Turn by Dole Appears to be Backfiring," *New York Times,* October 22, 1996, A1. Also see interview with the author by Mara Liasson, "Clinton Attacks Dole, Too, but Subtly," *National Public Radio Morning Edition,* October 22, 1996.

13. Hillary Clinton is quoted in Francis Clines, "1,000 Friends Help Cheer Up a Beleaguered Mrs. Clinton," *New York Times,* April 27, 1996, 10. The Stephanopoulos quote comes from Berke, "Should Dole Risk Tough Image? Poll Says He Already Has One," *New York Times,* October 16, 1996, A1.

14. Helen Dewar and David Maraniss, "Morphing and Bashing in Madison," *Washington Post,* October 11, 1996, A14; and Robin Toner, "In Final Rounds, Both Sides Whip Out Bare-Knuckle Ads," *New York*

Times, October 21, 1996, A1. Also see Howard Kurtz, "Clinton Team's Early Offensive Blunted Effect of Dole Ad Blitz," *Washington Post,* October 25, 1996, A19.

15. Scott MacKay, "Reed Counterattacks GOP's Negative TV Ad," *Providence Journal,* May 17, 1996, B1; and M. Charles Bakst, "Saying It Straight: Political Attack Ads Fill Air with Garbage," *Providence Journal,* May 16, 1996, B1. Also see Eliza Carney, "Party Time," *National Journal,* October 19, 1996, 2214–2218; and Adam Nagourney, "For G.O.P., Northeast Is Becoming Foreign Turf," *New York Times,* November 14, 1996, B12.

16. Interview with Reed campaign manager J.B. Poersch on October 30, 1996.

17. "The Great Ad Wars of 2004," *New York Times,* November 1, 2004, A22.

Chapter 9: Ads in Congressional Elections

1. Ira Chinoy, "In Presidential Race, TV Ads Were Biggest '96 Cost by Far," *Washington Post,* March 31, 1997, A19.

2. David Beiler, "The Classics of Political Television Advertising: A Viewer's Guide," Washington, D.C.: Campaigns and Elections, Inc., 1986.

3. Ken Goldstein and Paul Freedman, "New Evidence for New Arguments: Money and Advertising in the 1996 Senate Elections" (paper presented at the annual meeting of the American Political Science Association, Boston, September 3–6, 1998).

4. Patrick McGreevy, "Rogan, Schiff Try Healthy Tugs to Woo Seniors," *Los Angeles Times,* November 2, 2000, B1.

5. Ben White, "GOP to Unveil Negative Web Site," *Washington Post,* September 27, 2000, A14.

6. John Hendren, "Social Security Weights on Gorton, Cantwell," *Seattle Times,* October 31, 2000, A10.

7. Dionne Searcey, "Cantwell, Gorton Trade Barbs on Mine," *Seattle Times,* November 3, 2000, B2.

8. Lynne Duke, "How Hillary Got Her Groove Back," *Washington Post,* November 13, 2000, C1.

9. "Tight Senate Race for Clinton and Giuliani," www.InsidePolitics.org, November 5, 1999.

10. Adam Nagourney with Marjorie Connelly, "Mrs. Clinton Rolls Ahead of Giuliani as Senate Choice," *New York Times,* April 7, 2000, A1.

11. Adam Nagourney with Marjorie Connelly, "Poll Finds New Opponent Fails to Lift Mrs. Clinton," *New York Times,* June 13, 2000, A1.

12. Randal Archibold with David Chen, "Lazio and Clinton Take Each Other to Task over Health Care Efforts," *New York Times,* October 24, 2000, A26.

13. Felicity Barringer, "Spending So Much to Sway So Few," *New York Times,* October 8, 2000, 31.

14. Adam Nagourney, "New York Senate Race Ends in Nasty Brawl over Narrow Turf," *New York Times,* November 5, 2000, 41.

15. Adam Nagourney and Marjorie Connelly, "Poll Finds Little Voter Movement in Race for Senate in New York," *New York Times,* October 30, 2000, A1.
16. New York Senate exit poll found at www.cnn.com, November 19, 2000.
17. Charles Babington and Helen Dewar, "8 Senate Races Key to Democrats' Hopes," *Washington Post,* October 18, 2004, A1.
18. William Welch, "Senate's No. 1 Dem Also Its Most Threatened," *USA Today,* October 25, 2004, A12.
19. Ibid.
20. Babington and Dewar, "8 Senate Races Key to Democrats' Hopes," A1.
21. Karen Crummy, "Eco-group Launches Major Attack Against Coors," *Denver Post,* October 22, 2004, B4.
22. Graeme Zielinski, "Michels Makes Case with Images from 9-11," *Milwaukee Journal Sentinel,* October 19, 2004, A1.
23. See Darrell M. West, "Advertising and Citizen Voting Behavior" in Doris Graber, ed. (Washington, D.C.: CQ Press, 2008).
24. CBS News/*New York Times* national survey of 1,084 adults completed October 27–31, 2006.
25. Sylvester Brown, "Some Voters Will Buy into Misleading Political Ads," *St. Louis Post-Dispatch,* October 29, 2006, D1.
26. Michael Shear, "Vitriol Fills the Air and Airwaves," *Washington Post,* November 3, 2006, B2.
27. Ibid.
28. Ira Teinowitz, "No Shortage of Mudslinging in Midterm Run-Up," *Advertising Age,* October 31, 2006.
29. Alessandra Stanley, "Scary, Like Funny Scary," *New York Times,* October 29, 2006, Section 4, 1.
30. Adam Nagourney and Megan Thee, "With Election Driven by Iraq, Voters Want New Approach," *New York Times,* November 2, 2006, p. A1.
31. Jonathan Weisman and Chris Cillizza, "Campaigns Set for TV Finale," *Washington Post,* November 3, 2006, A1.
32. David Espo, "Dems Counter Bush Attack with Iraq Ads," CBS News.com, October 31, 2006.
33. Rupert Cornwell, "Republican Advert Banned over Racial Slur," *The Independent,* October 27, 2006, 44.
34. Drew Jubera, "Corker Holds GOP Seat in Tenn.," *Atlanta Journal-Constitution,* November 8, 2006, 16A.
35. "Out of Steam," *Los Angeles Times,* November 1, 2006, A18.
36. "Candidates Fight Dirty in Battle for Congress," *The Independent,* October 30, 2006, 2.
37. Jim Kuhnhenn, "Millions Spent on Negative Political Ads," CBS News, October 31, 2006.
38. Robert Kaiser, "In Senate Battlegrounds, Fusillades of TV Ads," *Washington Post,* October 28, 2008, A1.
39. "Sen. Dole Makes Issue of 'Godless' Group," *Washington Post,* October 31, 2008, A7.
40. Robert Kaiser, "In Senate Battlegrounds, Fusillades of TV Ads," *Washington Post,* October 28, 2008, A1.

Chapter 10: Advertising and Democratic Elections

1. John Dryzek, *Discursive Democracy* (Cambridge: Cambridge University Press, 1990); Jeffrey Abramson, Christopher Arterton, and Gary Orren, *The Electronic Commonwealth: The Impact of New Media Technologies on Democratic Politics* (New York: Basic Books, 1988); and Robert Entman, *Democracy without Citizens* (New York: Oxford University Press, 1989).
2. Joseph Schumpeter, *Capitalism, Socialism, and Democracy* (New York: Harper and Row, 1942), 250–268.
3. Nelson Polsby, *Consequences of Party Reform* (New York: Oxford University Press, 1983).
4. Morris Fiorina, *Retrospective Evaluations in American National Elections* (New Haven: Yale University Press, 1981).
5. Richard Merelman, *Making Something of Ourselves: On Culture and Politics in the United States* (Berkeley: University of California Press, 1984). Nancy Rosenblum also has made this point in a personal communication to me.
6. Benjamin Barber has made a useful distinction between strong and thin democracy in *Strong Democracy: Participatory Politics for a New Age* (Berkeley: University of California Press, 1984).
7. Diana Mutz, "Mass Media and the Depoliticization of Personal Experience," *American Journal of Political Science* 36 (1992): 483–508.
8. David Mayhew, *Congress: The Electoral Connection* (New Haven: Yale University Press, 1974).
9. Barbara Hinckley, Richard Hofstetter, and John Kessel, "Information and the Vote: A Comparative Election Study," *American Politics Quarterly* 2 (1974): 131–158; Kim Kahn, "Senate Elections in the News," *Legislative Studies Quarterly* 16 (1991): 349–374; and Kim Kahn, "Does Being Male Help? An Investigation of the Effects of Candidate Gender and Campaign Coverage on Evaluations of U.S. Senate Candidates," *Journal of Politics* 54 (1992): 497–517.
10. Benjamin Page and Robert Shapiro, "Educating and Manipulating the Public," in *Manipulating Public Opinion*, ed. Michael Margolis and Gary Mauser (Belmont, Calif.: Brooks/Cole, 1989), 307–308.
11. Martha Moore, "Political Ads Practice Art of Half-Truths," *USA Today*, October 26, 2000.
12. Floyd Brown's fakery is described in Mike Robinson, "Clinton Camp Denounces TV Ad," *Providence Journal*, October 24, 1992, A1.
13. Spencer Hsu and Ellen Nakashima, "J. Warner's Ad Alters Photo to Cast Democrat as Insider," *Washington Post*, October 10, 1996, A1; and Spencer Hsu, "John Warner Fires Consultant Who Altered Challenger's Photo in Ad," *Washington Post*, October 11, 1996, B1.
14. Jim Rutenberg, "Bush Campaign Replaces Ad That Had Doctored Images," *New York Times*, October 29, 2004, A20.
15. Joe McGinnis, *The Selling of the President* (New York: Simon and Schuster, 1969); and Robert Spero, *The Duping of the American Voter* (New York: Lippincott and Crowell, 1980).

16. J. Gregory Payne, John Marlier, and Robert Baukus, "Polispots in the 1988 Presidential Primaries," *American Behavioral Scientist* 32 (1989): 375.

17. When strong prior beliefs are present, the danger of advertising decreases dramatically. But, of course, in a rapidly changing world in which traditional moorings are disappearing—witness the collapse of communism on the world scene—even prior assumptions are being challenged. For a discussion of constraints on ad influence, see Elizabeth Kolbert, "Ad Effect on Vote Slipping," *New York Times Week in Review,* March 22, 1992, 4.

18. Critics have also complained about the effectiveness of ad targeting on underage youths by tobacco companies, such as through the cartoon figure Old Joe Camel.

19. The classic Supreme Court ruling in the campaign area was *Buckley v. Valeo* in 1976 (424 U.S. 1). This case struck down a number of finance regulations as unconstitutional encroachments.

20. A more extended discussion of reform proposals can be found in Darrell West, "Reforming Campaign Ads," *PS: Political Science and Politics* 24 (1992): 74–77.

21. Laurence Parisot, "Attitudes about the Media: A Five-Country Comparison," *Public Opinion* 10 (1988): 18–19, 60.

22. Kathleen Hall Jamieson, "For Televised Mendacity, This Year Is the Worst Ever," *Washington Post,* October 30, 1988, C1; and David Broder, "Five Ways to Put Some Sanity Back in Elections," *Washington Post,* January 14, 1990, B1.

23. Media scholar Jamieson has been instrumental in encouraging these ad watch efforts.

24. Race, of course, has been a controversial subject in many areas of American life. See Edward Carmines and James Stimson, *Issue Evolution: Race and the Transformation of American Politics* (Princeton: Princeton University Press, 1989); and Paul Sniderman and Edward Carmines, *Reaching beyond Race* (Cambridge: Harvard University Press, 1997).

25. Quoted by Kathleen Jamieson and Karlyn Kohrs Campbell in *The Interplay of Influence,* 2nd ed. (Belmont, Calif.: Wadsworth, 1988), 55.

26. For an example of this thinking, see L. Brent Bozell and Brent Baker, eds., *And That's the Way It Isn't* (Alexandria, Va.: Media Research Center, 1990); and Elizabeth Kolbert, "As Political Campaigns Turn Negative, the Press Is Given a Negative Rating," *New York Times,* May 1, 1992, A18.

27. Howard Kurtz, "Are the Media Tilting to Gore?" *Washington Post,* September 25, 2000, A1.

28. John Harris and Jim VandeHei, "Why McCain is Getting Hosed in the Press," Policio.com, October 28, 2008.

29. The media rating was in response to a question: "So far this year, would you say the news media have done an excellent, good, fair, or poor job of covering this presidential campaign?" The press bias question also was asked in the survey: "In your opinion, has news coverage of this year's fall presidential campaign been biased against any individual candidate? If so, which candidate received the most biased

coverage?" The figures on television coverage come from Howard Kurtz, "Networks Stressed the Negative in Comments about Bush, Study Finds," *Washington Post*, November 15, 1992, A7. The longitudinal evidence on the party leanings of reporters is discussed by William Glaberson in "More Reporters Leaning Democratic, Study Says," *New York Times*, November 18, 1992, A20. Also see Elizabeth Kolbert, "Maybe the Media Did Treat Bush a Bit Harshly," *New York Times Week in Review*, November 22, 1992, 3.

30. Pew Research Center, "Voters Impressed with Campaign; But News Coverage Gets Lukewarm Ratings," October 24, 2004, press release from www.people-press.org.

Appendix: Memorable Ads, 1984–2008

1. L. Patrick Devlin, "Contrasts in Presidential Campaign Commercials of 1984," *Political Communications Review* 12 (1987): 26.
2. Ibid.
3. L. Patrick Devlin, "Contrasts in Presidential Campaign Commercials of 1988," *American Behavioral Scientist* 32 (1989): 390.
4. Ed McCabe, "The Campaign You Never Saw," *New York Times*, December 12, 1988, 32.
5. Author's transcription from 1992 Clinton primary ad tapes.
6. Author's transcription from 1992 general election ad tapes.
7. Ibid.
8. Ibid.
9. Ibid.
10. "Clinton Unleashes a Fierce Attack on Dole," *New York Times*, September 25, 1996, A18.
11. Adam Nagourney, "An Attack in Black and White on Clinton's Drug Policy," *New York Times*, September 21, 1996, 8.
12. Howard Kurtz, "Ad Watch," *Washington Post*, September 28, 1996, A12.
13. James Bennet, "Republicans Return to a Tested Weapon," *New York Times*, May 18, 1996, 8.
14. Kevin Sack, "Organized Labor Fires Back on Medicare," *New York Times*, August 30, 1996, A16.
15. Peter Marks, "Commercial Attacking Bush Is Most Hostile of Campaign," *New York Times*, November 3, 2000, A22.
16. Peter Marks, "Focusing on Gore Hyperbole," *New York Times*, November 2, 2000, A27.
17. Richard Stevenson, "A Focus on Lost Jobs and Higher Costs," *New York Times*, October 11, 2004, A20; and Howard Kurtz, "In Ad Battle, GOP Unleashes Wolves, Democrats Use Ostrich," *Washington Post*, October 23, 2004, A6.
18. Author's transcription from 2004 general election ad tapes.
19. Ibid.
20. Ibid.
21. Author's transcription from 2008 general election ad tapes.
22. Ibid.
23. Ibid.
24. Ibid.

Index

DATE DUE